Also By Mike Pannett:

Now Then Lad

YOU'RE COMING WITH ME LAD

Tales of a Yorkshire bobby

MIKE PANNETT

HODDER

First published in Great Britain in 2009 by Hodder & Stoughton
An Hachette UK company

First published in paperback in 2010

12

A CIP catalogue record for this title is available from the British Library

ISBN 978 0 340 91877 7

Typeset in Sabon by Palimpsest Book Production Limited,
Grangemouth, Stirlingshire

Printed and bound by Clays Ltd, St Ives plc

Hodder & Stoughton policy is to use papers that are natural, renewable
and recyclable products and made from wood grown in sustainable forests.
The logging and manufacturing processes are expected to conform to the
environmental regulations of the country of origin.

Hodder & Stoughton Ltd
338 Euston Road
London NW1 3BH

www.hodder.co.uk

With love to Alex, Kate and Georgia

With special thanks to Alan Wilkinson

Contents

The Moors

the DALeS ←

Rosedale

Farndale

Newtondale

Bilsdale

Bransdale

Cropton

The New Inn

Thirsk

Kirkbymoorside

Helmsley

A 170

River Derwent

Hovingham

Castle Howard

HARrocAte ←

A 64

York

Whitby

A169

Scarborough

Pickering

Filey

The Wolds

Malton
Norton

Leavening
The Jolly Farmers

Drffle
LD

Stamford bridge

The story of my first year as a North Yorkshire country bobby is told in *Now Then Lad*. In *You're Coming With Me Lad*, as in the first book, all the cases I deal with actually happened. I have changed the names of the characters – police as well as villains – and altered the locations only when absolutely necessary to protect people's identities.

Policing procedures are always being updated; what you read here accurately reflects the way we operated at the time each event took place – which in every case is within the last ten years.

Mike Pannett
North Yorkshire
June 2009

Chapter 1

Welcome to Yorkshire

OK, so I'd moved out of London in search of a quieter life. Perhaps a simpler life. I'd left behind the streets of Battersea and a career in the Metropolitan Police to come home to my native Yorkshire as a rural beat bobby. I didn't expect to end up living with a retired farmer in a remote cottage on the Yorkshire Wolds, but when you find yourself on your own, without a place to stay, and someone offers you a spare bedroom you jump at it. Well, I did. Some months later, when I found myself taking the teabag out of my mug, squeezing the juice from it, and placing it on the Rayburn next to one of Walter's in case I fancied a drink later on – well, that's when I decided it really was time to think about moving on. Much more of this and I'd be picking up more of his tips on household economy: washing my clothes in the dirty bath water; stashing my loose change in a jam jar every night; smoking half a cigarette and sticking the rest behind my ear.

It had all started out the previous springtime as a stop-gap arrangement, a few weeks' respite till I got myself sorted. Now here we were about to enter a new year and I was still lodging in his spare bedroom, sitting by his fire on a night toasting crumpets over the hot coals. I'd heard of cabin fever. But it wasn't until Walt nodded off in his chair one night and I started up a conversation with Tina, his old black Labrador, that I realised precisely what it meant.

As for paying him, he wouldn't have that. No, he said, I invited you in; you're my guest. So I'd had to be a bit canny, nipping over to Scarborough and bulk-buying the groceries from time to time. Not that he needed much help: he had an endless supply of game, and always seemed to be fetching home vege-tables and fruit from various friends around the neighbourhood. So I just did what else I could, like paying to have the odd load of logs delivered, and making sure there were always a few bottles of beer in the pantry. And of course I tried to do my share of jobs around the place. But whenever I raised the subject of rent he insisted that just having me there was payment enough. 'The way I see it,' he said, 'this is t'best insurance policy I've ever had.'

'How d'you mean, Walt?'

'Why, break-ins and the like. Local villains daren't come near me with you on t'premises.'

It was true. He'd had one or two burglaries in the year or so before I moved in. Nothing too serious, but they'd nicked a few odds and ends from his garage and had a go at the back door. Waste of time that was, with his three separate locks. One of them dated from his grandad's time. Even the locksmith strug-gled to get through that the time he lost his keys, and if I hadn't come home when I did and found my spare they'd have ended up battering it down. Once I moved in though, the excitement had all stopped. At first I wondered how everyone knew he had a copper living with him, but when I thought about it it was pretty obvious. They always say that every time the landlord at the Jolly Farmers pulls a pint and makes polite conversation with a stranger, someone will be listening. And by the time the stranger has drained that first glass his name, place of origin, occupation and description will be circulating around the village and reaching out across the hills, courtesy of the bush tele- graph. And there I was, a regular. Part of the furniture, in fact. They all knew me, and where I lived, and what I did for a living. But no matter how secure Walt felt, the fact was he'd made a policy of living alone all his adult life. I needed to move on.

It was a Sunday morning, and I was sitting at the kitchen table in my dressing gown. I'd never worn one of those in my life, but when the weather turned cold and everyone else in the civilised world reached for the thermostat, the first thing Walter did was pile on a waistcoat, a cardigan, a pair of those gloves with no fingers like bus conductors used to wear, a cravat to make sure he didn't get a chill in the throat, and as a final resort that old hat of his. Then, if he was still shivering, he'd take a deep breath and crank up his rudimentary central heating – not that it ever penetrated the recesses of the upper floor where I slept. It was a point of pride to him that he'd filled up his oil tank three winters previously and never had another delivery since.

Still, he was a great believer in stoking the inner fires, was Walter, by which he meant getting plenty of food inside you. And today he was treating me to a late breakfast. Well, call it an early lunch, because it was well past noon. I enjoy a good fry-up when I'm working the afternoon shift. It sets you up for the day. You never really know when you'll get a chance to eat on those turns. Could be as early as four o'clock, but if you get

3

tangled up in a difficult case you can go right through till ten and never find time for more than a quick drink of coffee from your flask.

'Walt,' I said, as he shovelled the dry-cured bacon onto my plate and went back to the stove, 'It's time I found a place of my own, maybe down in the village.'

'You'll enjoy these,' he said, sliding two enormous fried eggs from his blackened cast-iron frying pan. 'Them's duck eggs. I just fetched 'em from my pal Gideon.'

'Gideon? What kind of a name is that?'

'His dad were a preacher at t'old chapel in Pickering. Had seven or eight lads and named 'em all from Old Testament. Clever as a cartload of monkeys, they were.' He put the pan back on the stove, sat down opposite me and shoved that rumpled cap of his to the back of his head. 'There was Amos and Caleb. I went to school with them. Twins. Used to sit right in front of me. Always chittering they were, and every time the teacher threw the chalk at 'em they just ducked and left me in t'firing line. Then there was Enoch and Jacob. They were a few years older. Set up their own haulage business later on, over at Kirkby. Made a fortune, and I'll tell you how they did it some day. How's that bacon I cooked for you?'

'Hey, I tell you what, Walt, it's good.'

'Aye, that'll be Abel.'

'Who's he? Another of Gideon's brothers?'

'No. Abel is t'owd pig he had slaughtered last back-end. Probably the last one we shall have to deal with.'

'Why's that then?'

'Why, Gideon isn't as young as he used to be. Reckons to be through with livestock. Matter of fact he'll be coming round later. He's been ailing. Doctor says it's a hernia. Been waiting for an operation this last month or two. And his old lass isn't so well either. Age, you see . . . '

Once Walt got onto the woes of old age there was no letting up. So I didn't get to broach the subject of me moving out that morning. By the time I'd ploughed my way through the fry-up – and a pile of toast smothered in his lady friend's homemade marmalade – it was time to get into my uniform and make tracks.

Sunday's always been a special day to me. We didn't do much in the way of church-going when I was a lad. Maybe Armistice Day, Harvest Festival, Christmas Eve and the like but we did try to keep it as a day of rest. Back then there wasn't a lot to do on the Sabbath. No shops, nothing much on the telly, and if you ever found yourself in town the streets would be pretty well deserted. As for the villages, well, you might see someone clipping his hedge with a pair of shears on an afternoon, but that was about it. And most likely he'd have his slippers on. If we made too much racket playing outside it wouldn't be long before someone would be out telling us to quieten down, or clear off and play somewhere else and didn't we know it was the day of rest?

Things have changed since then, of course. The leisure industry, the pubs, professional sports: they all run seven days a week. And the shops, God help us. But when you're out on the rural beat, Sunday still has a certain feel to it, especially in the winter months. It's a well-known fact that there's a rise in the divorce rate at Christmas, with a surge in what we call domestic incidents. In my experience the same thing applies on a smaller scale to Sundays. Whether it's that people have spent all their money and are fed up, or they're bored with each other's company, I don't know. Booze will have a bit to do with it, I suppose, blokes coming back late from the pub and getting into trouble because their dinner's ruined, that sort of thing. Or maybe they've had the in-laws round. But the point is that by Sunday afternoon a lot of otherwise well-behaved people are at each other's throats.

I got to the station nice and early. I was hoping to get all my paperwork out of the way, but I'd no sooner sat down at the desk than I got a call. Would I go out to Rillington to check on some youths who'd been seen larking around in the school grounds? I'd had dealings over there before. It's only a primary school, but you get the odd group of older kids who like to congregate in the field at the back with a bottle of cheap wine. Trouble is, when the drink gets to work they start getting daft and spray-painting anything in sight, or otherwise vandalising the place.

As I drove east along the main road grey clouds were scudding across a wintry landscape, and a few drops of rain were falling on my windscreen, washing the muddy film that was thrown up by the Scarborough bus as it pulled out in front of me. It had been a horrible back-end. Rain, rain and more rain. The fields were a patchwork of green where the winter wheat had survived and huge yellow stains where it had been waterlogged. Would it recover? Time would tell.

When I got to the old school the rain was coming down in earnest. Not surprisingly, there was no one to be seen. Even underage drinkers would drift home on an afternoon like this. But I made a mental note to ask around and get it sorted. I won't have that sort of behaviour on my beat.

Sunday bloody Sunday. Who said that? I think it was a film title. I'd had a look around and was just getting back into the car when I got the call. *'Domestic incident, central Malton.*

Neighbour reports an argument, female shouting. Husband may have assaulted her.'

'Righto, show me dealing,' I answered, and straight away I felt that shiver of something low down in my back.

As I sped back along the deserted A64 I got onto the control room. 'What have we got on the occupants?' It's the first thing you want to know. Have they got a criminal record, and if so what is it? Are they likely to be violent? Do they take drugs? If there's one thing all of us hate, it's dealing with these domestic bust-ups. You go in to protect a family from some nutter who's threatening them with destruction, and as soon as you lay hands on them the rest of the family will turn on you. Wife, kids, the lot. Trust me, it happens all the time. One minute you're riding to the rescue, the next you're the black-hatted villain.

'Have you got a name yet?' They had, and soon as I heard it I swore out loud. Wood. We knew him OK. He wasn't from around our area. York, I think it was. Married a local lass. A couple of the lads had had a run-in with him just a few weeks ago. Fuelled up with booze on a Friday night and fighting mad. Decided he'd take on the locals, all at once, dishing out verbal abuse, challenging everyone he came across to a fight. Nasty piece of work by all accounts, but the lads managed to calm him down before he did too much damage. There were minor charges that night, and we were interested to discover that he'd done time for assaulting some poor sod with an axe. You don't forget a man like that in a hurry.

I called control again. 'Any firearms held at that address?'

'*Nothing registered.*' Well, that was a relief – always providing he hadn't got hold of something illegally. Because that's getting easier, year by year.

'You got any backup sorted?' I was into Norton now, driving

fast along Commercial Street, down past the car showrooms. I crossed my fingers as I approached the railway. I've lost more than one villain there when the crossing gates have come down right in front of me. But there was no train today to slow me down. Over the other side of the river I swung into Sheepsfoot Hill. I still hadn't had an answer from control about backup and was just going to get onto them when they radioed in. They'd got a dog handler on his way from Scarborough. God knows how long he'd be, but one of the other PCs on our shift was on his way from Sheriff Hutton direction. Gary Ford. New lad. Only recently completed his probation, but he was on the ball. Good in a scrap. Not one of your shrinking violets.

It was already getting gloomy, but the place was easy enough to spot. There was a ground-floor window, the rising sash pulled right up, lights blazing. Across the road stood an elderly couple, huddled under an umbrella, peering towards it through the spiked railings that guarded the front of the house. I stopped the car a little way up the street so that I could approach on foot, nice and quiet. I always try to do that. You can learn a lot just by stationing yourself outside a place and listening.

I was out of the car and putting on my body armour when Fordy pulled up behind me.

'Now then. You fit?'

He patted his midriff. 'All suited up and ready to go, matey.' He was a short, stout lad and with all the kit on he was like a little barrel.

I slipped my jacket on, checked I had my Asp on one side, and gave the CS gas a good shake.

'What do we know about this guy?' Fordy asked.

'Nasty bit of work,' I said. 'Assaulted a man with an axe not so long ago.'

'Bloody hell.'

'So we treat him with extreme caution. Yes?'

'Yes.'

As we approached the house we heard our man for the first time.

'Don't you give me that, you f***ing bitch!' he bellowed. 'Just once more, that's all. I'm warning you!'

Through the open window we could see him quite clearly. In fact, we could see the whole scene. He was standing there, shaven headed, in a pair of jeans and a red football top, legs apart, fists clenched. Early twenties, I should say. Opposite him, her back pressed against the wall, stood a woman, shorter than him, younger, maybe still in her teens, blonde ponytail, her eyes half closed and her right arm raised as if to protect her face.

'See that?' Fordy was pointing. I wiped the raindrops off my glasses and followed his gaze.

'I don't believe it.' There on the settee, right beside his mother under a standard lamp, was a baby, all wrapped up in white with a bonnet on its head. Fast asleep. Quite oblivious to what was going on.

'I told you before, you f***ing bitch!' Wood screamed, the veins on his neck bulging. 'What I do when I walk out that door is my f***ing business. You got that?' She didn't answer him; just flinched as he raised his fist. He was well built. Very angry. Very frightening. 'Any more from you and I'll f***ing kill you!'

He fell silent for a moment. Above the sound of the rain spilling out from the guttering I heard Fordy talking to control. '*Aye, and there's a baby in there with 'em.*' The woman must have heard him too. She glanced our way, her mouth open. Wood turned towards the window.

'Oh, you fetched the f***ing law did you?' He was snarling now, his face contorted in anger. 'Well, I know how to deal with them lot. You just f***ing see if I don't.'

'Now then, Mr Wood,' I called out, as he loomed at the open window. 'Let's just calm down and talk this over, shall we? You don't want to be—' But as I spoke he turned round and went across to the sofa. For an awful moment I thought he'd lost the plot, that he was about to do something really terrible. Then I saw him reach across the baby and stretch his arms up. On the wall was an ornament, or that's what I'd thought it was: a long, curved, ceremonial sword of some kind. He pulled it down, strode back to the window and drew the blade out of its sheath.

'Nah then,' he snarled, 'I'm gonna f***ing 'ave you, copper.' Clasping the weapon in both hands, he stood there, his face reflecting the orange streetlight as he swayed from left to right, brandishing the weapon. All that stood between me and the vicious-looking steel edge was the row of spiked railings.

Fordy was standing beside me. 'Bloody hell, Mike. We going in after him, or what?'

'I don't know what we're going to do, buddy. But we are *not* taking him on while he has that thing in his hands. You got your CS gas handy?'

He patted the canister on his hip. I saw he had his Asp in his other hand. 'If he comes at us, we empty the gas in his face, then whack him – and I mean whack him. You got that?'

'You're the boss.'

At that precise moment I wished I wasn't. Wood was just a couple of feet back from the window, still swinging the sword. He handled it deftly, as though he'd been practising in the mirror for his big moment. Some of them do that. They think they're starring in their own movie. He was eyeballing me now, his lips wet and twisted, his eyes narrowed. I wondered what was fuelling him. Amphets? Speed? Too much lunchtime booze? Sometimes it's just rage.

'Come on, you f*****. Make your f***ing move.'

It's at times like these that I'm mightily glad of the experience I gained in the Met. I'd had plenty of stand-offs with cases like this young fellow, which is not to say my heart wasn't in my mouth as I stood there and watched the blade swishing to and fro. I was thinking, I was sweating, I was genuinely fearful as to how it might turn out. Firstly, I needed to keep things as low-key as possible. He was inflamed enough as it was. The last thing you do in a situation like this is to crank it up. My mind was racing as I played through all the possible scenarios. What if he went for the wife or child? How the hell was I going to stop him? If I tried to go through the window I'd most likely impale myself on the railings. So what about the door? It was an old panelled thing with a big brass handle, pretty heavy by the look of it. Would I be able to kick it open? And then, supposing I did get in, how would I tackle him?

'Listen,' I called out to him, 'you've got a bit excited. Fair enough.' As I spoke I slowly lowered my right hand, pulled my radio out of its pouch and pushed my thumb on the transmit button. I needed to let control know just what I was dealing with here, but I didn't want him to know what I was up to. I spoke in measured tones, loud and clear, emphasising the key words. 'Now, why don't you put that *sword* down. *Great big blade like that*, you could soon *chop someone's head off* if you aren't careful. You don't want to be waving that about with *the baby* in the room, do you now? How old is it, by the way?'

'F*** off, you piece of shit! This is my f***ing house and I'll do as I f***ing like. Try coming in here and I'll f***ing kill ya – and yer f***ing mate. Teks more'n a couple of coppers to frighten me.'

As he raved on I heard control coming through. You get to know them all after a while, and they get to know you. I recognised Julie's voice on the other end, and she knew who I was straight away. '*Yes, Mike, got that. ARV on its way.*' In London you could whistle up an Armed Response Vehicle in five minutes. They're never more than a mile or two away. Ours could be anywhere: York, Scarborough, Harrogate. It could take them forty, forty-five minutes to get through. And more. But the good news was that they were on the case. '*Also got an ambulance on way and I've let the duty inspector know. ETA of ARV about twenty-five minutes.*'

'I'm waiting. I'm ready.' Wood was silhouetted in the window frame. Wound up as he was he now seemed almost calm. He'd adopted a sort of kung-fu fighter's stance. He must have spent a lot of time in front of that bedroom mirror. 'Come on copper,' he snarled. 'Let's be 'aving you, eh?'

I can't say you don't get scared in these situations. You do. I was shaking with nerves. And I was still thinking. All sorts of things. How would Fordy stand up if it turned nasty? What if Wood tried to get across the railings to us? He looked crazy enough to try it. Was he just trying to show the wife what a hard case he was? And what in God's name was a man with a record like his doing with a three-foot-long blade in his possession? What possible need was there for anyone to have such a thing in the house? Why wasn't there some sort of law against it?

'Look,' I said, 'I can see you've got yourself wound up, but you don't want to be putting your lass and the little 'un in danger.'

'They've nowt to do wi' this. This is you and me – and yer f***ing pal there.'

'Look, you're upset. I understand that. But it's gone far enough. Nobody's hurt yet. We can sort it all out if you'll just put that sword down.' Sometimes it galls you, having to talk so calmly and reasonably, so civilly, to someone like that. A part of you wonders why the hell you should bother. Does he deserve it? But of course there's the safety of others to consider. The thing is to remember your training and what you're there for – to keep the peace. And the softly-softly approach is the one that gets the result, by and large. 'Now, come on,' I said, 'Don't be daft.'

'It's always the bloody same wi' you!' The woman was on her feet now, standing behind him, screaming in his ear. 'You're always t'bloody same. You get a few drinks down you and you go frigging barmy. Look at you. You're three sheets to t'bloody wind.'

'Oh Christ.' I turned to Fordy. 'Just when you think you're getting somewhere, the wife decides to have her two penn'orth.'

Wood turned into the room, the sword held high above his head. For just a moment it really looked as though he was going to attack her. Here goes, I thought, and made a move towards the street door although God knows what I would've done had I got inside. But before I got that far she'd backed off and he was shouting at me again. And something in his manner encouraged me. It just didn't have quite the same grating edge to it.

'Come on,' I said, 'you're only going to get yourself into trouble.' When a person's as enraged as this you just know he's either going to blow completely or he's going to cool down. They're on a kind of high, and there's no way they can sustain it indefinitely. If they're on drugs, well, you have a problem, but if you can start some sort of dialogue then the longer you can keep it going the more chance that they'll calm down before they do something really daft. 'Look,' I said, 'why not put the sword down and let's talk this through, shall we?'

But he wasn't listening. He'd turned on the woman now and was raging about money. It was him who put the hours in up the bacon factory, not her, so who was she to tell him how to spend it? And who'd paid for that holiday in Spain she had with her sister?

'Well,' Fordy said, 'he probably feels better for getting that lot off his chest.'

'Let's hope so. Get on the radio, will you. Give them an update and make sure they have a door-entry team geared up as well. While you're on get an ETA.' For the first time I was aware that we had attracted a gaggle of onlookers. Ten, maybe a dozen of them. Some were passersby with shopping bags and umbrellas. A young couple had come out from a neighbouring house and were standing there with coats draped over their heads. I looked at my watch. 'Where the hell's – shit!'

There was a crash from inside the room, then a scream. The woman was on her knees, the lamp was lying across the arm of the settee, and our man was back at the window, all wound up again, leaning right through the opening into the rain. He was barely six feet from me, and his broad shoulders seemed to fill the opening. 'Are you going to f*** off, or am I gonna come and get you? Eh? What's it to be? In here or out there? Cos one of us is going down.' The sword was in his right hand, still tucked behind him. He tried to get it through the window but as he swung it round it clanged against the frame. He clenched his left fist and thrust his jaw towards me. 'You f***ing coming or what?'

'Right,' I said, 'enough of this.' As he tried to work the sword through the opening I took a deep breath, leaned forward and let him have it. One . . . two . . . three full seconds, smothering his face and chest with CS gas spray before I stepped back a foot or two. All I had in mind was to give him a shock, take the heat out of the moment and hope against hope that it would calm him down. I didn't know what else to do. It was just a gut reaction. But it worked. There was a clatter as the sword fell to the floor behind him. 'You bastard!' he gasped as he staggered back into the room, screwing up his eyes, coughing, pawing at his face and ripping his shirt off. 'You . . . bastard.'

As he tried to shake the pain out of his eyes, I waited. As hyped up as he was I couldn't be sure that the gas would incapacitate him for more than a minute at best. What would happen next there was no telling. It affects different people in different ways. Some come like lambs. Others don't. 'It's no good rubbing your face, mate,' I called through to him. 'You'll only make it worse. Look, if you'll just come out now we'll get you cleaned up.'

He was mopping his face with the T-shirt now. Breathing deeply, spitting on the floor, blinking, eyes streaming, shaking his head, like a boxer who'd taken a fall but was determined to wade back into the fight.

I stepped away from the railings and looked around. Fordy had been doing a good job, summoning help while I kept me-laddo talking. He'd got the traffic stopped and the end of the street blocked off. He'd got the onlookers well out of the way, and now behind me I saw the firearms team, maybe twenty yards away in the shadow of a parked van. There was something very reassuring about seeing those lads. They looked more like a couple of squaddies with their black trousers tucked into their combat boots, their short Hechler and Kock rifles at the ready.

There was a third officer with them, holding a baton-round gun. That was good. A single rubber bullet from him and our friend would be disabled instantly. I suddenly felt a lot more confident and reassured. I felt myself able to breathe properly again.

Fordy was beside me, nudging me and pointing to another new arrival. I recognised an inspector from York, a negotiator. Well, I thought, who knows? Maybe he can talk the guy out. But for the moment he stayed back. As he caught my eye he gave me the thumbs up. He was leaving me to do the talking. 'I've filled him in,' Fordy said. 'He reckons to be weighing up the options.'

'I just hope he keeps out the way for now,' I said. At this stage, the fewer police that were visible the better as far as I was concerned. I had a gut feeling that we were dealing with the sort who might just blow completely if he thought he was trapped. A death-or-glory type who'd go down with all guns blazing. But you never know. None of us really, really know what we'd do in such a situation, and I'd have been willing to bet that matey was now into unknown territory, acting on blind instinct. I couldn't imagine that he'd ever been this far out on a limb before. As I pondered the situation, he kept rubbing at his eyes, swearing, whacking his head with his open palm as if his brain was fogged and he was trying to clear it.

'Go on,' Fordy said under his breath. 'Hit it a bit harder. Might knock some bloody sense into it.'

I called through the window again. 'Y'know, if you'll just come out we can get this sorted,' I said. 'Think of the young 'un on the settee there. And your missus. How are they going to feel?'

'Ask her. It's her f***ing fault.' It was the first time he'd actually spoken, rather than just shouted at me. And he shivered as a gust of wind spattered his bare chest with rainwater that was spilling out from above his head. My experience of this kind of case was that if someone's going to do something really stupid – or violent – they'll generally do it sooner rather than later. Once they consent to talk to you it generally means they're going to calm down. So at this stage I was starting to feel just a little bit hopeful. I was able to start thinking about what we were trying to achieve, which was quite simple: to get him out of the house and disarm him, and to remove the woman and her child from any possible danger.

'Look,' I said, 'why not put your shirt back on? You're gonna feel like crap when you cool off. Looks to me like you've had a few beers at lunchtime. You won't be feeling the cold yet, but you're gonna make yourself ill, stood there with nowt on.'

For a full minute he remained quite still, eyes half closed, looking at the ground. It seemed we were getting somewhere at last. I carried on talking. I tried to draw him on what was troubling him. Was it money? Had he got a problem with the wife? Was it to do with work? The longer I could keep him there, the better the chance that whatever he had taken would wear off, that the adrenaline would drain away. And in the end he'd start to feel the cold. He had to, because all the time he stood there the rain was running down his upper body and soaking into his jeans.

I kept asking questions, but I now realised he was no longer listening. He had his head bowed, and was taking deep, low breaths like a weightlifter. If you could imagine someone clenching his nostrils, that's what he was doing. Building up a head of steam.

'Now listen, mate . . .' I didn't like the look of this. I'd thought he was about to calm down, but now it was as if he'd stopped, had a think and slung himself into reverse gear ready to launch one more assault. He was pulling himself up to his full height now, walking deliberately over to where his wife was sitting. There was no way of telling what was on his mind.

He leaned behind the settee, slow and deliberate, and pulled out a baseball bat. Not a wooden one as far as I could see, but a sort of metallic blue effort that glinted under the bare light-bulb that hung from the ceiling. And now he was back at the window, snarling. 'You.' He was barely seven or eight feet away and I could see the colour of his eyes. Brown, and bloodshot. You never feel comfortable being that close to a villain. You can go home feeling dirty some days.

'You f***ing gassed me,' he shouted. 'And you told me to come out. Well, guess what? I'm gonna come out, right? And I'm gonna knock yer f***ing head off. I'll teach you to f***ing gas me.'

In cold print the words sound ugly, and they sound threatening. But what I always remember about that incident is that I suddenly found myself saying to Fordy, 'You know what? This guy's all bluster and hot air. I don't think he's got the balls to do more than stand there and shout the odds at us. It's all show. And anyway looking on the bright side of life, at least it's only a baseball bat, not a sword.'

As he stood in the window shaking the bat and mouthing off about what he was going to do to us, I held my hand up. 'Whoa,' I said, 'hang about. Now listen, you've had your say, but let me tell you – d'you see those lads over there?' That got his attention. He actually looked where I was pointing. I could see him half-crouch as he tried to make out the shadowy figures down the street. I noticed the dog handler had shown up too. He wouldn't like that. They never do.

18

'Those,' I said, 'are firearms officers. Crack shots. I'm telling you, those lads can shoot a sparrow out of a tree at a hundred yards. No trouble at all. Now, you try anything daft, like coming out of there with that thing in your hands, and as sure as I'm standing here they will shoot you. They'll try not to kill you, but they will shoot you. And trust me, matey, the bullets they fire will stop an ox.'

He stood there, quite still; just a ghost of a shiver. You could almost hear his brain ticking over. Then his shoulders sort of slumped, as he lowered the bat. 'Tell you what,' he said, 'why don't you come in and tek me away?'

'No no,' I said. 'That's not how it's going to be.' By now I'd had word from the negotiator, the inspector who'd come from York. He'd told us exactly how he wanted the endgame to be played. 'What's going to happen,' I said, 'is you are going to walk out of the door onto the street with your arms raised above your head so that we can be quite sure you're unarmed.'

'Nah, I'm not 'aving that. You come and get me.'

We started wrangling now. No, I'm not doing that; oh yes you are; well, how about if I do this . . . ? It was a pain in the rear end, because Fordy and I were wet, cold, and starting to feel the strain. But the fact that our man was arguing was a good sign. We knew that. Ever so slowly, Wood was climbing down. He was finished, and he knew it.

'Tell you what,' he finally said.

'I'm listening.'

'I'll come out through 'ere.'

There comes a point in these negotiations when you have to throw up your hands and accept that the bloke's beaten, so what the hell if he does get to act out one last part of his fantasy? Whatever the reason, he'd got it into his head that he wanted to come out through the window, and if that made him feel better did it really matter all that much? People who do this sort of thing are usually attention-seekers. They play to the crowd – if they can muster one. The height of his ambition might have been for us to fetch in helicopters, arc lights, TV crews. Our aim was to keep it as low-key as possible. From his point of view he was a hero in his own video game. From our point of view he was . . . well, let's say I could think of better ways to spend a Sunday afternoon. So, I thought, if it speeds things along let's give him a little something. The inspector was standing just a few yards away now, listening to every word. And he was giving me the thumbs up once more. We'd get the result we wanted and nobody would be hurt. The only question was, how would he get across those railings and onto the pavement?

He had the answer. He grabbed a mattress from behind the sofa, dragged it out, all striped and stained, and shoved it through the window so that it hung over the railings.

'Right,' I said. 'If that's the way you want to come out. But let me tell you what you're going to do.'

'Aye, go on,' he said. Funny, but once a bloke like that calms down the first thing you notice is how he looks a lot smaller than when he's all pumped up. When he was waving that sword about he really did look dangerous. Now his shoulders were more rounded, you could see he had the beginnings of a beer belly, and as he started shivering he looked young, not much more than a lad. Three or four years ago I could've been talking to him about hanging around in school fields drinking lager. He was just a big overgrown kid really. And he was hanging on my every word.

'You're going to come out nice and slow, and you're going

kneel on the pavement with your hands above your head. No –
don't be putting your shirt back on. Just come as you are.' In
situations like these you don't take any chances at all. Even a
wet T-shirt can be used to conceal a weapon.

As I spoke his eyes were darting this way and that, from me
to the street and back again. He was frightened now. 'Them
firearms lads,' he said, his voice shaky and low. 'What they
gonna do to me? They ain't gonna shoot me are they?'

'You've been watching the wrong kind of TV shows, buddy.
This is North Yorks, not New York. You do just as I'm telling
you and I guarantee you we won't harm a hair on your head.
Now come on, have a care for your family. The quicker you're
out of there the quicker we can get the missus out. I should
think the baby'll be waking up and wanting its bottle in a minute.'

Still he hesitated. 'No,' he said. 'I know what you're after.
You're after shooting me, aren't you? Then you'll say it's self-
defence. I've read t'f***ing papers.'

And so he went on, for another five minutes. What he'd seen
on the Net, what he'd seen on TV, what he'd heard about from
a mate of his who was doing time for armed robbery. It was
just a matter of waiting until he'd used the last dregs of his
pent-up energy. Then, when he'd had his say, he came like a
lamb, a wet, tremulous, half-naked lamb, part walking, part
crawling across the mattress before sinking to his knees on the
rain-slicked pavement. He had the satisfaction of one or two
mobile-phone cameras popping off from the crowd at the end
of the street, but his big day was over. The dog handler moved
in, Fordy held his shaking wrists while I put the cuffs on, and
a minute or two later we were on our way to Old Maltongate.

Later the inspector called in and had a word. 'They asked
me to come over and conduct any negotiations,' he said, 'but I

have to say I thought you handled it perfectly. You did a hell of a job there. Wouldn't have done it any different myself.'

You would've thought that an incident like that would lead to a custodial sentence. After all, we were charging the lad with a raft of public-order offences, and with making threats to kill. But no, he was bound over to keep the peace for six months, and given a community-service order. As to the baseball bat and the sword, I was all for taking them out the back of the police station, busting them up and binning them, and I said as much. 'Oh no,' I was told, 'you can't destroy private property.'

'Why the bloody hell not?' I said. 'How can we trust a nutter like him with weapons like these?' But no. I wasn't allowed to touch it. And it got better. Three weeks after the incident, and just a day or two after his court appearance, me-laddo showed up, bold as brass, to ask for his sword back – and got it. Someone tried to explain the legal technicalities of it all to me, that there had been a cock-up between the police, the court and the Crown Prosecution Service over our request for confiscation orders, but after a while I stopped listening. Common sense and the law don't always talk the same language. I later heard that Wood had gone back to his wife. Yes, she loved him after all. It's amazing how often you hear that. He's a good lad really, just that when he gets a bit of drink in him . . . Not surprisingly, we weren't through with her hubby yet. He'd be making another bid for stardom later in the year – but that's another story.

Somewhere along the way I'd missed my meal break, of course, and by the time the paperwork was in order it was half past nine. One or two of the night shift had come in early, so the duty sergeant said I might as well call it a day. Driving back to Walter's, I found myself going back over the day's events. What was on my mind was all the what ifs. What if he'd killed the baby, or the wife, or me or Fordy? Sure, we'd brought it all to a peaceful conclusion, but there had been one or two moments there when it had all hung in the balance, when it could easily have gone the other way. It's not so much what happens in these cases that keeps you awake at night; it's what might have happened.

Well, from the sublime to the ridiculous. I got home and found Walt on his knees in the kitchen surrounded by a scene of bloodshed and carnage. There were skinned rabbits, plucked pheasants, joints of unnamed dark red meat, whole raw livers, a couple of hearts and a few kidneys, all strewn about the place. Luckily they were all frozen solid.

'Walter,' I said, stepping over a slab of tripe, 'are you going to tell me what's going off — or have I to guess?'

'It's Gideon. His hernia's playing up.'

'And? No, don't tell me. You're rummaging through the freezer looking for a spare part. That it?'

Walt liked that. He sat back on his haunches and laughed. 'Don't be daft,' he said. 'No, t'owd quack reckons he should put sommat cold on it, reduce the inflammation like. Like a packet of frozen peas.'

'Well, hasn't Gideon got any frozen peas at his place?'

'Gideon? Why, they don't have no kitchen appliances. They're living in t'Dark Ages down yonder. Still salt their vegetables and bottle their fruit. If you think my place is owd-fashioned you want to go down there some time. Any road', and he started putting the various packets of meat back in the freezer, 'I've no peas either by t'look of it. Just meat.'

'Well,' I said, picking up a rabbit. 'What's wrong with this? This'll do the job, won't it?'

'Aye, you're right. Should fit nice and neat across his stomach.' Walt stood up. 'Right then, I'll pop down to his place now. He'll be pleased with this, will t'owd lad.'

'Till it melts.'

'Aye, till it melts – then I'd best fetch her back.'

'Can't you just give it him? '

'Give it? By 'eck no we're having this bugger for our tea tomorrow.'

24

Chapter 2

In With a Bang

'I hope she's worth it.' Walt shook the raindrops off his tatty old gabardine raincoat and hung it up above the Rayburn.

'Hey, go easy,' I said, as I rummaged through his box of boot brushes. 'Those are my best shoes you're splashing.'

'Don't know that I'd go to all that trouble for a lass,' he muttered. 'Here'. He pulled out an old wooden-handled job and shoved it in my hand. 'This'll put a shine on 'em. Pure horse-hair that.'

'If we were talking about any other lass I might agree with you,' I said, buffing away. 'But not this one. This one's special.'

'Aye, so you said, and you know what that means. She'll have a queue of fellers after her. Women like that, they can pick and choose y'know.'

'The thing is, Walt, you've never seen me in action. When I turn on the charm, they don't stand a chance. You wait. She won't know what's hit her.'

As I polished I digested what I'd just said. I was getting carried away with myself, and I knew it. The fact was I hadn't stopped thinking about Ann all over Christmas, and asking myself questions. I kept remembering what Chris Cocks the desk sergeant had said, that she was out of my league. Was he right? Had she really wanted to come to the party with me, or was it a case of not knowing how to turn me down? Maybe she'd do what that lass in London did one time: call me and say she'd had a better offer. But then I remembered that goodnight kiss in Malton marketplace. That answered a lot of questions, surely.

'Anyway,' I said, looking Walt up and down, 'what are you wearing to the party?' He had on a pair of baggy brown cords and a chunky off-white sweater, the kind I'd wear to go deep-sea fishing in. 'I see you've managed to find a matching pair of laces at least.' I pointed at his trusty black boots. That first time I'd met him, he'd had one brown and one red as I recall.

'I've pushed the boat out for this do,' he said, 'being as it's up at your mate's big house yonder.' He lifted his sweater to reveal a broad black leather belt. 'Got it at Yates's,' he said, 'and this' – he patted a shiny steel buckle in the shape of a Harley-Davidson – 'I got in Pickering. They have a shop there, specialises in 'em.'

'And that's it? That's your New Year's party outfit?'

'Why, it cost me a bloody fortune did this lot.'

'Aye, in about 1973. Anyway, just so long as you're not planning to make a grand entrance with me and Ann, you scruffy . . .'

'No, I shall come along later. I've to pick up me brother first, and t'other feller.'

His brother, Cyril, I'd met a few times. The 'other feller' would be Ronny, a retired RAF fitter who had a single topic of conversation: the life and times of an RAF fitter. The three of them would get together in the Jolly Farmers, or on a summer night they'd sit on an old wooden bench on the roadside outside Walt's house and sup beer while they watched the world go by. I called them the Three Wise Monkeys, among other things. Good company for half an hour or so. And not the sort of lads to miss out on one of Algy's parties, where the beer flowed free.

Thinking of Algy reminded me I needed to ask him about that cottage of his. The one he rented out. It must have been a month or two since he'd first mentioned it, and I was sure he'd said it would come vacant in the new year.

'Well,' I said, 'you three'll liven the place up.' I handed back the brush and held up the shoes for him to see. 'By, that did the job OK. You can see your face in them.'

'Aye well, it's quality is that brush. Belonged me dad.' He took it from me and ran his hand across the thick, soft bristles, looking thoughtful. 'Got this when he signed up with t'East Yorkshires. Eighty, getting on for ninety years old.'

'That's a hell of an age for a soldier, Walt.'

'I'm talking about t'boot brush, yer daft bugger. He took it off to t'trenches in his kit-bag. That'd be early on, 1915 or thereabouts.'

'There we are.' I had the shoes on now. They were positively gleaming. 'What do you reckon?'

'They'll do,' he sniffed. 'But I wouldn't cross that yard in 'em. Standing water and mud everywhere you tread.'

As soon as I opened the door I could see what he meant. It was a wild old night, the rain lashing down, the sycamores bending before a westerly gale, the roof of the garage creaking as the wind got under a loose corner of corrugated iron and tugged at it. But at least it was mild. I put the shoes in a plastic bag and went to find my wellies. 'And take this too,' Walt said, handing me an old black brolly.

'What about you?'

'I'll manage. I'm not escorting a lady tonight, am I?'

'Hey, that's a point. Where is your lady friend?'

'Cruising.'

'What, in Old Malton?'

'Enough of that. I told you before. She's in t'Med, on a luxury liner, with her daughter.'

'She says.'

'Aye, she says. And I've no reason to doubt her.'

'Right then.' I opened the door. 'As someone once remarked on venturing out into the wilds of Antarctica, "I may be some time".'

All the way to Ann's place up at Thornton le Dale I rehearsed what I might say. Lovely weather for ducks? Hope Father Christmas brought you something nice? Your carriage awaits?

I might as well have not bothered. As soon as she came to the door I dried up. Opened my mouth and nothing came out. She looked an absolute picture. And when I finally loosened my tongue I told her so.

'Why, thank you,' she said, as she ducked under the umbrella, her hair brushing against the back of my hand. 'And you don't look so bad yourself.' She was wearing what women call a little black dress, had a light coat thrown over her shoulders, and her face was illuminated by a broad smile. She smelled divine.

'Pity it's not properly flooded,' I said, as I opened the car door for her and watched her step gracefully over a large puddle.

'Why's that?'

'Well, I would've had to carry you.'

She paused, half in the car and half out. 'Who knows? If it keeps raining like this you may have to by the time the party's over.'

I hadn't got an answer for that. I just got in and drove off in silence.

'What's he like, this mate of yours? Algy, isn't it?' I was leaning forward in the driving seat, peering through the windscreen as the tall thorn hedges loomed over us on either side. I'd never approached his place in the dark before, and I wasn't quite sure how far down the lane it was.

'Well, for a start he's loaded. More money than you or I'll ever see. And he's a one-off.'

'Meaning?'

'Ah, here we go.' I recognised the holly trees that stood either side of his entrance. 'Well,' I said, as we scrunched our way up the gravelled drive and the car lights swept across the lawn to illuminate the white rose ensign that fluttered proudly from the flagpole, 'there's your first clue.'

'Oh, him. Wasn't he in the *Yorkshire Post*?'

'He was.'

'And wasn't he ordered to take it down.'

'Indeed he was.'

'So why's it still there?'

'Like I say, he is not as other men. Last I heard he was on his way to Strasbourg with it.'

'Strasbourg? With a Yorkshire flag?'

'Aye, Court of Human Rights or some such.'

I parked under the copper-beech tree and walked around the front of the car to let Ann out. She took my arm and I escorted her across the drive to the front porch. 'Very grand,' she said, looking up at the fluted pillars as we climbed the worn stone steps. I was just about to hit the brass bell-push when the door opened and there was our host, in his black dinner jacket and red-white-and-blue dickie bow, a glass of bubbly in his hand, his head silhouetted against the light of a chandelier.

'Michael, old boy. And I say, what a delectable companion!' He took Ann's hand, bowed and kissed it. 'Miles Waring. Delighted to meet you, Miss—'

'Barker. Ann Barker.'

'But call me Algy. Everyone else does. Well, look, do come inside and let me pour you a drink while—' he looked me up and down '—while Michael here gets out of his wellington boots.'

'Oh heck,' I said, and scuttled back to the car. Shoes, shoes . . . plastic bag. I glanced in the back. Not there. Then I lifted the hatchback. They weren't there either. I opened a door and had a closer look among the stuff on the rear seats; an old anorak, an empty carrier bag and a couple of newspapers. Then I got on my knees and felt about under the front seat, pulled out a torch and had another look. Nothing. I'd left the buggers at Walt's.

When I went back inside Ann was standing with a glass of champagne in her hand, listening to Algy as he leaned forward, his right arm stretched out against the wood-panelled wall. He was in full flow, telling her about his younger days in the Guards. When she saw me she tilted her head to one side, a smile starting to flicker about her mouth. I brushed a few bits of wet gravel off my knees and shoved the torch into my jacket pocket. 'Here,' she said, reaching out and wiping a smudge off my forehead with the tips of her fingers, 'you're looking a bit flustered.'

'No luck, old boy?'

'I had 'em, Algy. I had 'em all polished to bu— well, let's say they were nice and shiny.' I looked at Ann, who was grinning broadly. 'You know what I've done, don't you?' She nodded. 'I've left them in a bloody carrier bag on Walt's kitchen table.

Should I go back or what? I don't want to make a mess of your floors.'

'No problem there, old chap,' Algy said. 'Rolled up all the carpets yesterday. Bare boards good enough for this rabble, don't you think?' He looked around him at a sea of heads. 'Put the silver cutlery away too, ha ha. Plastic plates and plastic knives and forks . . . Hmm, that's a song, isn't it?' He looked at his empty glass. 'Well, quite so . . . Just a little joke. Refill, anyone?'

'It'll be juice for me,' Ann said. 'I'm at work tomorrow morning. Six o'clock start.' She looked at me. 'But by the look of him this man needs something a little bit stronger.'

'How come you're working?' I said.

'Thommo's gone sick and I've been brought in to cover the early shift.'

'That's a bit harsh.'

She shrugged. 'It's how it goes, isn't it? Anyway, no reason why you shouldn't have a drink. Why don't you let me drive you home?'

'That's very good of you, Ann, but I'm not sure you'd fancy Walt's spare bed.'

'I didn't mean I'd stay over. I was thinking I could drop you off, take your car back to mine and then we'll swap them over tomorrow after I've finished my shift.'

'Sounds a bit complicated to me, but it's a plan.'

I was about to put in an order for a glass of bubbly when a hand grabbed my shoulder, and from behind me came a familiar voice. 'Now then, me old cock-bod! I see you've got your wellies on. We off fly-fishing or what? I could've brought me rod if you'd told me.'

'Soapy!' He had the usual jeans on, the red bandanna round

his neck, but instead of the Def Leppard T-shirt he wore a smartly pressed denim shirt. Behind one ear, on Ann's blind side, was a big, fat, hand-rolled ciggy of dubious origin. 'How're you keeping?'

'Middling fair, cock-bod, middling fair.'

'You won't have met Ann,' I said. 'Ann, this is Soapy, he's Algy's – um . . .'

He nodded a greeting, grasped Ann's hand and shook it. I waited for him to let go. 'I'm his right-hand man, sweetheart.' He looked her up and down and said, 'And I reckon you'll be in t'same line as matey here, eh?' He let go of her hand, reached up to remove the cig and slipped it deftly into his breast pocket. 'Tell you what, Mike, she can put the cuffs on me any time she likes. Strip search, you name it.'

'How about a whack round the head with my truncheon, Soapy?'

He ignored my comment and looked at the wellies again. 'So, you're all kitted up for t'main event then?'

'What d'you mean, mate?'

'Why, the old galoshes. All ready for – you know, the going-on at midnight.'

I looked at him blankly.

'You know . . .' He threw his arms in the air. 'Ka-boom!'

I turned to ask Algy what he was on about, but he was already leading Ann to the bar.

'What happens at midnight?'

'Ah, well . . .' Soapy gave me a look I'd seen before, halfway between a wink and a shake of the head. It usually meant he was up to something. 'That's for me to know and you to find out, sunshine.' Then he reached into his jeans and nodded towards the door. 'Just popping outside.' I looked at him blankly.

Funny thing about Soapy: he always seemed a jump ahead of the action. 'Behind t'old bike-sheds, like.' He held a lighter up to my face and flicked it into life.

'Oh, aye. The bike-sheds. Of course.'

'And you'd best chase after your lass before them rugby players find her.'

Ann was in safe hands for now. And if I was going to fight off the attentions of Algy's mates I'd do better with at least one drink inside me. Above the sound of laughter and raised voices I heard the sound of a cork popping, and set off in the general direction. I'd never been to a party quite like this. For a start there was the music. In the first room I passed through he had what you'd call proper party tunes playing, stuff you'd dance to – and Algy's public-school mates were doing their best – but where the drinks were being served, in what he called his drawing room, it was all classical: not what I'd have chosen for a New Year's do, but it seemed to fit in with the floor-length velvet curtains, the gilt-framed portraits, the candy-striped chairs and the farmers' wives sitting around the edge of the room. And it was tuneful: you could say that about it. As for the guests, well, the rugby lot were hogging the bar and I had to fight my way through a scrum to get myself a drink. What a set-up. He had two types of bitter on tap, a cask of lager, a selection of wines, white, red and rosé, and a whole row of ice-buckets, each with a bottle of champagne in it. There was no barman. It was strictly help yourself. I poured a glass and went in search of Ann.

Instead I bumped into Algy once more. 'I say,' he said, 'aren't you the lucky one with that splendid young lady of yours. You must bring her over some time when we can have a more intimate get-together, a dinner party. You moved in with her yet?'

'Steady on, Algy. I've only known her a few weeks.'

'Oh, so you're still living up the hill with the old fellow are you?'

'I am.'

'That's right . . . and I was going to fix you up with a place on the estate. We must have a talk about that.'

'Well, no time like the present, as they say.'

But he was off. Mingling. As Soapy said, back from the bike-sheds now and looking very perky indeed, 'You can't keep his attention for long. He'll be wanting to chat to everyone. He's got all sorts here, you know. You should've seen the invitations he sent out. Millionaires and farm hands. Gamekeepers and poachers. Scarlet women and bishops.'

'Bishops?'

'Aye, he's had one or two of them over here to visit, you know. Reckons he went to a choir school or some such, and them's his old pals. Sounds dead dodgy to me, like, but there you go. Teks all sorts.'

It was indeed a weird and wonderful collection of people. I recognised two local schoolteachers, several farmers from around and about. There was at least one vet, three or four gamekeepers chatting with a fellow I knew for certain did a bit of poaching on the side. There was a lad I'd arrested not so long ago. Drunk in charge of a moving vehicle, which in his case was a bicycle. I never saw a bishop, but I did spot a vicar with a woman who wasn't his wife, according to Soapy, and a lad I knew who burned charcoal up Howsham woods. Then there were a couple of fellows he introduced to me as merchant bankers from Argentina. But I couldn't speak Spanish and they were struggling with Soapy's version of Yorkshire. I was enjoying myself, circulating, but I realised the clock was ticking.

Ann would want to be away soon after midnight. By the time I caught up with her she was trapped in the corner by some sheep farmer, who was bending her ear.

'So I said to t'salesman, I said if a four-wheel drive were good enough for that bugger down the road it'd be good enough for me. I just wanted to know, would it stand up to t'job. Cos I don't want it looking all scruffy and banged about. Oh don't you worry, sir, he says. They're sturdy enough. Why, that paint-work'll stand up to whatever you throw at it. What about sheep shit, I says? Cos I'm a plain talker, me. I don't beat about the bush. Once the sun gets on that stuff, I says, it bakes it. Teks some shifting does sheep shit. Tell you what, I says, I'll tek her on trial for t'weekend, when we round t'flock up for dipping. Course, he weren't having none of that . . . '

Ann needed rescuing, and this was no time for standing on ceremony. 'Last orders for champagne!' I shouted. The old fellow looked at his empty glass. 'I should get yourself over there before they run out,' I said. As he headed for the bar I turned to Ann. 'Enjoying yourself?' I asked.

'I was until our friend there cornered me.'

'So what d'you reckon to this set-up then?'

'Amazing. You got any more contacts on your patch like this?'

'Mmm – none quite in this league. Unless you count the Colonel . . . Anyway' I said, 'let's forget about them for the time being. I was wanting to talk to you about your . . . availability.'

'I beg your pardon! That's no way to talk to a lady.'

'I mean shifts. The way they run we're going to be hard pushed to see much of each other, if you'd like to, of course.'

She gave me an awkward look. 'I'm glad you raised that,' she said, 'because there is a slight – problem.'

'What's that? Not someone else, is there?'

'No no – nothing like that. No, it has to do with work.'

'Go on.'

'The vacant sergeant's post.'

'Yes?'

'I've got it. Temporarily.'

'That's good news, isn't it? Well done you.'

'Well, it's good and it's bad at the same time.' She was looking at me and she seemed to be genuinely upset. 'Think about it. Sergeant Barker.'

'Oh,' I said. 'Right. I see what you mean.'

In the police force they don't encourage officers of different ranks to date each other. It's just not on the cards. If you're duty bound to take orders from a supervising officer, how will it be if you're going out with her? Or him? But of course it happens. It always will. And normally people just keep the relationship under wraps until they know where it's going. Then, if things become serious, one of them will get a move to another station.

'So, what are we to do?' I asked, putting an arm around her shoulders.

She sighed, and leant her head against my chest. 'There's only one thing for it,' she said, looking up at me through half-closed eyes. 'We're going to have to be as cunning as a pair of foxes. Or as cunning as your friend Soapy.'

I liked that. She seemed to be telling me we were in this together. Yes, I liked it very much.

Just then the DJ blasted out a Robbie Williams number. 'C'mon,' I said, 'even I should be able to dance to this.'

'I thought you'd never ask. I love this guy.'

Asking Ann to dance was one thing. Finding space in which to do it was another. We could barely move. Guests of all ages – and all sizes – were moving and shaking in a variety of dance styles going back over the past forty years and more. But no sooner had we got going than the DJ slipped a Kylie Minogue number on, and dispersed the crowd at a stroke.

'This is more like it,' I said. 'Get on down!' For one awful moment I thought Ann was taking me seriously. Then she cracked up.

'Right, Sarge,' I said, 'let's make sure we've got something in our glasses to drink to a great new year.'

Ann looked at her watch. 'We've got fifteen minutes.'

In fact we had even less, because Algy was already going from room to room, ushering people towards the main door. 'Ladies and gentlemen,' he boomed, 'it'll soon be time to see out the old year and welcome in the new. Those of you who have graced the old pile with your presence in previous years' – he rubbed his hands with a schoolboy glee – 'will know I like to see it in with a bit of a bang.'

'What d'you think he's he got planned?' Ann said.

'No idea, but knowing Algy, when he says "bang" he means it. I don't think we'll be disappointed.'

'If you're man enough to brave the elements you can assemble on the lawn, the rest of you – the frail, the sick, the lame . . . the ladies, God bless 'em, well, my advice is not to stand too close to the windows. They're older than any of us, and they might not be up to it.'

'What's it to be then?' Ann said. 'Inside or out?'

'Well, I'm all right; I've got my wellies.'

'Ah, a real old-fashioned gent.' She slipped off her shoes and stuffed them in my jacket pocket, then waited, grinning, while I took my wellies off.

'They're way too big for you,' I argued.

But she was already stepping into them. 'Roomy,' she said. 'But anyway, it won't harm you to get your feet wet.'

Before we got to the door we bumped into Walt, standing on his own with the remains of a meat pie in one hand, a carrier bag in the other and a half-empty champagne bottle sticking out of his trouser pocket. 'Been looking for you all over,' he said.

'I bet you haven't. I bet you and your mates have been stood in the kitchen scoffing them hot game pies of Algy's.'

'Well, seeing as I supplied him wi' pheasants, and t'rabbit – and a haunch of venison . . . '

'Now, Walt, when you say supply . . . '

'Aye well, money did change hands as you might say. Anyway, that doesn't explain where the pair of you've been all night. Canoodling in a corner, I shouldn't be surprised.'

'Walter, do we look like the kind of people who'd canoodle?'

He ignored the question. 'Here,' he said, 'I've a present for you,' and he handed me the bag.

'Oh, me shoes. Walt, if you weren't so bloody ugly I'd kiss you.' I popped them on and we went out onto the drive.

I always said Algy should have been in showbiz. He was a natural. There he was, on the front lawn in his shirt-sleeves, with a deerstalker hat perched on his head. As he walked to and fro, supervising the entertainment, Soapy scuttled after him with a huge umbrella, even though the rain had now stopped and a half moon was shining through the bare branches of the copper beech. It was, of course, fireworks, and he had them all lined up ready to go. But if *they* looked impressive, the centrepiece, when it was wheeled out, brought a gasp from the brave souls who stood there, glasses charged and ready, their breath coming in clouds.

'Is that what I think it is?' Ann said.

'Hellfire. It looks like a bloody howitzer.'

As Algy explained to us, it was in fact a cannon, two or three feet long, mounted on a wooden base with little metal wheels.

'I've heard him talk about this,' I said. 'I thought he was just romancing.'

'Ladies and gentleman, this venerable field-piece dates from the mid-eighteenth century. It never saw any action—'

'But we will, won't we Algy? Before we head for t'lifeboats.'

'You tell 'im, mate!'

'What did you say back there? You want me to start again?'

'Gerron wi' it!'

'As I was saying, it never saw the heat of battle, but it was used in peacetime to start regattas and the like, and, in later years, horse races on the Knavesmire – and, I believe, the Kiplingcotes Derby.'

'That'd get a horse galloping all right.'

'Not if I'd backed it, it wouldn't.'

'Quite so, quite so. Now, I call upon my right-hand man here, Soapy, to hand me my—'

'Balls! That's what you put in a cannon, isn't it?'

'No no – we're saving them for when the Revenue chaps come for the Yorkshire flag here. Soapy will put a fuse in place, ram a small charge of gunpowder up the barrel and tamp it in with his little rod.'

''E told us it were a big 'un!'

'And as the clock strikes midnight we will apply the lighted taper.' He looked around as Soapy did his tamping. He was loving this. 'Time, somebody?'

'Time to light her up and get back indoors! We're bloody freezing here.'

'Ten . . . Nine . . . Eight . . . Seven . . . Six . . .'

Algy held the lighted taper to the fuse. It sparked, then fizzed, casting a pale blue light onto his face.

'Three . . . Two . . . One . . . '

There was a moment's silence, broken by a half-hearted 'Happy New . . .' Then – KA-BOOM! followed by the sound of tinkling glass.

'Ooh 'eck, is that the conservatory?'

'No, it's me bloomin' champagne flute.'

As the smoke cleared, Algy took a bow, and we all linked arms to sing 'Auld Lang Syne', followed by a rendition of 'For He's A Jolly Good Fellow'. Then up went the rockets and everybody ooh-ed and aah-ed before we started to drift back indoors to toast the new year as 'Land of Hope and Glory' belted out from the sound system.

We didn't stay much longer after that. We went to find Algy, to thank him and say goodbye.

'And what did you think of my *piece de resistance*, Mike?'

'Algy, it was spectacular – but I wouldn't have expected anything less. It's been a cracking night.'

'And what are you two hoping for in the new year – as if I couldn't guess?'

'Ah. That'd be telling,' I said.

'I'm asking your good lady, not you.'

'And I'm saying nothing either.' Ann looked at her watch.

'I know,' I said. 'Work in the morning.'

'But before you go,' Algy said, 'weren't we supposed to be having a chat about my little cottage?'

'Aye, you did say something.'

'Well look, why don't you pop by in the week. I've a super little place tucked away in the woods. Suit you down to the ground.' He glanced at Ann and winked at me. 'A proper little love nest.'

By the time we'd got into the car it had started raining again. It was only a few minutes' drive back to Walt's place, but we stopped the car on Leavening Brow. The view from up there is one of my favourites, one of the best in the country if you ask me. All over the valley, in among the twinkling lights of the towns and villages we could see fireworks going off as people celebrated the new year. We got out of the car and stood there in the rain for a minute or two, taking it all in.

'Looks like we have a bit of thinking to do,' I said. 'This promotion caper could put a spanner in the works, couldn't it?'

'Well,' she said, 'there's an old saying.' She got up on her tiptoes and kissed me lightly on the lips. 'Love will find a way.'

Chapter 3

In at the Deep End

You get into some strange situations in this business. We always say anything can happen, and it usually does. The worst of it is, there's always somebody there to witness your most embarrassing moments. There was the time I was photographed crawling across Ganton golf course on my hands and knees looking for – well, that can wait: I dare say I'll tell that story in due course, even though it's an embarrassment to me. Then there was the occasion in Battersea when I nearly fell off a ladder, and this is no word of a lie, when a corpse came back to life. No, that one will have to come later as well. And now I found myself on County Bridge in the middle of Malton, rain sheeting down, clambering over the wall with a piece of chalk in one hand and a six-inch ruler in the other. If this had been London, sure, people would have seen me; but they wouldn't have said a word. They would've just walked on by, absorbed in their own little worlds. They see far stranger things every day of the week, and besides, for Londoners, being curious just isn't cool. In North Yorkshire, on the other hand, the minute you do anything that looks the slightest bit odd, there's going to be somebody there giving a running commentary. That's when the crowd forms.

After several days of heavy rain and strong winds the river was higher than I'd seen it in a long while, and as I lowered myself carefully onto the last bit of bank that was visible above the water an old tree swept past, stripped of its bark and all tangled up with a plastic crate and a knot of straw and weeds. Out in the middle a huge limb from a willow was wedged against the pale stone pier, buffeted this way and that by the force of the water. I'd just reached the water's edge and was leaning forward to draw a horizontal chalk-mark on the buttress.

'Hey, we've enough bloody graffiti around town without you lot scrawling your names on public buildings.'

Sometimes, if you ignore them, they go away. Sometimes they don't.

'I said, we've enough of that – bloody hooligans spray-painting everything in sight.'

I was determined not even to look up. You make eye contact and it's fatal.

'What you up to, any road?'

I put a large number '1' next to the line, offered up my trans-parent plastic ruler, and drew another, six inches above it.

'You're wasting your time, you know. T'water's still rising. You want to be out chasing them muggers and rapists, not drawing bloody diagrams. It'll be washed away by teatime. You see if it isn't.'

As I reached out to write a large '2' my foot slipped and I got a bootful of cold water.

'And you wanna watch them stones too. Right slippery are them. Soon have you in t'river if you aren't careful.'

I carried on chalking, and measuring, and numbering, and finally he got it. 'Ah,' he said, 'I was only saying to my missus this morning I said, they want to be marking t'levels. That's what they want to be doing – then they can see how she's rising. Keep an eye on her.'

There really are advantages to growing older. You learn to take things in your stride. Ten years ago I'd have been up that bank and at his throat. Because he was definitely asking for it. He really did deserve to die. Instead, I carried on chalking.

We'd had floods before in Ryedale. Well, what we called floods. I mean localised events causing minor inconveniences like the odd car that gets stranded when some driver out on a country lane underestimates the depth of a big puddle, and as we help them out we crack that old joke about it only coming halfway up the ducks. Usually it's the waterways that meander over the flat valley between the moors and the wolds, streams and rivers that most people don't even realise are there. Not until we get a proper downpour, that is. Costa Beck, Marrs Beck, the little river Seven and so on. You ask most people and they'll be scratching their heads. They've heard of them, but they can't quite locate them, except for farmers, and fishermen. As for real emergencies, some of the lads remember the various floods in York over the years, although we were never involved with them. The way the TV news covered them you'd think it was a winter sideshow for the visitors who roll up their trouser legs and stand up to their knees in water in the King's Head, down a quick pint, then go home to tell their friends about their big adventure up north. Them Yorkies can cope, we'd say. Especially since they built that huge new barrier back in the early eighties. They'll be fine. Safe as houses. As for our neck of the woods – well, when was the last time we'd had a flood? When had the Derwent properly burst its banks? Some time before the war, they reckoned.

As it happened, I'd had a word of warning from an old boy I

met up at Walter's one afternoon when this current wet spell had just started. His name was Arnold. He was an old River Board man, used to work along the Derwent. He'd retired to Leavening, and liked to stroll up the hill to Walt's place to chew the cud over a pot of tea. I don't know how we got on to talking about the river, but once he started he was away. 'It's a right mess,' he said. 'And I'm sorry to tell you it were us lads as started it. On t'Board, must've been thirty years ago. Before we started meddling, it meandered all over. There was water meadows, shallows, boggy patches, little ponds. And waterfowl galore. You'd get a wet spell and it'd change course. Then another one and it'd go back to where it was before. The Derwent, d'you see, it were like a great big sponge that absorbed the rain and then let it back out nice and steady. You never got no rush of water roaring through Kirkham and such places every time there was a downpour. Then somebody had a bright idea. What if we straightened her out, and dredged her? Mek a canal of it. Well, what it meant was, with all t'water draining off the hills this new river carried it downstream all the faster. We've been lucky, last thirty, forty years. Never had no proper wet years. But back before the war there was a hell of a flood. Thirty-one, I think it were. You go to County Bridge on t'Malton side, you'll see they've got the levels all etched in stone. And the date.'

As the rain kept falling I picked up on an air of disquiet as I went out on my rounds. I heard country people grumbling about the rising water table, about good land being eroded, about livestock getting foot rot. At first I joked about it. Why, I said, you farmers, you're always moaning. Last year it was drought. Next year it'll be sommat else. But with no let-up in the weather we all started to take these warnings seriously. I was coming to work on an afternoon turn, and I'd stopped in Castlegate to get a newspaper. I had a bit of time in hand so I decided to take a walk down to County Bridge and see what was happening. I actually stopped at the bottom of Sheepsfoot Hill and looked at the historic marker old Arnold mentioned. He was right with his dates. There were two high-water marks there, carved in stone; the lower one from 1878, the other, just a couple of inches above it, dated 7 September 1931. As to the river, a quick glance told me it was rising – rapidly. I walked over the bridge towards the level crossing and stood there, right opposite the signal box, and watched the waters swirling past, flooding the riverside park and gradually encroaching onto the little wooded island that stands midstream. And still the rain kept falling. Later that day the inspector called me back from my rounds and told me to take another look around town. I was shocked to find quite a crowd of people gathered on the bridge, and the press, and a lad from Radio York. The entire riverside area was under water, and it only needed another foot or two before it would be spilling into Blackboards, the road that runs parallel to the railway. From there it would soon be on the line itself.

There was a CCTV camera that overlooked the crossing, and at a pinch it could be manoeuvred to face the foot of the bridge. If I could make a few marks on the stonework we'd at least have an idea as to how fast the water was rising. That was my thinking, anyway, and that's what had taken me down there with my little ruler and my chalk, to the delight of my heckler friend.

'Aye,' I said to him as I stepped back over the wall, waggling my piece of chalk, 'this is the new low-tech police force, making your Council Tax go further than ever.'

While he chewed that over I got on the radio to the station. 'See if you can swivel that camera round to face the bridge, will you?'

'*I already did.*'

'And what did you see?'

'*Some plonker in a pair of wellies defacing public property.*'

'Yeah yeah yeah. What about me marks? Can you see them?'

'*We can indeed.*'

We now had a reference point. It was a step in the right direction. The fact is that with no recent experience of flooding, we had no master plan in place. We had schemes for dealing with civil unrest, with pestilence, with war – nuclear or conventional – or with a major event like a train crash, an explosion or a chemical spillage. But flooding? Nowt. We were staring disaster in the face and we hadn't a clue as to how we were going to handle it. For years we'd been more preoccupied with drought.

'But hey,' I said to the desk sergeant, when I got back to the station, 'this is Yorkshire. We'll figure it out.' Optimistic, you see. You have to be in this job.

As afternoon turned to evening it became a very quiet shift – out on our patch, that is. Too wet for villains, was the general opinion. At the station you could hardly move for bodies. There were five of us on duty, as I recall, plus Chris Cocks on the desk and the inspector prowling up and down, and one by one all of us beat officers found our way back to base with our various stories of flooded fields, rising waters, and people preparing for the worst. I'd had another look around at the bridge, tying to work out which properties were the most vulnerable. I wasn't short of advice, as a steady stream of sightseers and worried local residents came to see what was happening. 'It'll be them old folk,' someone said to me, pointing to the flats that looked onto the river just below the bridge. I could see they were probably right, but I wasn't convinced we needed to evacuate anyone just yet. Besides, we had no provision for evacuees, nowhere to take them. We'd be hoping that most of them had relatives or friends nearby.

Later that shift when I took another tour around my patch in the Daihatsu four-track, what I called the Puddle Hopper, the inspector decided he'd come with me. Not everyone rated Inspector Finch. He was a peacemaker, and a peace-lover. His attitude was that if one of his officers got into a row with another one he'd leave them alone to sort it out themselves rather than try to get to the bottom of it. I was OK with that. If someone starts to get up my nose I know how to deal with it. I tell 'em. Not aggressively, just a quiet word. And a firm one. But it seems that's the old way now. The new way is to get everyone together, drag in one of their volunteer counsellors and have what we politely call a beanbag session. The trouble with Inspector Finch – Birdie to the lads – was that he was happy with life. He was born and bred in Ryedale, had family all over North Yorkshire, and had done well in the force. He knew he wasn't going to rise any higher, much as he'd like to, because there was no way he was ever going to leave the area.

Out on the road we soon saw that things were deteriorating. We hadn't got far along the Pickering road when we hit standing water at Howe Bridge where the Rye had burst its banks. 'Won't be long before the cars are struggling to get through this lot,' I said. Birdie agreed. 'Let's get on to Highways and tell them we needed signage and diversionary routes put in place,' he said. Then he had a think and added, 'Y'know, Mike, we need to sort out some kind of co-ordinated flood control centre. Either at the police station or at the council. This could get serious. I mean, there's a lot more water to come down off the hills yet.'

As we made our way back towards town we saw a huge area

of farmland under water. Here and there cows and sheep were making their way to higher ground. At one stage we had to manoeuvre our way past a miniature lake where a beck had spilled over onto the carriageway; further on we found water bursting up from an overladen drain. In one or two places there were jagged cracks in the road surface where the pressure of water coming up from long-dormant springs had burst through the tarmac. Back in town there was water gathering at the bottom of Sheepsfoot Hill, and for the first time, as we went to cross the river, we splashed through an inch or two on the road. And still it rained, and still the river kept rising.

'I don't think we've ever had anything like this,' Birdie said. 'I tell you what,' – we were parked up outside a row of low-lying houses facing the railway crossing, and through the open window we could hear the church clock strike eight – 'I'm going to call the night shift out. I can see us doing a few emergency evacuations before long. These'll be well in the firing line, don't you reckon?'

I did. The rate at which the water was rising was now alarming. The river had already swallowed up two of my chalk-marks and was lapping at the third. 'Looks like a case of all hands to the pump,' I said.

'Aye, and you lads won't be going home at ten either,' Birdie added as we swung round and splashed our way back through town to the station. 'It'll be twelve hours all round, and cancel your rest days.'

Back at the station people were starting to ring in, frightened by the rising water levels, asking about sandbags. While we handled the calls, Birdie deliberated over his next move. For the next four hours we were going to be mob-handed. We'd have ten officers available, plus the fire brigade, who'd called out their part-timers, and their volunteers. If we were going to make a real difference, now was the time to get stuck in.

By the time the night shift showed up the rain was easing slightly, but of course the river would keep rising for a good twelve hours yet, maybe longer, and the news from the Environment Agency wasn't good.

'Can you believe it?' Chris Cocks had been on the phone to them. 'They're trying to get the sluice open at the top end of the Derwent, get some of the water away to the coast through Scawby Cut, right?' We waited. 'But guess what?' he said.

'Er – the bloke with the keys is having a week off?' Ed said.

'What are you, psychic?'

'No, but I can read your mind, Cocks. And the look on your face.'

'Well, you're close enough. He's not at work and they can't get hold of him.'

He was interrupted by Birdie, who was getting everyone together in the parade room for a briefing. It was quite plain that he viewed this as a serious situation. 'Not good' was the phrase he used. 'The water levels haven't been this high for as long as anyone can remember, and we have no emergency plans in place. So we're setting up a flood control scheme with the council, and the superintendent is on his way in. I want you to get out there and do two things. First, patrol your communities and reassure people as well as you can. Second, report back to flood control with what you find. We need to know what the situation is out there, and only you can tell us.' He looked around at us and paused. There really was a sort of wartime, backs-to-the-wall feel about it. 'All right, ladies and gents, we will disperse when I've said one more thing. Do not get your vehicles stuck. If the water looks too deep, stay where you are and give Mike a shout. He has the four-wheel drive. We're trying to get the other one over from Helmsley just in case.' With that we were dismissed, and sent out to save Ryedale from the rising waters. In pairs. All except me: I was on my Jack Jones.

It wasn't long before the first proper emergency overtook us. It was, as we'd expected, the old people's flats near the bridge, and I was already kicking myself that we hadn't acted earlier. I shot down there to see what I could do. The problem was the four or five ground-floor flats nearest the river. The water had already got into the parking area and was now inching up towards the downstairs windows. I got on the radio.

'1015 to flood control.'

'*Yes, Mike.*'

'I'm at the flats, bottom of Castlegate. We need to get these people, out, sharpish. I'm standing in a foot of water right now.'

'*Are you on your own?*'

'Yep – spare man. Everyone else is paired up.'

'*Right, I'm sending Ed down to join you. We'll get the fire brigade on the case as well. Ambulance?*'

'Aye, get them too. Some of these folk might be distressed – bugger!' A council lorry loaded with sandbags roared past, sending out a tidal wave that broke over the top of my boots. I took my wellie off and tipped the water out of it. I was still wringing the sock out when Ed showed up.

'Right, buddy. Where we going to start?'

'Well,' I said, as I leant on the first doorbell, 'I'll wake 'em up. 'You carry 'em out.'

'I'll carry the good-looking ones.'

I rang the bell again. The place was still in darkness. Finally an upstairs window opened and there was a white-haired lady leaning out.

'Ooh my goodness.' She was looking right past us at the streetlights, their orange glow reflected in the still water. 'Have we to abandon ship?'

'I'm afraid so, madam.'

'You sure? The rain seems to be stopping now.'

'Aye, it is, but they reckon the river'll keep coming for a few hours yet. And there's heavy showers forecast.'

'Just let me make myself decent and I'll come right down and let you in.'

She closed the window and disappeared. We waited, me with one foot drenched and the other one freezing cold. She seemed to be taking an age. 'Come on,' Ed said. 'What's up with her?'

'All right for you, mate,' I said. 'At least you've got dry feet. I've had them bloody cowboy sandbag merchants roaring past. Straight into me wellies. It's waders tomorrow for me, I'm telling you.'

Finally, the door opened and there she was in her dressing gown. 'I've got the kettle on,' she said. 'You look as though you could do with a drink.'

'Matter of fact,' I said, 'we've been supping tea all night. I'd like to use your toilet if that's OK.'

As we went inside she said, 'I thought I'd be all right, being upstairs. Are you sure we have to get out?'

'I'm afraid so, love. The electrics, you see . . . Any time now you could be without power and heating, and then you really would be in a pickle.'

'Well, can you give me a few minutes to get dressed?'

'Course we can. Can't have you trailing about the streets of Malton in your nightie now, can we?'

She packed some clothes while we knocked on the rest of

the doors. There must have been getting on for twenty in all.

'Where are you taking us?'

'Good question,' Ed said. 'You can go home with Constable Pannett here – but only if you promise to behave.'

'Ooh, I haven't had an offer like that in quite some while.'

'Now then, what have you got? Dry clothes, sommat warm?'

'Aye, there's me new winter coat I got for Christmas.'

'Packed something to read?'

'Oh, that's an idea. I'll fetch the book off my bedside table.'

'Glasses – you'll want them too, won't you? And before we set off, is there anybody you ought to be ringing?'

'I'll call me daughter.'

'Oh, and is there any medication you need to take?'

'I have that right here in my sponge-bag, look. I wish you knew where you were taking us.'

That was the big worry. So far all we could do was ferry them to the police station. But first we had to get them across the car park, which was under a foot or more of water.

'Oh, I'll never get across there.'

'No, you won't,' said Ed, 'but my mate here's kindly volunteered to carry you.'

The old lady looked like a startled rabbit. 'You aren't going to do one of them fireman's lifts, are you? I've never liked the look of them.'

'No, it's not very dignified, is it? Still, you're nice and light.' I scooped her up in my arms and carried her across to the Daihatsu. 'Ooh,' she giggled, 'it's been a long time since I was swept off my feet by a handsome young man. Wait till my daughter hears about this.'

All this time her next-door neighbour had been watching from upstairs.

'You needn't think I'll consent to that,' she said. 'Carting her off like a sack of taties. 'Tisn't right, not at our age. You go and rescue those that want rescuing. I'm nice and dry up here, thank you very much.'

I soon got her down. I put it to her that her friend would be miserable on her own. 'She'll only worry about you,' I said. 'And what'll you do if the lights go out? We may be forced to take you out then, and the water could be even higher. You'll have to swim across the car park. Now come on, and we'll carry you. I'll give you a piggyback if you like.'

'Every time you open your mouth you talk yourself into trouble, you do,' Ed said as we waited for her to pack up her things and find her way downstairs.

'How d'you mean?'

'Have you seen the size of her?'

He was right. When this lady talked about being carted around like a sack of spuds she wasn't far off the mark.

It was one o'clock by now, and I was starting to wilt. Back at the office I hung my socks on the radiator. They might not dry, but at least they'd be warm.

'You should be off home,' Birdie said when he came through to find me supping a mug of hot chocolate.

'I will be, sir, just as soon as I know we've done all we can.' That's the thing with this job. You don't just do your eight hours – or twelve – and call it a day. You do what has to be done, regardless of how long it takes. You're trained for emergencies. The public are relying on you. Besides, you have to balance times like these against the days when you'll come to work and find there's not much doing. Swings and roundabouts. Good days and bad.

* * *

It must've been about an hour later that the decision was made. This was now, officially, a major incident. A major incident can be called by any of the emergency services. It basically means that due to the risk of death or harm to a substantial number of people, or of people being made homeless, there is a clear need for special measures. That was all very well, but as yet there was still no emergency plan, and we knew it. We were batting blind, playing it by ear. We got onto the council, and they called out their planners and environmental officers. We were lucky here, having their offices right next door to us. As the cars started arriving and the lights of Ryedale House came on one by one, I popped across to see what they were up to. I found a bunch of bleary-eyed staff in casual dress, some of them pulling maps out of filing cabinets and opening fat folders while others got on the phone to talk to the emergency services. You have to hand it to them: they didn't hang about. Within an hour of them showing up we had a flood hotline, a number people could use to contact us if they were in trouble or could offer help. While that went out on local radio the inspector assembled an emergency planning team in the council offices. The flood control centre was going to run twenty-four hours a day. There was one of our officers manning the police radio, there were the Environmental Agency, emergency planners and housing officers, as well as the fire brigade, ambulance and highways staff. At the same time senior police officers, including our superintendent, met with the relevant partner agencies to set the strategy and oversee contingency planning. They were soon in contact with their opposite numbers in York, where flooding was a regular problem. It was a start, but we knew it was still a wing and a prayer job for us.

I finally left the station just as the early shift were coming in, and by the time I got up to Walt's day was breaking. It was hard to imagine, up on the hill there, that things were so bad down in the valley. The clouds had blown away, the moon was still just visible against a pale blue sky, and the rooks were starting to argue up in the sycamores. Walt was up and about offering me tea and sympathy.

'Oh hell,' I said, wringing out my thick fisherman's socks for a third time and spreading them across the stove, 'I don't think I want another cuppa till about next Thursday. No, I need to get myself off to bed.'

'What time you up?'

'Half ten, eleven. I'm back in at twelve.'

'I'll have some breakfast ready for you, lad.'

'That'll be great.'

I grabbed a few hours' sleep, wolfed down my grub and was back at work for midday. This time I was prepared, waddling into the station in my waders, much to the amusement of my fellow officers. The first thing I noticed was that they'd managed to move on all the pensioners and other people who'd been evacuated during the night. Some had been taken to Ryedale House, but the majority of them had been taken in by relatives and friends.

When Birdie briefed us he had good news and bad news. The good news was that with flood control up and running and several more officers drafted in from around the region, we had a full-time canteen on the go at Ryedale House. Yes, it was set up to feed the evacuees and emergency staff, but we knew we wouldn't be turned away. Even better, it was free. The bad news was that the river was still on the rise, and now we were under attack, so to speak, on both sides of town. In Old Malton it had overflowed just a few hundred yards from the station, right by the old abbey. The Environment Agency were on the case now. Another foot, they told us, and we'd be evacuating people from the cottages that backed onto the river down there. 'So,' said Birdie, 'we're on standby for that.' There was one other bit of news. Ben Blackstone, a sergeant on another shift, had been flooded out of his house in Church Street, right next to the level crossing. He'd taken his family to stay with relatives and come to work as normal. 'There's nothing I can do at home,' he said. 'The damage is done.'

Over a cup of tea we put the telly on to get the latest news. Down in Norton the railway line was now under water. The trains had long since stopped, and they showed a dramatic shot across a sea of water, with the station manager standing on the platform and leaning on a broom. With a flight of seagulls wheeling above the roof he looked like a harbourmaster waiting for a boat to come into port.

We settled into a pattern now: twelve-hour shifts, no rest days, and all leave cancelled. At first it had all seemed like a bit of local excitement. The adrenaline had seen us through those first few hours as the river rose and we started to realise what we were in for. Now we felt we were likely to be overwhelmed at any moment. It was like being under siege. As we evacuated one lot of people we'd get a call to say that water was bursting up in someone else's backyard. At first it was all a bit puzzling. Some of these properties were well above the floodline. Then I went down to the newsagent in Castlegate and there, across the road, was a house with its letterbox right at the bottom of the front door, just above the front step. The flap was sticking straight out and a stream of water was gushing through it, forming a graceful arc across the pavement. It reminded me of those gargoyles you see on old churches, the ones that spew water out of their mouths every time there's a storm. I could see what was happening now. All the time we were watching the river, the rain and run-off had been seeping into the higher ground and now it was as if the waters of the deep were opened. Long-forgotten springs that had been dormant for a hundred years were bursting out from the sodden earth.

We were firefighting now, dashing here and there to respond to emergency calls, getting around as well as we could to gather information about who was under threat, who was stranded, who was cut off. While the Derwent continued to rise, its tributary streams were running fuller by the hour, and backing up. As more run-off cascaded down from the moors there was nowhere for it to go. It was the water flowing in from a swollen Costa Beck that had caused the Rye to spill out onto the main Pickering road at Howe Bridge. Next it was Hovingham, where Marrs Beck was seeping into back kitchens and outhouses. I was just about to set off and see what I could do for them when I got a call from the Malt Shovel. Both they and the Worsley Arms were flooded out, and so was the village shop. I grabbed a few boxes of teabags, some Max-Pak coffees, a carton of milk, and delivered them to the village hall where the locals were doing what they could for the victims. I'll always remember how grateful they were; and I'll always remember reflecting on all the bad things I'd said about the much-maligned Puddle Hopper. It had got me through where an ordinary car would have failed me.

By the time I got back to town the river had finally cut Norton off from Malton. You could no longer get a car across. Halfway down towards the bridge a small crowd had gathered.

'Now then,' I said, as I got out of the Puddle Hopper. 'What's happening?'

And there was Nick the gamekeeper in his waders and deer-stalker, grinning at me. 'Why, we're waiting for the ferry service.'

'Ferry? What you on about?'

He took his cigarette out of his mouth and pointed towards the bridge. 'Here she comes now.'

And there was a big blue tractor nosing its way through the water, pushing a bow-wave ahead of it as it came around the bend. Behind it was a sturdy red trailer, and in the trailer were a dozen or so passengers in rain hats and flat caps.

'That's a hell of an idea,' I said. 'Who's put that on?'

'Yates's, mate. Started it up this morning. Been to-ing and fro-ing since about ten o'clock. Doing a roaring trade.'

'Trade? They're never charging folk, are they?'

He shook his head. 'No, but I tell you what, they ought to be. Most of them riding on that wagon, why, they've no intention of going to the shops. They're there for the crack.'

He was right. When the tractor pulled into the supermarket car park half the passengers stayed on board. There were old fellows smoking pipes and telling the tale, a couple of women with Thermos flasks. It was like a charabanc outing. They'd even got a row of straw bales each side to make seats. One of the lads was supping beer. He'd come out from the Derwent Arms and hopped aboard with a pint pot in his hand. When the half dozen or so genuine shoppers had got off I climbed aboard – and there was Walt.

'Budge up,' I said, squatting next to him.

'By, I thought we wouldn't have to wait long before you showed up,' he said. 'Come to keep an eye on things, I suppose.'

'It's a Health and Safety issue,' I said. 'Needs the strong arm of the law, a situation like this.'

'How's that then? Do we need safety belts or sommat?'

'No, but this lot . . . ' I patted the straw. 'Needs watching, does this stuff. Big fire hazard.'

'Go on with you,' he laughed, 'you're just wanting to ride across the river.'

He was right, but I wasn't going to tell him. 'Anyway,' I said, 'never mind me. What are you up to?'

'Me?' he said. 'I'm offering my services.'

'You sure you don't need a licence for that?'

'You never know when they might need a helping hand, lad. I mean, there might just be some damsel wants rescuing from her bedroom . . .'

'You've missed the boat where that's concerned, Walt. I spent most of last night carting distressed females across the car park.'

'Did you now?'

'Aye, and they were in their nightwear too. How does that grab you?'

The driver was back on board now after helping the next lot of passengers climb up with their shopping bags. 'Any more for the *Skylark*?' he shouted. 'Right then, gentlemen hang on to your lifebelts, and ladies, grab hold of a gentleman – if you can find one among this rabble. Next stop the Derwent Arms.'

I leaned across to the lad with the pint pot and said, 'Aye, and I think you should go back in with that, don't you?'

We hit the water well before we got to the bottom of the road. As we swung right towards the bridge one of the passengers let out a gasp. Only the middle third or so of the bridge was showing above the water. Below us the islands were now almost completely submerged, and when we got to the far side the water stretched a good seventy or eighty yards up the street. The garage forecourt was a lake. The glass front of the showroom was perfectly reflected in two and a half feet of still water. Right up as far as the post office, almost to the public baths, was awash. It was a mess, and a lot of people were going to need a lot of help.

We pulled up outside the pub, as advertised. 'Right,' said Walt, 'I'll see you later. I'm off to ride t'other conveyance yonder.' He pointed across to the far side of the car park, from where there emerged a second tractor, also pulling a trailer – and at the wheel, wearing a vintage flying jacket, a pair of goggles and a white silk scarf, was Algy.

He seemed delighted to see me. 'I say, old bean. Can we offer you a trip across the river in our superior conveyance?' He pulled a red lollipop from his pocket and handed it to me. 'With free in-flight snacks?'

'Algy,' I said, 'what the bloody hell are you up to?'

'Spirit of Dunkirk, old boy. We may have our backs to the wall, we may be hemmed in by rising waters, but do we panic like the French? No. Do we run like the Italians? No. Do we mobilise our entire armed forces and call out the marching bands like our American allies? No, by Jove, we grit our teeth and set our faces against a sea of troubles, like true Brits. Algernon is here to fly the flag. For Harry, England and St George!' He lowered his voice and leaned towards me. 'And to make sure that when the press come with their cameras they know that these are Yorkshiremen standing proud against the tide. By the way, what do you think of the jacket? It's the real thing, y'know. They issued them to Spitfire pilots. Cost me a packet, I can tell you.' Saying which, he delved into one of its pockets and pulled out his white rose flag.

'Algy,' I said, 'I've been wearing these glasses since I was a nipper. And you know why?'

'I'm making a shrewd guess, Michael, m'boy.'

'I reckon you are. Cos my eyesight's not so hot.' I took them off and put them in my top pocket. 'Now, I haven't seen any flag. And I don't intend to. But I will accept a ride back across the river if you're heading that way.'

And off we went, with Walt in the back entertaining the old ladies, and Algy at the helm. As we pulled up in the supermarket car park and I climbed down from the trailer he said, 'Oh by the way, you remember that cottage I mentioned?'

'I do. I have high hopes of it.'

'Well, I think it's time you started packing up your effects and ordering the pantechnicon. My tenant has flitted.'

'Well, hadn't I better have a look at it first, Algy?'

'Quite so, quite so. Just swan by some time that suits and we'll give it the once over, eh?'

Back at the station I was chewing the cud with Chris Cocks when Birdie came in. He had news for us. We were about to be visited by a representative of Her Majesty's Government.

'Who's that?' I asked.

He took a deep breath. 'None other than the Deputy Prime Minister.'

'Two Jags? Coming here?'

'His name, Sergeant Cocks, is Prescott. Mr Prescott to you and me.'

'Yes sir – absolutely.'

'And you, Mike, are going to show him round. Let him see what the situation is and how we're coping. He'll be here tomorrow morning. Ten o'clock.'

'Right sir.'

'So, no need to tell you that we will be smart. Freshly pressed uniform. Nice close shave . . .'

'Maybe a drop of cologne?' said Chris. 'He still stinks of river water sir.'

'And talking of rivers, Mike.'

'Yes sir?'

'We will wear shoes. Nicely polished uniform shoes. Not wellies, and not waders. Got that?'

'Yes sir.'

'And your vehicle will be spotless.'

I came on duty at eight o'clock next day. I'd stayed late the night before giving the Puddle Hopper a thorough cleaning, and I'd been up at six ironing my shirt, polishing my shoes and scrubbing the muck off my wellies. Because, despite what Birdie had said, there was no way I was setting off on a tour of my patch without a pair of waterproof boots to hand, government dignitary or not.

It was quiet around the station. I don't know if everyone was keeping out of the way or if they were cruising their various beats. So when Chris took a phone call from a lady out at Nunnington who said she was stranded by flood water he had nobody but me to call on.

'Chris,' I said, 'I've got the Deputy bloody Prime Minister coming by in an hour and a half. Nunnington's way over yon side of Hovingham. Can't you get anyone else?'

'I've tried 'em all, matey. Ed's at an R.T.A. on the A64. Jayne's had to go to court in Scarborough, Ed's pulling drowned sheep out of a ditch at Foxholes. So that leaves you.'

'Great.' I got in the sparkly clean Puddle Hopper and set off on the Helmsley road. I hadn't got past Swinton when I got stuck behind a tractor that sprayed me with mucky water and kept flicking clods of earth onto my windscreen. At Appleton le Street I had to drive through a puddle a foot deep and fifteen yards long, and at Slingsby I had a sugar-beet lorry coming the other way, well over the speed limit, spraying me with mud as it hurtled past a flooded gateway. I was on the radio to Chris, giving him grief, when I hit the standing water at Hovingham. 'What is it?' he asked.

'Whatever it was, Chris, it's too late now. I give up. I really do.'

The lady at Nunnington was distraught. There she was, in two feet of water, sobbing her heart out. I could see where she was coming from and was totally on her side, until she told me what had happened. 'I saw it was flooded, but this tractor went through and it didn't look very deep, and I was so worried.'

'What were you worried about, love?' I was still standing on dry ground at this stage, deciding whether I could get through with my wellies or whether to roll my trousers up and do it barefoot. I was imagining at the very least she'd lost a dog, or a child, or her house was on fire.

'Well,' she sniffed, 'I have a hair appointment and if I'm late it'll be another three days till Nigel can fit me in and it's our girls' night out in York tonight, and . . . ' She was about to burst into tears and for an awful moment I thought I was too. An hour ago I was all spruced up for a royal visitation, well ahead of the clock, and everything tickety-boo. Well, I was buggered if I was going to wade through two feet of muddy water to rescue her. I gunned the Daihatsu's engine, kept the revs high, and backed it slowly up to her car. 'Right now, you slip your shoes off and hop across,' I shouted above the roar of the engine.

'But I'll get my feet all wet.' From the look on her face you'd have thought I'd just asked her to swim through an alligator-infested swamp in full combat gear.

'Well,' I said, pressing my foot down on the accelerator – if the water gets up my exhaust that'll be two of us stranded – 'try and think of it as an adventure, something to tell the girls on your night out, eh?'

She didn't answer, and by this time I too was lost for words. The water – foul, smelly and icy cold – was seeping into the footwell and lapping at the bottom of my newly pressed trousers.

You try not to be old-fashioned or patronising when dealing with women – but in the end, somehow, they always appeal to your sense of what a gentleman is. Yes, I admit it. As the tears ran down her cheeks I got out. Yes, I stepped into two and a half feet of foul water, and yes, I carried her the whole four feet from her car to mine. And I'm ashamed to say that I even agreed with her that it was truly, truly tragic that she would miss her hair appointment and have to go on the Micklegate run with her mates looking like an absolute dog.

I wasn't late for the Deputy Prime Minister, but I was far from calm when I arrived back at the station. It was a quarter to ten and Birdie was pacing up and down looking at his watch. 'Where the hell have you been?' he asked me as I stepped out of the Daihatsu in my bare feet. 'And what the bloody hell have you been doing to get the vehicle in that state? And – for God's sake, look at you!'

I turned away from him and reached into the back seat. 'Ah, but look at these, sir,' I said, holding up my shiny black shoes. 'How about them?'

Birdie knew where I'd been, OK. Chris had explained to him. And I kept quiet about the daft girl with her hair appointment. As soon as I mentioned the three magic words 'woman' 'alone' and 'stranded' he calmed down. He's very old-school, is Birdie. And in any case he didn't get the chance to say anything more, because at that moment Prezza's car arrived. I just had time to slip the shoes onto my bare feet as he stepped out, flanked by two Close Protection Officers.

Funny thing about important people. Deep down you know they're no different from anybody else, but no matter how much you tell yourself that you're as good as they are, it gets to you.

As I stood there waiting to be introduced I kept thinking to myself, 'Don't call him Two Jags, call him Mr Prescott . . . don't call him Two Jags, call him Mr Prescott . . . .'

Birdie was speaking ' . . . And this is PC Mike Pannett who'll be showing you round the area, sir.'

He held out his hand. 'Now then officer.'

I held out mine. 'Now then John.' Out of the corner of my eye I could see Birdie's eyes widen, but before he could say anything my mate John had taken control.

'Right then, let's crack on, shall we? You must have a lot to show me.'

I can only say that the man was courteous, intelligent and above all concerned about the plight of the people who had been made homeless, or were otherwise suffering, as a result of the floods. I took him down to Yates's hardware store, I took him down to the bridge where he met both ferry operators and talked at length to residents and to the press, and promised that the government would help in any way it could. And then I took him out into the country and showed him some of the practical problems we were having to deal with, as when I pulled up on the Pickering road to show him a couple of dozen sheep that'd got caught in the rising water and drowned, their fleeces waterlogged. And when it was over he thanked me and shook my hand.

The real emergency lasted four, maybe five days. The river reached a peak a good foot above the previous record before it slowly subsided, leaving a lot of mud, a lot of stranded vehicles and a number of temporarily homeless people. I spent most of my time now going around the villages on my patch, 'flying the flag' as the inspector put it. There were no further evacuations, but we needed to reassure the public that we were on the case, and that they could count on us. And we doled out advice, reminding people to wash their hands and feet thoroughly after they'd waded through flood water. They were all alert to the perils of sewage escaping into the waterways, but very few were aware of the dangers from Weil's disease, released into the water from rats' urine and posing a deadly threat. So we had a public-health role to play, as well as our routine policing. It was a good feeling, going from village to village, calling in at isolated farmhouses, asking people if we could do anything to help. It reinforced that sense I've referred to before, about being part of a community, all pulling together. Some days I found myself able to assist people in a very practical way, helping them remove sodden carpets from their houses, or setting up hot-air blowers as they made a start on drying out. And when the residents of the riverside flats moved back in I made a point of going down to see that they were all right. They'd all found temporary accommodation with family or friends in the area, which in itself reflected the close-knit community we police in North Yorkshire. And what impressed me was that during the entire period of the emergency, for a week or ten days, despite scores, maybe hundreds of properties standing empty and unguarded, we didn't have a single burglary reported.

A week later, as the firemen hosed down the pavements in Malton and Norton, the newshounds went back to where they'd come from, and the people who had ridden the trailers to and fro across the river found other things to do with their time, I finally had a day off. I got up late, had a pot of tea, and went down to Yates's to buy some new wellie socks. Someone had found the old ones drying out on the radiator at work and slung them in the bin. After I'd finished in there, and got a haircut in a little place up

Savile Street, I decided to have a quiet lunchtime pint and a bite of grub. I'd forgotten it was market day. The Spotted Cow was heaving, but there was Walt shuffling along his seat to make room for me.

'Now then,' I said. Here was an opportunity I'd been waiting for. 'Walt,' I said as I sat down next to him, 'I doubt I'll ever be able to pay you properly for what you've done these last few months.'

'Aye, go on then.' He handed me his empty glass. 'Reckon I've time for another.'

'That's not what I had in mind,' I said, but of course I had no option. When I brought him his refill I started again.

'No,' I said, 'not many people would've done what you did, putting me up, feeding me – aye, and entertaining me by your fireside on a night.'

'Why,' he said, 'anybody with a heart would've taken pity on you. But I s'pose you're going to tell me you're moving in with that lass I met at the New Year's do, am I right?'

'Steady on, mate. We've hardly got to know each other yet. When she finds out the truth about me she might have second thoughts, y'know.'

'Now you're talking sense.'

'No, I've started to look for a place to rent – and Algy says he might be able to help.'

'I see.'

'So I may be getting out of your hair before long.'

'Ah. Right you are then.'

I left it at that. I couldn't read his thoughts. I'd imagined he'd be glad to see me moving on. Now I wasn't sure.

Chapter 4

A Moving Experience

If you weren't looking for it you'd never know Keeper's Cottage was there. It's just down the hill from Walt's place, barely five minutes' walk from Leavening and the Jolly Farmers, but tucked away, deep in the woods. Even most of the locals were unaware of it, according to Algy, and I certainly was. When the trees were bare, as they were that balmy afternoon in March when he first took me to see it, you could just about make the place out if you crouched down and peered between the lower limbs. Once they came into leaf, as they would within a month or two, and once the fringe of cow parsley came into flower, it was going to be completely secluded.

There was a long track leading up to it, stony and full of potholes, with a larch wood to one side and a mixture of mature, broad-leaved trees to the other. I saw oak and sycamore, the red buds of a linden, the black of the ash, and a couple of wild cherries looking as though they only needed a few more warm days to burst into bloom. It was the sort of wood you don't see so much these days, sort of old and neglected, but very much loved by those who have the good fortune to know them. Under the trees were the remnants of the year's snowdrops, with a scattering of wood anemones starting to poke through the carpet of dead leaves.

The house I was going to rent stood in a clearing, about a quarter of an acre of rough grass with a few scattered shrubs and a thicket of gooseberry bushes tucked away in a corner. To one side was a dyke, full of water but half buried under a tangle of elder and blackberry. Along the far end of the plot, right outside the back door, ran a little beck, and beyond that was a thorn hedge and a grass field dotted with dead thistles and the odd patch of nettles. Away in the distance, where it sloped towards another wood, was a rabbit warren. I wondered whether Walt ever got over that way with his shotgun. I'd have to ask him.

The cottage itself was painted white. It had a red pantiled roof – well, two separate pitched roofs in fact, with a valley between them. According to Algy, it used to be a pair of bothies – estate workers' dwellings – built in about 1800, possibly earlier. Each of them had been a one-up one-down affair, but at some time during the last hundred years or so they'd been knocked through to make a place for the estate's gamekeeper and his family. An old lean-to scullery or wash-house had been incorporated as a kitchen, and what had once been a coalhouse had been converted to form a downstairs bathroom. To one side of the drive was an old asbestos-roofed garage with a crooked up-and-over door at one end and a broken window at the other.

Inside the house were a living room and a dining room, each with a bedroom above, both of which had its own staircase, steep and narrow, with an old-fashioned door at the bottom, like you'd find on a pantry or an understairs cupboard. 'I like it,' I said, as Algy showed me around the place. We were standing in what he called the master bedroom, although as far as I could see it was no different from the other one. 'But there's a problem, isn't there?'

'What do you mean, old chap?'

'Well, how am I supposed to get my bed and so on up here?' Looking at the size of the room – and the sharp turn halfway up the staircase – I was wondering whether any of my stuff would fit. I had quite a few items stashed at my sister's place.

'Ah, see what you mean,' said Algy, looking around as if he'd never noticed how cramped it was. 'Well, you want to do what the chappy who was here before did. He managed rather well. Got himself one of those self-assemble thingies. You know the sort: a bundle of laths, a bag full of hardware and hours of fun with the jolly old instructions. Rather like an Airfix kit, except there's no glue involved. I used to get into terrible trouble with the glue. Always spreading it all over my clothes and—'

'You're talking about IKEA,' I said.

'Yes, that's it. Swedish chappies. I seem to remember we squeezed the mattress up the stairs and hoisted all the wood-work through here.' He bent down and brushed a cobweb from a tiny little dormer window set under the ceiling where it sloped down to within a foot or two of the floor.

'Aye, that's all very well, but what about my wardrobe? I can't take that apart. Used to belong to me grandmother.'

'Ah, I'll show you where he put his wardrobe.' Algy turned and walked back towards the stairs, and without a further thought I went after him.

'Argghh!'

'Something the matter old chap?'

I clutched my head and swore quietly. 'Who put that bloody lintel there?'

'Ah, you didn't see the sign then?' As I staggered down the

stairs rubbing my right temple, he pointed to the faded chalk lettering above the door behind me. 'DUCK DON'T GROUSE. Aye, very droll. It wants an illuminated neon sign, that's what it wants. And a piece of foam rubber.' I turned to follow him down the rest of the staircase and cracked my left temple against the frame of the living-room door.

'I tell you what, Algy.' I was checking my fingers for traces of blood. 'It's a good job I'm a well brought up sort of lad or I might be tempted to do some serious swearing at this point.'

'Oh, quite so. Or as our pal Soapy likes to say, "Let's have a round of f***s and we'll all feel better", eh?'

We were standing in the living room now. It was what you'd call cosy, the ceiling so low that I could reach up and put the palms of my hands on it. 'And watch that,' Algy said as I flinched away from the beam that ran from one side to the other.

'No, I should be OK in here,' I said, standing up straight and measuring myself carefully against the darkened wood. 'There's all of four inches clearance. Just so long as platform heels don't make a comeback, eh?'

'Or that pogo dancing. Did you ever try that? Ever such fun. Quite the thing when we were in the sixth form.'

'Algy,' I said, 'you have to remember. We never had a sixth form at our school. We were kicked out into the world after year five and told to get on with it.'

'Ah yes, the university of life and all that. So anyway, what's the verdict?'

Apart from the health and safety issues – and the business of furnishing my sleeping quarters – Keeper's Cottage was a super place. I'd already fallen for the living room with its lovely old stone fireplace and open hearth. 'No need to worry about that,' Algy said, as I got down on my knees and peered up the chimney. 'Had it swept just a few weeks ago. And I'll send Soapy round with a few logs to make you feel at home. I think you'll find there's still a box of kindling in the outbuilding – or there's plenty of sticks to be gathered in the wood there.'

I could see myself being very cosy here. When you live on your own a nice open fire makes all the difference. 'More interesting than the jolly old television, I'd say,' was Algy's opinion, and I agreed with him.

He showed me into the other downstairs room. 'Now this is where your predecessor – if you take the place, that is – had his wardrobe. Trifle unorthodox, I suppose, hanging your shirts and trews up in the dining room, but needs must. And he still had room for a table and chairs.'

'That's no problem,' I said. 'I'm happy to eat off my knees in front of the fire.' I went back into the living room and looked out through the window. A cock pheasant was meandering down the driveway, and from the trees I heard the sound of a woodpecker at work. 'It's great, this. Way better than I expected. If you've no other contenders, I'll take it.'

'Tell the truth, old chap, I had you in mind the minute the place became vacant. Just say the word and you can move in as soon as you like.'

'Well, I'm on nights tonight. I'll have a think, check the old diary and give you a bell tomorrow, after I've had a few hours in bed.'

I felt good as I drove back up to Walt's. Better than good. Elated. The weather had held and as the sun started to sink it shone on fields that wore a cleaned-up, springtime look. The winter barley was starting to turn a brighter shade of green, the leaves of rape that had been battered into the earth by the winter rains had shaken off the mud and were reaching upwards, and the neat hawthorn hedges, freshly scalped, showed a first hint of colour as the buds started to swell. In the distance the Vale of York was a hazy blend of greens and browns, while away to the north the moors were capped by a line of puffy white clouds.

I found Walt at his garden fence, admiring the view from behind the house. At least, that's what I thought he was doing as I walked up behind him. 'D'you know, I've always had a fancy for a pond,' he said, thoughtfully, pointing across the pasture with his stick.

'Oh aye? Stocked up with fish, I suppose?'

'Aye, I could have a few carp I s'pose. But I tell you what I'm more interested in.' He clambered over the sagging wire fence and into the field. I followed him across the tufted grass, stepping over the fresh molehills, until he came to a slight hollow and started pacing around it. 'See, I reckon if I had a little pond here in this dip I could maybe put a decoy on it and get some of them birds to land.'

'You mean duck and suchlike?'

'Aye.' He narrowed his eyes and looked around, as if he expected a flight of mallards to come in over the treetops as he spoke. 'Then I could just' – he raised his stick as if it were a shotgun and squinted down the imaginary barrel – 'pick one off as I needed it.'

'Only one problem,' I said, turning up my coat collar. The sun was behind the trees now, and there was a distinct chill in the air. 'I mean, what makes you think the landowner wants a pond in the middle of his field?'

'Oh, don't worry yourself about that, Mike lad. You're looking at the landowner. I bought this field years ago.'

'You did?'

'One of them recessions they go on about. Farmland – why, they couldn't give it away. I offered cash and the bugger near bit me hand off. Aye' – he turned and walked back towards the fence – 'I never really had a plan for it, apart from renting out the grazing, like. It brings in a few bob every year and the odd lamb for my freezer. But now me mind's made up. I shall have me pond after all. Before I get too old to enjoy it. I'll borrow one of them diggers and fetch in some clay to line her with. Then you and me, mate, we'll be dining on wild duck whenever we feel like it.'

'I can't wait,' I said, as we headed back to the house. 'Only thing is, though, I shan't be here.'

'And why's that?'

'I've found a place of my own to rent.'

'Oh you have, have you? Is it far?'

'No, just down towards the village in them woods. One of Algy's places.'

'I know the one you mean. Used to be a keeper lived there – till his missus ran off with a lad from the village.'

'Oh aye?'

'Aye. Captain of our darts team. We never saw him no more.' He stopped at the back door and cleaned his boots on the black iron scraper he had there. 'So when are you off?'

'Soon as I can, really. It's all clean and ready to go. I just have to fetch my furniture from my sister's place.'

'Well, I shall be sorry to see you go. You've been good company to me.' He opened the door and I followed him into the warmth. 'You'll call in for a cup of tea when you're passing, won't you?'

'Walt, I count you as a friend.'

'So that means I shan't ever be rid of you, eh?'

'Precisely.'

'Aye, I reckoned as much.'

Walt seemed to have taken it in his stride, about me leaving. To tell the truth I think I was more upset than he was. After all, he'd be getting his home back to himself, the way he'd lived for thirty years or more since his dad passed on. I'd got used to his company, his ways, and his food. But I was excited about my new place, and was already planning to make the move towards the end of the week if I could get one or two of the lads to give me a hand. Yes, life was good. Spring in the air and changes afoot.

The mood lasted until I got to the station that night, a little after half past nine. Even as I drove down to town my eyes were feeling heavy-lidded, and I couldn't stop yawning. It's always the same, that first shift. Your body is expecting to go to bed, but here you are, sandwiches packed, flask filled, preparing for eight hours' work. Takes me two or three nights to get into my stride.

'Ah, been waiting for you.' It was Chris Cocks, the desk sergeant.

'Go on,' I said, 'make my day. But remember – I'm not on duty till ten, so if it's bad news I've still got time to come over all queer and take a sick day.'

He didn't say anything, just shuffled through a sheaf of papers on the top of his desk. He was playing this for effect, I could tell he was. Finally he looked up, and waved a bundle of half a dozen sheets at me. 'Five separate complaints,' he said. 'Looks like we have an outbreak of diesel thefts.'

'Not another one.' There had been several in the past few months. People having a few gallons, maybe half a tank full, siphoned out of their domestic heating tanks, farmers too from their yards. Hovingham, Terrington, Sheriff Hutton, out that way mostly. 'So where is it this time?' I asked.

'Thornton-le-Clay.'

'Hmm, same area, then.' I yawned. 'Got to be the same person, hasn't it?'

'By God, there's not much gets by you ex-Met types.'

'Chris, I was thinking aloud. And I'm not being paid for it, remember?' I glanced up at the clock on the wall. 'I'm not on duty for another twenty minutes.'

'Yeah well. Question is, can you have a look at it?'

'Course I will, mate.' As it happened this wasn't part of my dedicated beat, but on a night duty you had to cover the entire Ryedale area. 'I'll get word out to my Country Watch people. I can do that before I go out on patrol.' It wouldn't be difficult. When we started with Country Watch we'd set up a 'ringmaster' system, which allowed me to send the same telephone message to all the members, telling them what was happening and asking them to report in with any useful information they might pick up, or to report sightings of anything suspicious.

I didn't have a lot on that night. It was a Monday. Town was quiet, the roads mostly empty. It was a good time for the sort of thief who'd creep around a village and sneak off with half a tank of fuel, but of course people like him wouldn't be out until late on, most likely between half past two and four when everyone else was tucked up in bed and fast asleep. If I were planning to go on the prowl, that would be the time to do it.

I waited until all the pubs had turned out, made sure there was no sign of trouble around town, then set off on a tour of the northern end of my patch, concentrating on the villages. I went out past Eden Camp, where that old Spitfire they have by the entrance gleamed in the moonlight, then cut across country to Kirkbymoorside and Pickering. Nothing. The only sign of life was after I'd turned up towards Cropton, heading for Rosedale. A deer stepped out from the trees and glided across the road in two graceful bounds. Sometimes they move so swiftly you wonder whether you've actually seen them, especially at night. But there was no mistaking this one. The leaves it had disturbed on the wooded slope were still rolling out onto the road as I drove by.

From Rosedale village I carried on up the Chimney Bank on to Spaunton Moor where the road glistened with frost as it snaked its way between the heatherclad slopes. Dropping down through Hutton le Hole I worked my way towards Helmsley before doubling back on myself. One thing I'd learned in the Met was that a lot of villains will lie in wait for police cars on patrol, then get to work as soon as you've passed, the assumption being that you won't come by again for a while. More than once I'd got a result simply by retracing my steps. But tonight, even as I went back through Hutton, I knew I was wasting my time. It was just one of those shifts when nothing was going to happen.

I was back at the station for about half past one. I ate my grub, exchanged a few comments with the other lads back from their respective patrols. Two of them were almost total strangers to me, having been brought in to replace a couple of ours who were off sick, so the conversation was what you'd call sporadic. There was more yawning than banter. It'd be livelier later on in the week, when we'd all caught up on our sleep.

I was back on the road by ten to two. The A64 was more or less deserted, just the odd newspaper van, brake lights glaring red as the driver caught sight of me in the rear-view mirrors. I suppose I could have pulled them over for a talking-to, but I was busy thinking about our diesel thief. He – it could've been she, I suppose, but I somehow doubted it – seemed to be operating within a very tight area, probably not far from home. I turned off towards Sheriff Hutton, where the ruined castle was silhouetted against an empty sky. Where might a thief like this try next? Foston? Whitwell? Or how about Welburn, nice and handy for the main road? Perhaps I should try there, and Bulmer too.

Quite why I started at Bulmer I'm not sure. I'd like to say it was a gut feeling, a copper's hunch, but the fact is that as I drove through the village I had no great expectation of disturbing anybody, least of all a repeat offender. All the same, I was cruising nice and slowly, keeping the engine as quiet as I could. And then, I may as well admit it, I broke the law. I turned my lights off and drove by the moonlight. It was an old copper's ruse, one I'd used to good effect in the past. I also had my window down, so that with the engine on low revs I could listen out for any unusual noises, such as dogs barking. I was – there's no other word for it – on the prowl, and enjoying it. Cops and robbers. Well, why not? You may as well enjoy your work, I say.

Along the main street there was a pull-in on the right-hand side, and there, parked up, was an old red van. A vehicle like that tends to stand out like a sore thumb in a village such as Bulmer. Most of the people who live out there are pretty well-heeled. They don't run around in clapped-out Mark II Escorts.

I drove past and backed into a driveway, out of sight. I was sure there'd been something about a red van at briefing the previous week. I had a careful look to left and right. Not a soul. I got out of the car with my Maglite in my hand. The smaller Mags are only little things, maybe four inches long, but by heck they cast a powerful beam. They're also just about indestructible, which is a good job since I'd no sooner stepped into the road than I dropped the thing and trod on it.

Even as I approached the red van I could smell diesel, and there at my feet I could see where a few drops had splashed on the ground. And whereas the other cars I'd seen dotted along the main street were covered in frost, this one was clean. I peeled off a glove and put my bare hand on the grille. Still warm. As for the tax disc – nope, he didn't seem to have one. The van was actually parked right across the road from the churchyard, which was surrounded by a stone wall. OK then, if the driver was around I'd be waiting for him. I slipped through the gateway and ducked down behind a gravestone. The grass was thick with frost, the slab icy cold to the touch.

I got on the radio and quietly relayed the van registration number to control. When the answer came back it started to make sense. No current keeper, meaning it wasn't even registered, let alone taxed or insured, so if matey showed up and tried to drive it off I could have him for that. But there was more. There had been a report linking the vehicle to a youth named Leach. Just hearing his name made me grin. I knew Ronny from way back. Knew him even before I joined the police. I'm calling him a youth; in fact he was my age. He grew up not so far from me and made a bit of a name for himself as a tearaway. While I was pottering about on my brother's cast-off 50cc moped he had a proper bike, a 500cc job. Big, powerful, with a dodgy silencer. It dwarfed him: he was only slightly built. Always roaring through the village on it. He was mad keen on horses and had been a promising jockey as a lad. Managed to get taken on as an apprentice at one of the yards that operate in the Malton area, but he'd got in trouble with one of the stable lasses, started drinking, and eventually got the heave-ho. He was more of a wayward lad than an out-and-out villain. There were plenty of them when we were young. He was the one who never quite grew up. Now he was a bit of a sad case, living on benefits and bits and pieces of part-time casual work and indulging in the odd petty theft to feed his bad habits, which included drugs and – not surprisingly – backing horses. Losers mostly.

The other night car called in. They were double crewed. They would be making their way over from town to back me up. 'That's great,' I said, 'but just hang back a bit. Wait up at Castle Howard. I don't want you driving into the village just yet and disturbing our chum.'

I must have been behind that slab for twenty minutes or more, shivering, my legs cramping up as I crouched there out of sight of the road. As I waited I tried to trace the name that was carved on the stone, but time and the weather had more or less erased them. All I could make out was the date, 1840; or 1846, one or the other. Then, just as I was thinking about giving it up and going back to the car, I saw a peculiarly crooked figure waddling down the road towards me. His breath was coming in clouds, and I could hear a grating noise as if he was dragging something on the tarmac. As he came closer I recognised the fringe of long hair, the bowed legs exaggerated by his posture as he staggered towards his van with a five-gallon container, a length of plastic tubing trailing behind him. He was pausing every few steps to change hands.

I stood up and leaned forward across the top of the grave-stone, and waited till he was about to open the back of the van. I have to admit I made my voice a lot deeper than normal. And slower. I just couldn't resist it. Cops and robbers. The thrill of the chase. 'Ron-ny Lea-ach,' I called out.

I wish I could describe the look on his face. I can still see it, but I can't quite describe it. I hadn't meant to frighten the poor bugger, but I suppose I should have realised it would panic him, seeing a mysterious, dark figure rise up out of a cemetery at dead of night and call his name in sepulchral tones.

He dropped his can and stood there, mouth agape and eyes blinking as I shone the Maglite right in his face. 'Aye,' I said, stepping out from behind my slab and walking towards the gateway, 'it had to be Ronny, didn't it?'

'Oh bloody hell,' he gasped as I lowered the light and he caught sight of my face. 'I thought you was that Angel of Death come to get me.'

'No you didn't.'

'OK I didn't, but you put the fear of God in me.'

I got on the radio and let the other unit know that I'd stopped my suspect. '*Right,*' they said, '*we'll be on our way.*'

'What's this then, Ronny?' I tapped the jerry-can with my foot.

He gestured towards the van. 'I ran out of gas, Mike. Look, I just wanted a gallon or two to get me back home. I can put it back. I got the tube, see. I can siphon it back in. It's only that house back yonder. It'll only take a minute. Nobody'll know.'

'I can't let you do that, Ronny. You know I can't. Now come on, let's have a look in your van first. If it is yours.'

'This? No, I just borrowed it like. But my mate said he'd put me on his insurance.'

'No, I've already checked. It isn't insured. And don't tell me the tax is in the post. Cos it ain't.'

He stood there, wrinkling up his lips, then his shoulders drooped. 'Aye OK then. You copped me. What do we do next? Every time I get into trouble it's a different going-on.'

'That's modern policing for you, lad. We move with the times. We'll start by having a look in the back of the van, shall we? Open her up.'

'There's nowt in there.'

82

'Open up.'

You feel sorry for some people. You really do. It's like Walt said to me once about one of the young lads in the village who was always getting himself into scrapes. 'They just can't help it,' he said. 'They have this thing that drives 'em, that they have to go looking for trouble.' And poor old Ronny – he'd found it.

There were four more jerry-cans in the back of the van, all full. And Ronny didn't even try to come up with an excuse or explanation. He just stood there looking sorry for himself, and shivering. He only had a fake leather jacket on and a thin pair of jeans.

'Right,' I said, as I put the cuffs on him, 'now you're going to sit in the car with me while I drive back through the village, and you're going to show me the houses you've visited tonight. Every one of them.'

'You're not going to fetch 'em out to me, are you? The owners, like?'

I think he was worried that I'd force him to confront his victims – and there are times when I really wish we could do that. It'd do lads like him a power of good to see the distress they cause people. But all I had in mind was to leave notes through their letterboxes asking the owners to contact us. There were six of them altogether, and I saw no reason why they shouldn't have their fuel returned once it had been logged as evidence.

After that was done I had to take Ronny to Scarborough for locking up. He'd be charged in the morning and then most likely released on bail to await a court appearance. Right now, at that time of night, I could've done without the hassle. I'd be lucky to be back in Malton before my shift finished. The last thing I wanted was to be working overtime.

It was strange having him in the car, and I don't mean just the fact that he reeked of diesel and I had to drive with the window half open. It's not easy to keep up the official posture with a prisoner you've known since you were kids. For some reason we started talking about horses, and I said something about him blowing the chance of a decent career.

'No,' he said, 'jockeying's not much of a career, not unless you hit the big time. You have to love it, otherwise it isn't worth a light. Ninety per cent of jocks are working flat out, seven days a week. Anywhere from Carlisle to Exeter. You see the big names flying about in helicopters. Rest of 'em are batting up and down the motorways hoping their cars don't fail.'

'Aye, but they're getting paid for it.'

'Why, they hardly make a living. Specially them as has families. And don't forget – any day, any ride, you can get thrown off, trampled half to death or have your knackers trampled. Nah, the only time you get a decent payday is if you manage to get in on a good thing.'

'What d'you mean, good thing?'

'You know, when you get the word from the yard about a horse that's coming into its peak and you manage to slip a big bet on. I mean at a decent price, before word gets out to the bookies.'

'Did you ever get any?'

'Oh hell aye. I've had some right good payouts. Mind, you have to be canny. You can't go waltzing up to an on-course bookie and slam five hundred quid on a horse. He'll scrub the price right away and all the others'll follow suit. You've to spread it around, a lot of little bets before they cotton on.' He sighed. 'Still, it's one thing winning a pile of money . . . '

'Another thing hanging on to it, eh?'

'Aye, that's always been me downfall. Still is. I had a big win a few weeks since. Hundred quid on a thirty-three-to-one shot. Bolted home. Fifteen lengths, and I had three and a half grand in me back pocket.'

'Well, what happened to it?'

'Ah, straight down the pub and drinks all round. I had a great weekend – or so they tell me. There's still fellows coming up to me saying what a great time we'd had and I can't remember a bloody thing except going into the bookies on Monday morning and putting the last five hundred on a dog at Walthamstow.'

'Which lost, right?'

'It were leading into the final straight.'

'And?'

'God knows. Fellow next to me said it stopped for a piss.'

I could see him in the rear-view mirror, half smiling, half shrugging. 'You still get the odd tip then, do you?' I asked him.

'Oh aye, I keep my nose to the ground. Still have me mates around the stables. Why, do you follow the races?'

'Only the big ones.'

'What, Grand National? Gold Cup?'

'Aye, those that come on the telly.'

'Well, if I have any inside information maybe I can put you in the picture.'

'You could do better than that, Ronny.'

'How d'you mean?'

'Think about what you just said.'

'What? About inside information?'

'Yes.'

'You mean if I hear owt . . . ?'

'Look,' I said, 'you're not a malicious person. You're not going to go robbing old ladies in the street. I know that. Why were you robbing that diesel?'

'Cos I was skint.'

'And why were you skint?'

'Cos of that bloody greyhound, mostly.'

'No, because you're a gambler.'

'And a loser. That what you mean?'

I ignored the question. It wasn't my place to tell him what he already knew. 'Look,' I said, 'if you try to keep your nose clean and tip me the wink when there's anything going on that I should know about – well, who knows? It might do you some good.'

I didn't pursue it any further. He knew what I was on about. Police officers rely on information more than most people realise, and a guy like Ronny – a weak man rather than an out-and-out malefactor – he was the sort of contact who could help me keep on top of what was happening in my patch. So long as he could stay out of prison.

I got Ronny to Scarborough OK, did the paperwork, and got away about five thirty. The rest of my week was largely uneventful. In fact, it was so quiet it dragged. But when Friday night came and went without so much as a single punch-up in town I was thankful for it. I'd arranged to move into Keeper's Cottage at the weekend and I needed to be fresh.

Moving out of Walt's wasn't difficult, although it was a bit of a wrench. I'd got used to coming home off a shift and having a bit of company, someone to unwind with. But, as he said more than once over the few days after I broke the news to him, 'You know where I am, lad. Just pop in when you're passing.' And I promised him that I would. I mean, where else could I be guaranteed a homemade mince pie with my cup of tea, winter and summer?

A Moving Experience

When the day of the move arrived it barely took twenty minutes to get my things sorted and away. I'd arrived at his place the previous year with not much more than the clothes I stood up in, a suitcase full of bits and pieces, and my outdoor gear: hiking boots, fishing rod, waders and so on. Everything else I'd stored at my sister's house. My only major purchase over the past few months had been a one-hundred-per-cent-Hungarian-goose-down duvet, for which I'd taken out a small mortgage. But no complaints over that: it was worth every penny, although I drew the line at taking Walt's advice and buying myself a nightcap from Yates's. I was warm as toast in that icy spare bedroom of his. That duvet – and the things I had in store – was the sum total of my worldly goods, or so I thought.

It was Saturday afternoon. Walt and I were at the new place unloading the car. We'd just got the component parts of an IKEA bed base in through the upstairs windows and there he was, poking about in the outhouse. 'Plenty of room here for your meat,' he said, lifting the lid of the chest freezer.

'What meat's that?' I said.

'Why, remember when Gideon killed that pig last back-end and we went half shares?'

'Oh hell, don't worry about that, Walt. You've fed me like royalty these past few months. You hang on to it.'

'Oh no, you don't want to be leaving your pork joints behind. Not after you've paid for 'em. Why, you've a ton of space here needs filling. You need to stock up, lad. These things, you know' – he patted the freezer lid – 'they run cheaper when they're full. And you can take a few gamebirds off me hands too. I shot more pheasants than I could manage this year. I tell you what, I'll switch this on and pop back later. We'll soon get her filled up.'

'Any chance you could slip me some of your sister's mince-pies while you're at it?' I asked. But I knew from the look on his face I was pushing my luck there.

I said I didn't possess a great deal. That was about to change. It's a funny thing about being single. People always assume you can't look after yourself, that you'll be short of things. Let the word get out that you're moving into a place on your own and they immediately want to help fill it up. It's no good telling them you travel light, that you're just a rolling stone: they think you're making excuses for being hard done by. They assume you're living a miserable existence with nothing but a sofa-bed, a sandwich-toaster and a CD player. I've always liked my home comforts, but I try to draw the line at taking other people's cast-off junk.

First it was Ed on the phone. 'Mike, old buddy,' he said, 'I've got just the thing for you. You'll love it. Fireside chair. Be perfect for your place. I'll bring it round – and there's a few other odds and ends I can let you have too.'

'What sort of things you talking about?' I asked, warily. I'd been to Ed's house, and it seemed to be furnished entirely out of what his missus called antiques but the rest of us would call junk. I remember sitting on a sofa and sinking almost to the floor while his kids pulled the stuffing out of the cushions, along with the dismembered limbs of an Action Man. If he was talking about cast-off furniture – well, God knows what state it'd be in.

I was soon to find out. No sooner had Walt left than there was Ed scrunching down the lane in his Peugeot estate with a big old leather recliner strapped to the top of it. I peered into the car as he disentangled the ropes from the roof-rack. The rear seat was obscured by a stack of cardboard boxes. I walked round to the back and tried the hatch, but it was locked.

Whatever he'd got stashed under that pile of old blankets would remain a mystery for now.

'Well, what a cracking place,' he said, as we squeezed my new fireside chair through the back door. 'Nice and secluded. Proper little love nest.'

'Aye, it's not bad is it,' I started. 'Just mind your head on the—' But I was too late.

'Bugger!'

'On the lintel. And by the way—'

'Yes mate?'

'What's in those boxes in the back of your car?'

'Oh, just some stuff the missus wanted rid of – well, I mean, things you might find useful.' We set the chair down in front of the fireplace. 'Go on,' Ed said, 'try it out. You'll love it. There's a little lever down the side. I'll fetch the rest in.'

I was still trying to get the thing to recline when he came back with a drying rack, an ironing board, a plastic laundry basket and a hair-dryer. 'Steady on, Ed,' I said, as the chair lurched into horizontal mode and I lay on my back, legs in the air, wriggling helplessly, 'I'm a single bloke, you know – and I'm going bald. What do I want with that bloody lot?'

'Just because you're on your own there's no reason why you should live like a deadbeat, Mike.'

By the time I got upright again he was dropping a large cardboard box on the floor with an ominous chinking sound. 'She worries about you, does my missus. She's sent you a bit of crockery round.'

'Well, that's very good of her, Ed, but—'

He was off again, this time returning with three yards of electric cable and something bulky in a huge plastic bag.

'Ed . . .'

He dropped it on the kitchen work surface and shoved it in the corner. 'It's one of them slow cookers. She says it'll save you money. You put stews in and when you get back from work . . . ' He could see I wasn't happy. 'Look, buddy, you know what they're like. They want to mother you. If you don't need all this clobber, take it to a charity shop. Think of it this way: you're doing me a favour. Helping me make a bit of elbow room back at my place.' He was interrupted by the sound of an approaching car. 'Hey up, who's this then?'

I glanced through the window and saw a familiar little red Merc nosing its way long the track. 'Oh,' I said, nice and casual, 'looks like WPC Barker.'

'Ooh. Now then. This is interesting.'

'Don't stand there grinning like a bloody baboon.'

'Well, don't you stand there giving it "WPC Barker". You can't fool me.' I swear he would've nudged me in the ribs and winked if I hadn't already made for the back door.

'Ed,' I said, 'she's just bringing round some curtains, that's all.'

He was still peering through the window. 'In her tight-fitting jeans and sun-top? Yeah, right.'

'Yeah.' I gave him the hard stare. 'Right.'

When I got outside Ann was standing there with a camera in her hand. 'Hold it right there,' she said as Ed joined me.

'What's this in aid of?' Ed asked.

'Just thought it would be nice to record the scene,' Ann said. 'You know: major life events. Photographs.'

'Well, you just got here in time,' I said. 'Ed's on his way. He's unloaded all his surplus junk on me – and a rather nice recliner. Go on, Ed, crack on. You'll be wanting to get home, won't you? Don't want to be late for your tea.'

'Yeah yeah – two's company,' he said, as he delved into the back of his car and started tossing the blankets out onto the driveway. 'But we aren't done yet.'

'I'm sorry,' Ann whispered. 'Didn't expect anyone else to be here.'

'Just play it straight,' I said, grabbing the bundle of curtains she'd dragged out from the car. 'Not that he'd do owt to land us in it. I'd trust Ed with my—'

'Life?'

'Perhaps not that exactly. But he's a mate. He'll keep shtum. Come on, let's get these in the house.'

When Ed came back in carrying a coffee table, Ann was standing on a chair, hanging the curtains at the living-room window. 'Yep, looks as thought they'll just meet,' she said, reaching up to the rail and drawing them together while Ed stood there watching.

'Hey, is he admiring the curtains or my midriff?' Ann said, stepping down off the chair.

'Well,' I said, 'if I were a betting man . . . '

'I don't need you to stir it up, Pannett.' Ed took a look around the place. 'Well, just like home, isn't it?'

'Like your home, you mean. Your coffee table, your easy chair . . . But seriously, thanks mate.'

When Ed had gone Ann got back up to attend to the curtains. My goodness, she looked gorgeous, and I couldn't resist reaching up to put my arms around her. It's a good job I had no neighbours, because the scream she let out would have woken the dead. She fell off the chair and landed just where I wanted her. In my arms.

'What was that about?' I said. 'Spider?'

She squirmed out of my embrace. 'The *spiders* are no problem,' she started, 'but *that* is. She swept the curtain back and there at the window was a pig's snout. In fact there was an entire pig's head, minus its eyes and covered with frost. And behind it, his face stretched into a leering grin, was Walter.

'I've put your joints in t'freezer yonder,' he shouted, punctuating his words by tapping on the glass with his forefinger. 'Wasn't sure what to do about t'head.'

'How about frightening us out of our wits with it?' Ann said as I opened the window. 'God, you nearly stopped my heart.'

'Oh, I'm sorry, love. I didn't realise Mike had company.'

'What, you never noticed the Merc?' I said.

'I meant, you know, female company.'

'OK,' I said. 'Get yourself inside and I'll put the kettle on. I think I've some teabags somewhere.'

'Do you have to come in with that thing?' Ann said as Walt placed the offending part on the kitchen work surface.

'Why, Mike hasn't told me where to put it yet. Do you want it or not, lad? You can make a nice few pots of brawn with it. I can tell you how if you like. I brought it round specially for you.'

'I know all about making brawn,' Ann said. 'Used to help my mum when I was little. Go on – pop it in the freezer.'

Walt disappeared outside. When he returned he grabbed the recliner and sat himself down with a mug of tea. He apologised again for upsetting Ann, and I apologised for not having any cakes to put out. Then he dived into his jacket pocket and pulled out a paper package. 'Here y'are,' he said. 'You wouldn't buy one for yourself, so I decided to treat you.'

'Oh, thanks Walt. What a gent.' I tore the paper open and there was a bright red nightcap.

'Sommat to keep you warm in bed – if you need owt,' he said, winking at Ann.

'Yeah, cheers mate.'

'Aren't you going to try her on?'

'Not with you sat there staring at me.'

'Right then.' He drained his mug and got out of the chair. 'Reckon I'll leave you two love-birds to get on wi' it.'

After I'd seen him out I went into the kitchen where Ann was washing up the mugs. 'So,' I said, 'when are we going to tackle that pig's head?'

'Ah,' she said. 'Slight problem there.'

'What? Too busy just now?'

'Not that exactly. Just that when I said about helping my mum . . .'

'You were exaggerating?'

'Just a bit. She wouldn't entertain the stuff. Whenever there was a pig to be killed she'd send the head over to her auntie. Said she'd had enough brawn as a youngster to last her a lifetime. I didn't want to hurt Walt's feelings.'

'Even though he frightened you witless?'

She laughed. 'More of a shock than a fright. I mean . . .'

'OK,' I said. 'I'll leave it where it is. Find someone with a large dog to feed.' Just then a car horn sounded. 'Now who the hell is that?'

Out in the yard I found Algy, getting out of the Land Rover with Soapy. 'We've come to see if you want any assistance, old chap – and to give you a housewarming present.'

'Come on in,' I said, taking a large Harrods carrier bag from him. 'I'm just getting sorted.'

Ann dried her hands, greeted our visitors and followed us into the living room where I took two gift-wrapped packages out of the bag.

'Ah, that's great, Algy. Cheers.' He'd brought me a bottle of vintage red wine and a chess set.

'Something to keep you occupied on the long winter evenings,' Algy said, beaming.

Soapy glanced at Ann, turned to me and snorted. 'As if you'll need it, cock-bod.' Then he stood up. 'Any road, where's the old four-poster, Mike?'

'You what?'

'He means the IKEA self-assemble jobby,' Algy said. 'I told him you might need a hand with all those bits and pieces.'

'Ah, the bed. Aye, come on upstairs Soapy. And mind your head.'

Soapy stood in my bedroom scratching his chin while I spread out all the parts and sorted the bag of hardware into separate piles. He was deep in thought, pacing up and down, ducking under the sloping ceiling and stepping over the laths as I lay them in rows. Then he snapped his fingers. 'Aye, I'll need them Allen keys.'

'They're here somewhere,' I said. 'Ah, here you go.' I handed them over.

'Right,' he said, 'just you leave her to me. Piece of cake, these buggers.'

Downstairs Ann had lit a fire. Algy was in the recliner, easing the cork out of the wine.

'I'm afraid I need to be off,' Ann said, placing two clean glasses on the coffee table.

'No time to taste this?' Algy looked disappointed.

'She's on a night shift,' I said.

'Well, in that case you and I,' said Algy, pouring us a glass apiece, 'you and I can play a game with the new set.'

'Sounds good to me,' I said. 'I'll just see Ann out to her car.'

It took Algy about forty minutes to do what he generally does and tie me up in knots. Stuck in a corner with just a single

bishop, I surveyed the massed ranks of his encroaching army
and tipped the king over. 'You're too good for me,' I said.

'Ah well, that's what comes of practising all those years at
boarding-school. Have another drink, old chap.'

He topped up both glasses, passed me mine and said, 'Well,
here's to a happy tenancy at Keeper's Cottage.'

By the time Soapy came downstairs we'd almost finished the
bottle. 'By heck,' he said, 'they tek some fathoming do them
jobs. But I've got her beat. Just sling your mattress down and
you'll sleep like a good 'un. I've set her up perfect for you.'

'Right,' said Algy, 'we'll leave you to it. Soapy, you're driving
old boy.'

After they'd gone I drained the last half-glass of wine from
the bottle, sat and watched the fire, enjoying the silence for a
while, and soon felt myself nodding. Outside an owl hooted. I
peered through the window, hoping to catch sight of it, but all
I saw was a fat moon rising over the trees. I went upstairs,
yawned, pulled off my shirt, and sat on the edge of the bed to
take off my shoes. There was a nasty groaning sound as one of
the legs slid outwards, then a thump as the frame collapsed on
the floor, followed by a clatter as all the laths slid down to the
far end. As I picked myself up off the floor and banged my head
one more time on the ceiling I saw the note Soapy had stuck
there with an old galvanised nail. 'Happy Landings, Mike!'

Chapter 5

A Walk on the Wild Side

I've always liked rivers. I grew up splashing about in Bulmer Beck in my wellies and short trousers, learning from the big boys how to catch the brown trout that seemed to thrive in its waters. As I grew older I graduated to fly-fishing up on the Esk. I took my rod up there every chance I had: it was one of the things I missed so badly when I was doing my time in the Met, one of the reasons I was so keen to get back home. In fact, I've one or two good stories about my angling escapades, but they'll have to wait for another day.

I loved playing about in the beck with my mates. We used to pretend we were up the Amazon somewhere, hiding from head-hunters, chased by ferocious wild animals – ideas we picked up from films, comics and books. As a youngster I devoured anything about exploration, and used to drift off at night dreaming about the exploits of Victorian adventurers like Richard Burton looking for the source of the Nile, or Doctor Livingstone on the Limpopo. But for all that I was fascinated by those great African rivers, my favourite has always been the one I know best, the one that's right on my doorstep here in North Yorkshire.

The Derwent is only about eighty miles in length. It rises on the moors, not far from the sea. Looking at the map you'd think its natural course would be towards the coast. At one stage it's within three miles of the North Sea. There is in fact a man-made drainage channel that takes a lot of its water through a gap in the hills to Scarborough, but the river itself swings south, between the thickly wooded slopes of the Forge Valley and into the Vale of Pickering. Once again, you'd expect it to find its way eastward, to Filey, perhaps. But no, it flows resolutely inland, absorbing the waters of the Rye – another volatile river that floods at the drop of a hat – before winding its way south-west to Malton. From there it carves a route through the hills, down by Kirkham to Stamford Bridge, and out into the Vale of York where it meanders peacefully south to flow into the Humber estuary, just above Goole.

It's the upper reaches of this river that I know best. When I was in my teens and able to venture further afield on the bike I got to know the area pretty well. But until I came back to North Yorkshire it never entered my head that I might get to spend my working day exploring its banks. Now, as a newly qualified wildlife officer, there was always the possibility of being called out anywhere in Ryedale, or further afield in Hambleton, even into the Esk Valley, beyond the moors to the north. Not that every day was a wildlife day – far from it – but I now had to be prepared for anything.

It was a Sunday morning in April. I was on the early turn, which can sometimes be a quiet time after the excitement of a Saturday night. I'd spent a good half hour around the parade-room, sorting paperwork and exchanging intelligence with Ed. Well, let me correct that: we were actually discussing the latest crisis at York City and wondering how long their latest manager could last. And that led Ed onto one of his favourite topics, the history of Rillington FC, one-time winners of the Scarborough League Cup.

I love listening to Ed's stories, but this one was going to have to wait. 'Sorry, buddy,' I said, as he started on about the good old days when his dad turned out for the village team. 'I'm off for a walk in the country. I've got a wildlife job.'

'How do you manage it, Pannett?'

'Whaddayou mean?'

'Here's me stuck in the station with last night's drunks to process, and you're swanning off – where is it this time? Rosedale Abbey? Duncombe Park? Rievaulx?'

'Ed, do you remember a mad rush when they posted that wildlife course and asked for applicants? No. Did I have to elbow you aside when I went to sign up for it? I think not. So let's not be having any of your carping. You had your chance and you blew it. Now you'll just have to stand by while I take all the glamour jobs,' I said. 'Think of me while you're in the cells interviewing our Saturday-nighters. I'll be off to the moors. And Ed – try not to tread in the dried-up vomit down there.'

The call had come in from an unusual source, a Guide leader. 'I've got a group camping up here,' she said. 'We're on the head-waters of the Derwent. I didn't know whether to call you or not, but one of the girls was out along the river and she's found a trap, a sort of metal cage thing.'

'Aye,' I said. I knew the kind she meant. 'The keepers use them to trap mink. They're a flaming nuisance up there.'

'Well, this one's got an otter in it.'

'An otter? You're sure about that?'

'Oh, quite sure. I know my wildlife. The thing is, it's dead. Drowned, I should say. The trap's under water.'

'Has it been dead long?'

'Oh, I couldn't answer that. But it's not right, is it?'

'No,' I said, 'It's not. I'll need to get over straight away.' This wasn't good. Nobody had any right to be trapping otters. 'Whereabouts are you?'

That was where my problems started, because the Guides were actually on land belonging to a large private estate on the moors. They'd driven as far as they could up the valley and then backpacked to the campsite.

'The best I can do is meet you and lead you in on foot,' the woman said. 'We're a fair way off the road. Is that OK?'

'How far are you talking about?'

'It'll be a good mile.'

'Don't worry,' I said, 'I'll come prepared. How's the weather up there?'

'Oh it's a lovely morning, but it's still very wet underfoot.'

I packed my wellington boots and a pair of waterproof trousers into the back of the four-wheel drive, the Puddle Hopper, and set off, up to Pickering, then along the A170 towards Scarborough. As I turned off at West Ayton to drive through the woods heading north, I rolled the window down. Most of the trees were still bare, just a greenish fuzz on a plantation of larches and the occasional splash of white as I passed a blackthorn in bloom. Where the sun was breaking through between the trees it was pleasantly warm, but in the shade there was that cool, dank sort of smell you get in old woodlands. Damp earth, mingled with the occasional whiff of wild garlic.

After following the valley for a mile or two the road comes out into more open country where the river meanders through broad, low-lying pastures. A fresh southerly breeze rippled the new season's grasses, emerald green. It was a perfect April day, with white puffy clouds drifting across a pale blue sky, the sun warming my right arm. This is the life, I thought to myself. On a day like this I should be paying them.

I'd agreed a rendezvous with the woman who'd called me, and there she was, standing beside a Sherpa van in a white polo shirt and dark shorts. 'Is it Lesley?' I asked, as I pulled over. 'I was looking for someone in navy blue.'

'Er, I don't think we've worn that get-up since about nine-teen-seventy-something,' she laughed.

'No, you're right – I must have been thinking about my mother. She used to be a Guide leader.' I parked the car in the little pull-in and got my wellies out.

'You'll need them,' she said. 'It's very boggy along the riverside.'

'So how did you get the gear to where you're camping?'

'The hard way. We wanted the girls to have a proper outback experience, so they had to carry everything up from the road here.'

'Well, that'll keep 'em out of mischief I dare say.' I took out a little day-pack I keep in the back of the old Puddle Hopper. I always have a water bottle, a set of rainproofs and a few other odds and ends in it. 'Right,' I said, slamming down the hatch and checking the locks, 'lead on.'

'I'll have to take you towards the camp first,' she said. 'It's a bit of a long way round but I can't be sure of finding the exact spot from here.'

The walk took us along a narrow grass field, a proper little sun-trap. Flies, and even one or two bees droned past. Sand martins swooped out from their riverbank homes, dipping their wings as they darted past us to reveal their white underbellies. But as soon as we started climbing into the forestry the temperature dropped and everything was still and silent.

'Not very attractive, are they?' Lesley said. We were following a narrow path between rows and rows of conifers, the ground beneath them just a thick mat of dead, brown needles, the sun blotted out by the dense canopy.

'I don't think anything much lives in these plantations,' I said. 'You never see any birds, do you?'

'There's always these, though.' She'd was pointing at a mound of needles, three or four feet high and several feet across.

'What are they, anthills?'

'Wood ants,' she said, as I peered down to get a closer look at the scurrying insects.

'Can't say I've heard of them,' I said.

'No, they're not all that common. Good biters, though. As one or two of the girls found out yesterday.' She laughed. 'Thought these mounds would make a nice seat to rest on.'

We walked on and eventually started to hear voices through the trees.

'That'll be the camp,' she said, 'and if we take this right-hand path we should get down to where the trap is.'

'You seem to know this spot pretty well,' I said.

'I've been bringing girls here for twenty years and more.'

The path sloped down, out of the wood and into a tangle of young willows and dead bulrushes. Marsh marigolds were coming into flower and you could see the beginnings of this year's flags. 'You were right about the wellies,' I said, as I squelched through the black mud.

When we got to the river it was running a couple of feet deep and ten or twelve wide. Perfect for brown trout. Lesley had gone a few yards ahead of me, beating a path through the matted dry stalks.

'Here we are,' she said. And there, just protruding from the water, was a standard humane trap, a rectangular wire-mesh thing maybe two feet long and seven or eight inches square. It was the kind a gamekeeper would use to trap mink on dry land. All the animal has to do is step inside, trigger a lever, and bang! The door slams shut behind it.

Sunlight was dancing on the water, but through the ripples I could plainly make out the otter. No question it was dead – not that I'd doubted Lesley's word for a minute. From the trap a length of chain ran to a stout metal peg that had been hammered into the bank.

'Whoever set this has made a right dog's breakfast of it,' I said. 'That's the problem, isn't it?' I bent down to pull the trap from the water. 'Blooming chain's way too long. You trap a mink in this and it'll stay put, but an otter – why, it's bigger and stronger altogether. It'll drag one of these things, easily.'

'Trying to get back to the water, you mean?'

'Exactly. And with a chain that long it'll get there – and drown itself.'

It was not a pretty sight. The poor animal had obviously put up a hell of a fight. Its mouth was wide open, the teeth gripping the galvanised wire, and its webbed feet were poking through the bars where it had struggled to get some purchase.

'You say these are designed to catch mink?'

'Aye – they're a pest, from the gamekeeper's point of view. They eat fish and gamebirds, and if they get into a pheasant coop they'll go on the rampage.'

'But there's nothing to stop an otter getting caught in them?'

'You can't prevent, not entirely. But what you do is, you check 'em. The law states they have to be looked at every twenty-four hours. I believe it's twelve in Scotland, which makes more sense to my mind – but there we are. These are designed for humane killing. You trap the creature alive and then the keeper can deal with them when he does his rounds. This poor fellow – why, look at him, you can see where he's tried to claw himself free.'

'Tried to bite through the cage, by the look of it.'

'What a bloody way to die. It isn't right.'

I'm no expert, but it looked to me as though the animal had been dead a while. It was slightly shrunken, its half-closed eyes very dull. And it smelled. The crucial factor was, had it been dead more than twenty-four hours? If it had, then an offence had definitely been committed, and never mind the business of the chain.

I lowered the trap back into the swiftly flowing water. 'Why are you doing that?' Lesley asked.

'I need it to remain in situ and "preserve the scene", as we say. This may well constitute an offence under the Wildlife Act – which means the trap and its contents are evidence.' I got my radio out. 'I'll get onto our scene of crime officer, have him come and take some pictures.'

'Do you want me to stay here?'

'Up to you, really.'

'Oh well, if it doesn't bother you I may as well stay for a while. Be interested to see your photographer at work.'

'Who's minding the fort?' I nodded my head in the direction of the camp.

'Oh, there's two other leaders up there. They'll be busy sorting their lunch out by now.'

So she stayed with the trap while I set off back to the road. Stuart, the SOCO, was not a happy bunny when he showed up half an hour later. 'Took some bloody finding did this place,' he wheezed as he got out of his car and wiped the perspiration from his face. He was a big lad, not the fittest by any stretch of the imagination. 'Dragging me out to the back of beyond,' he muttered as he fetched his camera from the back seat.

'Sorry to tell you, sunshine, but we aren't quite there yet.'

'What do you mean?'

'Well, the river's over that way.' I pointed across the meadow.

'What, where them little bushes are?'

'Well, into the bushes, yes and then about a mile upstream. Take us a good half hour.'

'Half a bloody hour! I knew I should've stopped for my lunch.'

'Bring it with you,' I said, glancing up at the sky. It was clear blue now, not a cloud in sight. 'Grand day for a picnic.'

'But I haven't got anything. I was just going to grab a bite in Pickering when you called in.'

There's no pleasing some people. Here it was, the perfect spring day, and he was getting paid to take a nice walk in the country. But he didn't see it that way, especially when we were back in bulrush territory and he had a shoe full of black slime.

'Bloody nature,' he said. 'You can have it.'

Talk about a fish out of water. But once Stuart had got his camera out and started taking the pictures it was a different story. He concentrated a hundred per cent, never quibbled about crouching down and getting his knees all wet as he snapped away from every conceivable angle. I'd met him a few times before, and like everyone I tended to take the mick about his appetite. But as I stood there, holding the trap up for him to get a closeup of the dead otter, I saw a face that was alive with intelligence as he twiddled his f-stops and focused on the dripping corpse. I was screwing up my nose and half turning away.

He was a picture of concentration, totally absorbed in what he was doing, quite oblivious to the smell. It was like watching an artist at work.

'Now then,' he said, as he stowed the gear away in his black canvas bag and slung it over his shoulder, 'where are these Guides?'

'Only a few hundred yards up the hill,' Lesley said.

He looked at Lesley, a hopeful grin on his face. 'Not cooking, by any chance?'

'You what?' I said

He looked at his watch. 'Well, Girl Guides, campfires . . . Come on, Mike, don't tell me you aren't feeling a bit peckish.'

'Well, I have to lug this trap – and the otter – back to the car.'

'Don't you just bury it?' Lesley asked.

I shook my head. 'No, I need to get a vet to do a postmortem, establish how long it's been dead.'

'Well, you'd be welcome to swing by. I'm sure we can feed a couple of extra mouths.'

'OK then – and maybe the girls can have a look at this.'

As we got nearer the camp and caught the unmistakable smell of burning wood and scorched sausages I found myself lengthening my stride, but I still couldn't keep up with Stuart. 'Bloody hell,' I said, 'you were struggling and moaning across that field, and now look at you. Like a greyhound.'

'Ah well, it's all about incentives, Mike.'

I carried the cage up to the grass clearing on the edge of the woods and left it in the shade with my jacket over it. I'd let the girls have a look at it after we'd eaten, maybe take the opportunity to give them a lesson or two about what to do if they came across an animal caught in a trap like this. Meanwhile I sat down on a huge pine log and tucked into a good old-fashioned campfire meal.

'Reminds me of the old days,' I said as I prodded a blackened sausage with my fork.

'Why, were you in the Scouts?' Lesley asked.

'TA,' I said. 'Although as it happens I was at one time a Girl Guide.'

They both looked at me, mouths agape.

'Er, honorary.'

Stuart shook his head. 'Always said there was sommat odd about you,' he mumbled.

'Aye, I told you my mum was a leader, didn't I? She said I was too young to stay home alone, so whenever she had a camp like this she took me along where she could keep an eye on me. Set me up in my own tent with my best mate.'

'And how old did you say you were?' Stuart asked, his eyes narrow with suspicion.

'Oh, very young and innocent. Eight, ten, twelve, that sort of age. We used to join in with the fun and games sometimes. Sitting around the campfire singing songs. Other times we'd take ourselves off fishing. Then we got to an age where the girls wanted to invite us into their tents in the evening for midnight feasts. At which point my mum decided we'd better stay home.'

Lesley laughed. 'Good old Mum, eh?'

'Well, it's what they're for,' I said. 'Keep you out of mischief.'

When we'd eaten we let the girls see the trap – those that were interested – and showed them how to release it. After that I thanked Lesley and set off back to the road. Stuart went on his way and I drove over to Pickering. I wanted to call in at the police station so that I could get online. I was after a fellow I'd heard of. Brian something or other, chairman of the Otter League. They'd been trying to reintroduce otters after years of seeing them persecuted, and he was just the kind of contact I needed to be fostering if I was to be an effective wildlife officer. I needed him onside, as an ally and a source of information. And in return I would expect to keep him informed, as far as it was appropriate. It would be a matter of simple courtesy as much as anything else.

I gave him a call and explained what had happened. As I expected, what I had to say upset him. 'Aye,' he said, 'we did release a number of otters up there, in pairs. They've been doing really well. But trapped, you say? That can't be right.'

'Well, I'm afraid that's what's happened.'

'I'm disappointed, I must say. We liaised with the people up there. They knew what we were doing.'

'Let's not be jumping to any conclusions,' I said. 'It could be negligence rather than malice.'

'Aye, but does the poor old otter know that? Whatever's going on it wants sorting.'

He was right, of course. But it was a delicate situation. The countryside is under enormous pressure these days, with all sorts of conflicting interests: there's farmers, foresters, conservationists, hunters, anglers – and the wildlife of course. Mink, for example, are killers without a conscience. But that's their nature. Some people will want them left alone; others will want them eradicated. They have a point, because the mink aren't native: they've been imported for their fur but of course there were bound to be escapes, and now they're breeding in the wild, upsetting the natural balance of things.

Before I could talk to the person who owned the land where we'd found the trap, I needed to confirm that the otter had been dead more than twenty-four hours. And here I had a good contact, a lad who did veterinary work up at Flamingoland

Zoo, just outside Pickering. He was happy to open up his surgery and do a postmortem, even though it was his day of rest. And his opinion confirmed my suspicions. The otter had been in the trap some considerable time, four or five days minimum.

So, an offence had been committed, and I was into new territory here. I suppose a lot of policemen would have scented a 'result' at this stage. They'd have been straight round to the landowner, banging on the door, brandishing the evidence, and telling them they were on a charge. But that's not my style. Never has been and never will. The way I see it, rural policing's about working together towards the same outcome, a safer and more peaceful life for everyone, including otters. The more people you can work with, the more allies you're going to have when things get tough. And believe me, when the hunting ban came along a year or two later a lot of rural police officers around the country were in real danger of being caught in a crossfire. As it was, I would have friends on both side of the divide, which would make my job a lot easier than it might have been.

I needed to think this through. This was my first proper wildlife job and in political terms it was a big one. I was well aware that the landowners and moorland keepers are very protective of the countryside and very concerned for their livelihoods. Any sign of outside interference and, as you might expect, they'll be ready to close ranks. I needed to tread very carefully. My whole credibility as a wildlife officer, now and in the future, could depend on how I handled this business. I needed some advice and I knew just where to get it. But first I had to find a place to store the dead otter, which could still be required as evidence if we got as far as pressing charges. The best place I could think of at the time was the freezer at the station. Normally we only use it for things like DNA samples awaiting dispatch to the labs – and of course the odd ready meal when we're on a night shift. There was plenty of room, so in it went, wrapped up in a large, plastic, see-through evidence bag. Then I set off to call on a friend.

When I first met Nick, back in the early days of Country Watch, he'd been pretty wary of me. I didn't blame him for that. He hadn't had the best of times with my various predecessors, and I think he was suspicious of my proactive methods. But once Country Watch took off, he started to come around. I'll put that another way. I started to come around, for tea, coffee, a smoke and a natter, and whatever his wife happened to be baking in their little back kitchen.

'Come on in, you idle bugger!' he called out as I banged on the back gate and slipped my hand through the little hole to lift the latch. 'I s'pose you'll want feeding and watering as usual?'

'Ah well,' I said, as two plump Labradors came out to greet me. 'That's where you're wrong, Nick. You think you know everything but you don't.' I plonked myself down in an easy chair next to his solid-fuel Aga. 'I have just had a damned good fry-up, cooked on an open fire, in the woods, courtesy of the Girl Guides.'

'Spare us the details,' he said.

His wife Linda came in. 'Now come on, Nick, you've never known Mike to spare us the details, now, have you?'

He ran his hand back through his grey thatch of hair. 'It's all right for some,' he said, 'but t'bloody quack's got me on a diet. Nowt but a bowl of unsweetened muesli for my breakfast. Like bloody sweepings from a barn floor, it is.' He motioned to the pot that sat on the Aga. 'Go on, pour yourself a cup.

You may be fully fed, but I've never know you turn down a drink of tea yet.'

And so I told them the tale while Linda twisted my arm to try one of her rock buns, still warm from the oven. Then it was down to business. I was pretty sure about how I was going to handle this, but I wanted a bit of input from someone on the front line, so to speak. I was also hoping – because Nick had a wide range of contacts in that neck of the woods – that he might be able to prepare the ground for me.

'Aye, I know what you're getting at,' he said, sitting back in his armchair and taking a long drag on his cigarette. 'And I know the place you're talking about right enough. In fact I know the head keeper up yonder. Used to go beating with him on the Scampston estate, when we were lads.'

'Don't get me wrong, Nick,' I said. 'I mean, I want to know who's responsible, but I don't want to see some skinny-arsed eighteen-year-old underkeeper getting the bullet just because he's made a mistake.'

'If it is a mistake, and not pure bloody idleness, you mean.'

'Of course, but if we can educate one of those lads it's surely better than getting him fired and bringing in some other youth off the street who knows bugger all about the job. I mean, don't get me wrong, I hate cruelty, but I know how you lads feel about mink. We just need to make sure we're protecting these otters.'

'All right, Mike, leave it with me. I'll give my old mucker a bell and tell him to expect a call from the law.'

'Aye, and do tell him, won't you, that I come in peace. I mean, I'm here to make friends, not enemies.'

'So, you don't want me telling him what a bloody pillock you are?'

'That'll cost you another cup of tea and another rock bun, you cheeky sod.'

Before I made a move I got on the phone to the landowner. Courtesy again, keeping everyone informed. Because if you don't watch out you're liable to upset people, and start the old rumour mill turning. The man I spoke to was quite sharp in his response. He told me that if this got out it could really damage the estate's good name – and his personal reputation. That explained his manner: he was being defensive. None of these big estates want to be thought of as being unprofessional in their conduct, or badly managed, and they certainly don't want people thinking that they use cruel methods in attempting to control wildlife. 'That sort of thing doesn't go down well with our neighbours or our visitors,' he said. 'I'll find out who's responsible and see that he gets his cards.' Well, I said, before he made a decision, could I speak to the head keeper and establish the facts first? I wasn't enjoying this conversation. The man didn't know me and was very wary. You could hear the suspicion in his voice. I understood that: he was in a difficult position, and his reputation was on the line, but in the end he had no choice other than to trust me. Go ahead, he said, have a word with my head keeper.

Nick had been as good as his word and come up with a name. And I could tell he'd tried to pave the way for me. I wouldn't say the fellow I called welcomed me with open arms, but his manner certainly wasn't as hostile as it might have been. I explained that I needed to get to the bottom of what had happened and make sure it didn't happen again. That was my main concern. He asked me to give him half an hour to make some enquiries, but he was back on the phone within ten minutes.

'Aye, he said, 'I know who it is who set that trap. Will you be wanting to see him?'

'I'll have to. What sort of lad is he?'

'Well, for a start he's very upset. Nearly in tears when I spoke to him. He's a decent kid. Far as I can tell he's been forgetful. He knows he's done a daft thing, and he regrets it.'

'Tell you what,' I said, 'why don't we arrange a meeting, so that I can have a word with all your underkeepers. That way they'll know who I am and I can make sure they're up to speed on the law. I can have a quiet word with this lad in private at the same time.'

I went up there later in the week. By this time I'd got some copies of Stuart's photos, so I took them with me. The head man had gathered all the lads at his house, tucked away in the woods near the main gate to the estate. There were four or five of them standing outside the door, puffing on last-minute ciggies and casting sidelong glances at me. 'Come in and get a cup of tea,' he said. 'We've just mashed a big pot.'

I wanted to find out exactly what had happened before I made my final decision on how to handle this. As far as I could work out there were three possibilities. One, the lad had set out to kill an otter. Two, he was just bone bloody idle and hadn't bothered to check the trap. Three, he'd made a genuine mistake that was unlikely to happen again. I consider myself a good judge of character. Call it instinct, but I can generally sort out the decent lads from the wrong 'uns. The lad I interviewed was very nervous, but he struck me above all as an honest young underkeeper, keen to learn his trade and do a good job. He told me that he'd set a number of traps and now realised that he'd failed to make a proper note of where they all were. Which was how he'd missed this one out when he checked them. But had he checked the others every twenty-four hours, I asked him? He assured me that he had. This is where you trust your gut feeling – and my instinct was to believe him.

'OK,' I said, 'can we get all the lads in together?' We sat round the kitchen table, me, the head keeper and all the underkeepers. I kicked off by showing them the photographs, and asked them what was wrong with the way the trap had been set up. No answer. 'Well,' I said, 'look at the length of that chain. If that had been shorter,' I said, 'the trap would've stayed on the bank and one of those Guides could've released the otter. That was bad enough, but even worse, in my opinion, is the fact that it wasn't checked. Now that's a flagrant breach of the law, which states that you absolutely must' – I remember banging the table with the flat of my hand, and it didn't half make them jump – 'you absolutely *must* check those traps every twenty-four hours. More than that if you can. It's a horrible death for any animal. Think how you'd like it. Trapped in a cage and sinking into the river.'

The lads didn't have a lot to say for themselves after that. It was plain that the message had sunk in. I went on to explain a bit about what I did, and how we could help each other. As I packed up to go I said, 'You all know who I am now and I hope you feel you can contact me if you see owt that bothers you. The boss here has my number.' On the way out I asked him about the lad who was responsible for the whole thing. Was he to be fired? 'No, like I said, he's not a bad lad. He just got it wrong. He won't make that mistake again.'

As soon as I got back to the station in town I called Brian, the man from the Otter League. I explained what had happened, and that I'd had the chance to spell out to the lads on the estate how they were to treat their traps in future. I'd no sooner put the phone down on him than I had the newspapers to deal with. The *York Press*, the *Northern Echo* and the *Scarborough Evening News* had all got hold of the story, and they wanted to know everything. Whose land was the trap on, who was the culprit, and what were we doing about it? I played a straight bat to all their questions. 'Listen,' I said, 'there has been an incident, and regrettably an otter has been killed. It happened on the moors on a tributary of the Derwent. We know who set the trap, but as far as we're concerned the person in question made an error of judgement.' They tried and tried to get me to name names, but I wasn't having any of it. 'Look, a mistake has been made, but we've all learned lessons from it, and we've put practices into place to make sure it doesn't happen again. As far as I'm concerned that's all I need tell you.'

With the press off my back, I made a point of contacting the landowner and informing him of the outcome. Whatever else he was feeling, he was relieved. And so was I. This could easily have become confrontational, an 'us and them' sort of thing. But if there had been a barrier between us it had now been lowered a shade. Of that I was certain.

To wrap things up I made a point of calling Lesley, the Guide leader, and letting her know the result. I also thanked her. Without her call, none of this would have come to light.

It had been an unpleasant incident, yes – and a tragic one – but as I thought about it I came to the conclusion that some good had come out of it. Number one, I'd put those lads right about how they set their traps. Number two, I'd established a relationship with the head keeper on the estate, and maybe I could build on that. I think too I'd gained a bit of respect from him. He would know that I was serious about my job. I meant business. I was no pushover. But I think he also realised that I was a reasonable man to deal with.

A few days after all this the inspector called me into his office. 'Can I have a word, Mike?'

'Yes, sir. What's it about?'

'You had a case where an otter had been caught in a trap?'

'Yes sir. It's all dealt with now though.'

'Hmm, that's good. No – er – loose ends then?'

I had no idea what he was driving at. 'As far as I'm aware, no sir.'

'Quite sure?'

I looked at him blankly – and then he grinned. 'I've had nothing but complaints this last week, particularly from Jayne. Something unsightly bothering her in the – ah, the freezer?'

'Oh blimey – yes. That.'

'Yes Mike, the evidence. Time you got rid of it, I think.'

Chapter 6

Downhill Caravanning

It was a beautiful May evening, sunny and still. All the trees around my new home had come into leaf, and Keeper's Cottage was an island of white in a sea of green. What a place to come back to, footsore, sweaty and hungry after a day out. No wonder neither of us felt like getting changed and driving to work. But, as Ann pointed out, we should both be grateful. Just for once our shifts hadn't clashed. Here we were, both on nights, which meant we'd been able to spend the whole of Monday together. And we'd made the most of it. We'd put on our boots, shoved a couple of water bottles into our backpacks and set off nice and early, walking from my place up to the crossroads, then followed the winding valley road down into Thixendale. After an early lunch in the Cross Keys, we'd climbed up onto a section of the Wolds Way and down into Wharram Percy to visit the ruined church and deserted medieval village.

It was a perfect day for hiking: pleasantly warm, with a cool breeze coming in from the south-east. The grass was shimmering, the first swallows were darting across a clear blue sky, and the only trouble we had all day was with a herd of young bullocks, still getting used to the freedom of the open fields after a winter inside and a little too inquisitive for comfort. They can be a real nuisance when they decide to start following you. You turn and shoo them away, but where older cattle will back off the youngsters will only pause before pressing on. If you slow down they're on top of you; if you speed up they'll likely as not break into a trot. You have to be careful or you can soon have a stampede on your hands. I didn't tell Ann, but I was relieved when we'd put a five-bar gate between us and them.

From Wharram we somehow got it wrong. Well, I'll correct myself. I was the one with the map, after all. I thought I'd spotted a path along the top of the hills, but in fact there wasn't one. We had to drop down into Birdsall village, which left us a long climb, through the parkland that surrounds the stately home, and on up to Leavening Brow, before we made the final descent past Walt's place and home. But Ann was good-humoured about my mistake and, thanks to Ed's cast-off slow cooker, we knew we'd have a nice casserole waiting for us, a piece of venison Walt had dropped off the day he brought the pig's head round.

'God, you really have landed on your feet here, haven't you?' Ann said as we approached the house. She was trailing her hand through the cloud of cow parsley that lined the drive. I stopped, turned and put my arms around her. 'Landed on my feet?' I said. 'I reckon I've won the lottery.'

It was still light when we got into our cars and headed towards Malton. Ann had to be in before me to prepare for the shift briefing and get a handover from the previous shift sergeant. I needed to pop up to Algy's place before I went into work.

I found him standing outside his garage, wearing a pair of

spotless brown overalls and holding a clean yellow cloth in his hand. 'Well,' he said, 'what a coincidence. I was just this minute thinking, it's time I gave that new tenant of mine a call.'

'You don't need to worry about me,' I said, handing him my rent. 'I always pay me bills on time. It's the way I was brought up.'

'I haven't the slightest doubt about that, old chap.' He put the cheque in his top pocket. 'No, I was polishing a couple of the old bangers and I had a bit of a brainwave. I was thinking about you and that delightful young lady of yours, and—'

'Algy,' I said, 'you do realise that there is nothing between Ann and me – not officially anyway?'

'I see. So it's all intrigue and midnight assignations, I suppose.'

The way he put it I was almost sorry to disappoint him. 'Not exactly. But we do have to be discreet. I mean, we were out for a hike today and we called in at Thix for a drink. There we were, sat in the garden, and suddenly we realised – well, if anyone had seen us, anyone who knew who we were . . .'

'Quite so. Well, that makes my plan all the more pertinent to your situation. Come into the garage. I don't think you've seen these.'

Algy had three garages altogether, plus a couple of sheds out the back, and God knows how many cars. There were just a couple in this one. I recognised an MG roadster from the 1960s, but the other one was much older, and much bigger. 'By heck, Algy, it's straight out of *Brideshead Revisited*. Wire spokes, running board, brass headlamps – and look at that windscreen. Fantastic.'

'Ah well. This little beauty,' he said, 'is a Frazer Nash. Made in 1930. Cost me an absolute packet, but what a car! Chain-driven, you know. Goes like a rocket. I'll have to take you out in it some time. Trouble is, I hardly have time to keep them all turned over. These cars are like animals. They need exercising. I was going to take the little MG out last week, but the blasted battery failed on me.' He hesitated. 'I mean, you and this – what did you say her name was?'

'Ann.'

'Ah yes, lovely girl! You and Ann, you like the occasional trip out, I presume?'

'Oh, hell aye. It's just that we have to be careful not to be seen in this neck of the woods.'

'Perfect.' He tapped the side of his head. 'This where the Algernon brainwave kicks in, as they put it. What would you say to taking the MG here for a run? It needs a bit of a blow-through. Clean out the valves and so on.' He flicked his cloth over the radiator grille. 'Been parked here all winter gathering dust, and I dare say the old exhaust is clogged with soot.'

'I'd love to, but – are you sure?'

'Of course I'm sure, old chum. You'll be doing me a favour. In fact, have her for the weekend. Take the young lady out to the Dales and find yourselves a nice hotel somewhere.'

'Algy, I'm going to say yes before you change your mind. No idea when we'll manage a weekend off together, of course, but leave it with me.'

'Splendid.'

'Just one other thing, Algy.'

'Yes?'

'I haven't seen Soapy recently.'

'Ah, you won't.'

'Oh, gone away, has he?'

'No, he's about the place somewhere. But he's ah, he's avoiding certain parties at present.'

'You mean people whose bed he might have boobytrapped.'

'I believe there was talk of a practical joke, yes.'

'Well, perhaps you'd pass on a message to him.'

'Fire away, old boy.'

'I may take my time, but I will have him.'

'That it?'

'That's it, yes.'

I was actually singing as I arrived at the station. That's how good I felt, thinking about Ann and the possibility of a weekend away in Algy's MG. But I stopped as soon as I got out of the car. I'd just seen my partner for the night – for the week, most likely. I hadn't worked with Thommo in an age, and although I'd spotted his name next to mine on the roster the last thing I expected was for him to show up. Over the short time I'd known him I'd realised that Thommo had the worst attendance record of any police officer I've ever met, and trust me, I've met some idle sods in my time. When Thommo wasn't sick he was on a course. And when he wasn't on a course he was lurking around the office filling in forms to go on another one, or some seminar at a university somewhere. He'd done them all: drug abuse, illegal immigrants and sex trafficking; racism, sexism and homophobia; he'd even been off to learn about 'the politics of the workplace' and 'interpersonal relationships', although the general opinion was that he'd not learned a lot about either. And let's not get started on computers. If there was an IT problem, Thommo was certainly the man to sort it out – if you could find him. Whenever a computer course came up his name was first on the sheet. Basically, he would do anything except work a beat. His highest ambition seemed to be to make himself so well qualified that the force didn't dare risk him out there on the streets. I remember what Ed told me after he'd spent a few days working with him. 'Oh he's a special case, no doubt about it,' he said. 'He carries so much knowledge in that head of his he's like them old-fashioned computers they had thirty, forty years ago – you know, the ones that had to be kept in a dust-free atmosphere and you weren't allowed to shout or slam the door. Can't be let out of the building in case his wires short out.'

'What you mean,' I said, 'is he's an idle bastard.'

'Yeah, you could say that. But then maybe we'll get that way when we reach his age. What is he? Fifty-sommat?'

Thommo was indeed past fifty, a wise old bird who knew all the tricks. He once put in a sicknote saying he'd hurt his back throwing a soft toy for his dog. 'I mean, Ed,' I said, 'wouldn't you think a bloke would make something up rather than put down a daft thing like that? Even if it was true? "I was throwing a furry toy for me little dog and me back went"? Come on!'

'Maybe it was the old double bluff, buddy.'

'How d'you mean?'

'Well, "this'll look so bloody outlandish nobody'll dare challenge it", sort of thing.'

'Way too subtle for me, Ed.'

'That's what I'm saying. It's the sort of psychological trick he picks up at those country retreats and health spas. We're out there breaking up the Saturday-night punch-ups and he's got his feet up, absorbing the subtle art of bullshit. Mark my words, buddy. Another year or two and he'll be on the telly explaining why all us beat bobbies need to be replaced by psychiatrists. Then he'll retire.'

'If he doesn't have a heart attack first with all that junk food he shoves in his face.'

There was no doubt about it, Thommo was a challenge. But

if he had one redeeming feature in my book it was that he did, once upon a time, walk a beat. That was many years ago, when he was still in his native Glasgow, and in my book anyone who's patrolled those mean streets must have something to recommend him. He'd even survived a couple of stabbings, if you believed the hearsay. Not that he'd ever talked about it when I was around. But if it was true, well, perhaps he deserved to move over into the slow lane. When I was in the Met it was understood that experienced officers with long years of service had earned the right to take it easy. It was down to the younger officers to make the tea and deal with the more mundane jobs such as handling drunks, taking statements and so on. In Ryedale it was different: there were so few of us that we were all expected to muck in. Except Thommo. He was a special case.

'All right,' I said as we walked across to the car that night. 'Looks like it's you and me against the forces of evil. Just the two of us, shoulder to shoulder against the combined might of the Ryedale crime syndicates. Question is, are you up for it mate? Cos I am. Monday night and I'm raring to go.'

'Listen here, Pannett laddie, I want a nice quiet shift. Finish sharp on time. No roughhouse stuff. Ye got that? And no chases either. If there's any boy racers about we'll fetch the traffic boys in. I'm on a course Wednesday and I need to be fresh.'

'Thommo, I have a strategy in place. Don't you worry. We'll deal with anything they throw at us.'

'And what exactly is yer strategy, eh? What's the psychology behind it?'

'Simple, matey. A basic human emotion. Terror.'

'Terror, eh? I'm all ears.'

'Soon as we see trouble, you get out of the car and stand up to your full height. Once they set eyes on a big ugly bugger like you they'll come to us like lambs.'

'A comedian, eh? Listen, laddie, I'll get out of the car in an emergency. Otherwise I'm riding shotgun. That clear?'

'Aye, go on then.'

'Now, let's get on wi' it.'

As luck would have it, we'd only been on the road twenty minutes when we were called to a disturbance outside one of the pubs across the river in Norton. 'What's the matter wi' these people?' Thommo complained as we sped over the bridge. 'Can they no' wait till a Friday like civilised human beings?'

But to Thommo's great relief we got to the Derwent Arms and found a lot of fuss about not very much. There were half a dozen people out the front and a bit of a slanging match going on. It didn't take much to quieten them down, and it certainly didn't require Thommo to get out of the car. As soon as I appeared one of the youths involved – he can only have been nineteen or so – held up his arms. 'Whoa, lads. Hide your weapons and drop your stash cos here he comes – Dirty Harry!' It was a name I'd acquired after an incident a year or two earlier when I first arrived in Malton and announced that I was going to clean the town up. I'd got used to being greeted with it by the local youngsters, so I wasn't bothered by the lad's little joke. In fact, I was glad of it. It defused the tension right away. It seemed that the landlord had found one of his regulars trying to make off with a tub of flowers. It had got a bit physical, a couple of his mates had joined in, and one of the customers inside had called the police. Within five minutes of my arrival it was agreed that the whole thing had been a prank that got out of hand. Everyone was best mates again and the lads were back inside, signing up to sponsor the landlord on his half marathon the following weekend.

'Sorted,' I said to Thommo as I got back in the car. 'I'm in the wrong job, I reckon. Should've been a diplomat.'

'It wasn't exactly mayhem, laddie. What was the problem anyway?'

'Granny's birthday coming up, and the lads thought it'd be fun to make off with one of them windowboxes.'

'Nothing's sacred these days,' he said as we drove back into town.

'You're dead right there,' I said. And he was. We always say if it's not screwed down, someone'll have it; and if it is screwed down, they'll go and nick a crowbar. At various times in my career I've been sent out in search of anything from forty-ton lorries to scarecrows, grandfather clocks to collections of ladies' underwear nicked from washing lines. On one memorable occasion I found myself trying to trace a prize cockatoo and the roof of a Methodist church – well, the lead off it at any rate – on the same shift. But that was Battersea. When I moved back up north I expected to find a saner environment. In many ways it is saner, but when it comes to thieving, it may be on a lesser scale than the city but it's equally bizarre. I've had to investigate the theft of tractors, weathervanes, garden gnomes, pet dogs, stone troughs full of flowers, sheep . . . I once apprehended a lad who'd stolen a clutch of new-laid eggs from under a sitting hen. Mind you, that was after he'd burgled the house. Told me he hadn't any breakfast. And if ever I imagined that your rural thief was less canny than your city operator, I soon had that illusion shattered. That was when I dashed out of the police station to investigate a break-in at a supermarket in town. They'd got away with 20,000 cigarettes, and if they'd felt like it they could've tooted the horn as they drove by in their getaway vehicle, because when I went to the patrol car I found that they'd had the brass nerve to call by beforehand and let down my tyres.

Thommo and I left town shortly after midnight and took a slow drive eastward around the villages. We took in Rillington, Scagglethorpe, Thorpe Bassett, just scouting around for anything out of the ordinary. We went by the quarry at Knapton, had a look at the maltings down by the railway line, then over to Ganton to see that nobody was parked up by the golf club.

'Dead,' said Thommo. 'Nothin' doin'. And I'm starving, laddie.'

'Aye,' I said. 'Sort of night when you'd get a panther sighting, eh?'

Thommo looked at me. He couldn't work out whether I was having him on.

'Well,' I said, 'it's like UFOs. It only takes one sighting, mate, and you're a convert.'

'Food, laddie! Now! Before you start hallucinating. It's getting on for two, the countryside's deserted, and this old bobby's about to die of starvation. What's your plan?'

'Well, I've got a pack-up,' I said, 'but I know a place where we can get a decent coffee for nowt.'

'They sell grub there?'

'Aye, it's only at Staxton. Be there in five minutes. All-night petrol station. Sells sandwiches, pies, all that good stuff that you like. I've a mate there too. One of the lads off my Country Watch team.'

The lad was pleased to see us. 'Get bored out of my skull on these night shifts,' he said as I ordered a couple of coffees and Thommo went to rummage about among the groceries. 'Way too quiet. I've a job staying awake.'

'Is it worth you staying open?'

'Maybe till about midnight, one o'clock time – and we get a few customers about five in t'morning. But this time of night' – he glanced at the clock, which showed a little after two – 'I doubt we'll see another half dozen till the morning rush.'

'Anything to report on the roads?' I asked as he handed me the coffees.

'Few caravanners coming through, early on.'

Thommo was at the counter with his arms full of goodies. I took the drinks and made my way out to the car. There was a chill in the air and the sky was perfectly clear. There was no moon, so the stars were out in force but already, away to the north-east, there was just the first hint of paleness in the sky. Another hour and it'd be light.

'That's very good of you,' I said, as Thommo climbed into the car beside me.

'What d'you mean?'

I nodded to the stack of grub he had in his hands: two huge sandwiches, two bottles of cola and a large packets of crisps, plus a couple of Yorkie bars wrapped up in a magazine. 'I mean, you didn't have to do it, standing me supper. But I appreciate it. I really do.' I even reached across and tried to grab one of the sarnies.

'You said you'd brought your own grub.' He hugged his purchases closer to his chest.

'But you've got enough for two there, surely.'

'Maybe for two ordinary men, laddie. But I'm not ordinary.'

'No,' I murmured, 'you're heading for a heart attack buddy.' But the noise he made munching, he never heard me.

We parked up along the A64, near the Little Chef where we could observe any vehicles coming off the roundabout. It was deadly quiet – or it would have been were it not for Thommo tearing into his grub.

'Don't you ever chew?' I asked him.

'Hmph?' He'd got half the sandwich in his mouth and was shoving a few bits of trailing ham fat in after it.

'Don't you chew your grub before you swallow it?'

'Hey, never you mind my eating habits, Pannett. Just watch the road.'

We sat for twenty minutes or so, engine ticking over, lights off. A swathe of pale blue was tinting the sky on the eastern horizon. A handful of vehicles went by, mostly heading towards York. I doubt if any of them spotted us. Thommo yawned, checked his watch and burped loudly. 'Only three hours,' he said.

'Three and a half,' I corrected him, but he didn't respond. He was leaning back in his seat with his eyes closed. Then he started scratching his legs. At first I ignored it, but after a while I had to ask. 'What the hell are you scratching at, Thommo?'

'It's these bloody trousers, mon. Did I not tell ye? I'm trialing them for the force – being on the clothing committee we get first go at all the latest gear.'

'Clothing committee? You have to be joking.'

'Nae, laddie. It exists all right. And I'm on it. Here, take a look.' As I leaned forward he raised a leg towards my face. He was wearing thick woollen trousers with pockets on the side of the thigh, combat style.

'Thommo,' I said, 'this is the kind of gear the youngsters are wearing. They're all the rage, mate. Cutting edge of fashion.'

'Aye, the uniform for the twenty-first century.' He scratched again. 'But hellish itchy, mon.'

'You're a hero, Thommo. Only a man like you would volunteer to wear those.' I yawned. 'Well, I reckon we could take a slow drive back towards town,' I said. 'And maybe do a few of the villages again.' But even as I spoke I saw something that struck me as strange. 'Look at that,' I said, digging him in the ribs.

Thommo sat up and grunted. 'A caravan? What d'you expect on the coast road coming up to summertime?'

'Bit late to be on the move.'

'Or early. Depends on your point of view.'

'Aye, but look what's pulling it.' It was a Ford Mondeo, ten years old and burning oil.

'Fair point.'

'Did you see who was driving it?'

'No.'

'Couple of young lads.' I said, shifting the gearstick forward. 'They're not your average Caravan Club of Great Britain merchants.' We were no sooner on the road than it became clear that they'd seen us. They accelerated away towards Malton, sending out a cloud of smoke.

'1015 to control, vehicle check.'

'*Yeah, go ahead, Mike*'.

I gave the registration number on the caravan, and our location and direction of travel.

I tried to keep a reasonable distance. I didn't want to panic them, but they were cranking up their speed all the time. Fifty, fifty-five, sixty.

'*Control to 1015.*'

'Go ahead.'

'*That number is registered to a Land Rover at—*'

'Told you,' I said, as I put my foot down.

'Bloody hell, Pannett, how d'you do it? Everywhere you go you find trouble.' Thommo shoved the remains of a Yorkie bar into his mouth and threw the wrapper on the floor.

We were doing seventy now and still they were picking up speed, the caravan snaking left and right as they took the curves. 'Never chased one of these before,' I said. 'Weird feeling.'

'1015 to control, I need backup here. Suspect caravan is being pulled by a Mondeo, two up, travelling west on the A64 between Staxton and Ganton at high speed . . . ' I put on the lights and two-tones. 'And failing to stop.'

'Christ,' said Thommo, 'they're all over the place. Seventy-five . . . they're going to lose it.'

'Approaching red light at Staxton . . . eighty miles an hour.' I couldn't help myself, I had just had to add a classic Met phrase. 'They're all over the road.'

A car coming towards us braked, swerved to the side of the road and bumped the verge. 'Endangering oncoming traffic – straight through the red light.' As well as letting control know what was going on, and keeping any nearby patrol cars informed, my running commentary was serving another purpose. It was being recorded in the control room and would form part of my evidence if and when we pressed charges.

We were past Staxton when the caravan started to slow down to around 60mph. 'Now what?' I wondered aloud. 'Shit!'

We had reached a small side road on the left, and with no warning the suspects slammed the brakes on. As the car swerved left the van swung out to the right until it was jerked back into line. I wound the window down to get rid of the stench of burnt rubber.

'Now on the side road that cuts through to the Luttons. Caravan brake lights inoperative.'

Our speed had dropped to fifty. We were on a narrow road, and everything seemed to be happening much faster as undergrowth flashed by and the caravan, barely thirty feet ahead of us now, bucked over the uneven surface, swaying to left and right. As it negotiated a left-hander, the nearside caravan wheel left the ground completely for a moment. I held my breath and waited for it to tip over, easing off on the accelerator, fully expecting a crash. I was having visions of me and Thommo in a foot chase – and I didn't fancy it.

Just when I thought the van was going to topple over, the wheel dropped back down. I slammed the car into third. 'This is going to be interesting, Thommo. Either this lad knows just how far to push it, or he's very lucky.'

'Aye, but you can handle it, Pannett. I've every faith in you. And these.' He tapped the airbag compartment on the dashboard.

'It gets bloody steep up ahead.'

'Aye, and narrower. Let's hope they don't meet any oncoming.'

'*Control to 1015. We have backup approaching from Filey.*'

'Right. They want to be coming at us on the Foxholes to Ganton road. Repeat Foxholes to Ganton,' I said, and then to Thommo, 'That should stitch 'em up like a pair of kippers.' We were climbing now, into the woods, and our speed continued to drop. 'If the Filey boys can get through Foxholes before us we've got 'em.'

'What the hell are they playing at?' We were halfway up the hill, doing no more than twenty miles an hour and slowing all the time. Thommo had wound down his window and was leaning out, trying to get a look at the car. 'Can't see a bloody thing.' He swore and ducked back in as a stray bramble whipped across his face.

'Must be losing power,' I said. 'They're pulling a fair bit of weight.' I was in second gear, then first. We were barely moving at walking pace.

'They've stopped the bloody thing!'

'Right, I'm going after them!' Thommo opened the door and started to get out. God, I thought, I hope you're up to it. The thing with Thommo was, he may have been in the twilight of his career, he may have been a skiving sod, but when there was trouble his old copper's instinct was still alive and well.

'Whoa there!' The car door slammed and he was back inside, shouting at me. 'Back up, man! Back up!' As I slung it into reverse I saw what he was on about. The caravan was rolling back down the hill towards us.

'I don't frigging believe this.'

'Come on, mon! 'Fore it bloody hits us.'

'Christ, I hope there's nothing coming up this hill.' As the caravan lurched towards us we careered backwards at ten, fifteen, twenty miles an hour. Thommo was half out of the window, craning his neck, cursing as the leaves whipped the back of his head. 'Cannae see a bloody thing!' he shouted. 'Can you not go any faster?'

'No, I bloody well can't.'

'Aye well, they're only light, you know.' Thommo was watching the caravan as it bounced off one verge and then the other, still gaining on us. 'Proper flimsy. If it hits us it'll come off worse.'

'That makes me feel a lot better.'

'There she goes now.' The caravan had hit the embankment, climbed a few feet up it, and came to a juddering halt. As I slammed the brakes on it flopped gently over onto its side, completely blocking the lane.

'Right, let's have 'em.' I was out of the car with my Asp and my CS gas, squeezing my way between the caravan's roof and a clump of stinging nettles.

'Why the cheeky—!' I'd got past the van, half expecting to find an overturned car. In fact, there was no car at all, and certainly no youths, just the stink of burning oil.

'You know what they've done, don't you?' Thommo was at my side now, panting and wheezing. 'They've unhitched the bugger in motion.'

'That's about the sum and substance of it. They've slowed down and one of the little sods has got out.'

Thommo looked down the empty road. 'Still, I daresay your backup lads'll pick 'em up.'

'Don't count on it, Thommo. There's a little lane off to the left, just a few hundred yards or so. Takes 'em back onto the Driffield road. These lads have local knowledge or they wouldn't have found this road in the first place.'

It turned out I was right unless they'd slipped into a field and were waiting for the fuss to calm down. When the backup car arrived they told us they hadn't seen a single vehicle since Foxholes. So there we were, our way forward blocked by the caravan, and just to put the tin lid on it, we now had a newspaper-delivery van behind us.

We passed the information to control and they alerted Humberside as well as York. But of course we hadn't a clue where the Mondeo would be heading – if it was heading anywhere.

'Thommo,' I said, as we stood there weighing up our options, 'you've got to hand it to the buggers.'

'Aye?'

'I don't like to say it, but they've outsmarted us.'

It took an age to unravel everything. We had to wait a full hour to get a recovery vehicle from a garage in Scarborough. Meanwhile control came through and told us the caravan had been nicked from a site out near Cayton Bay. The residents were a couple of holidaymakers from the Midlands. They'd gone out to a club in Scarborough, come home about one o'clock after a few drinks and wandered round the site for twenty minutes wondering where the hell their van was.

'Could've been worse,' I said to Thommo as we drove back to Malton. 'I once had a couple over Whitby way, went to the shower block and came back in their dressing gowns to see the van disappearing through the gate.'

'It doesn't surprise me, laddie. Like I said, you attract trouble. Thank God I'm away on that course tomorrow.'

Chapter 7

Bank Holiday Blues

Bank holidays. Don't get me started. I hope I don't sound like a killjoy, but sometimes I wish they could be done away with. I really do. It's not as if people are short of leisure opportunities. It's not as if we're living in the nineteenth century when a trip to the seaside in a charabanc was the highlight of a working man's year. I mean, we can get in the car and pop over to Scarborough or Whitby any time we like now. You can drive across after work on a summer evening, have a stroll on the beach, a fish-and-chip supper and a pleasant drive back across the moors and still be home in daylight. As for shopping, if that's what you really want, you can do it seven days a week; and you can get away on a sunshine holiday any month of the year. The problem with doing anything on a bank holiday, as far as I'm concerned, is crowds: on the roads, in town, at the seaside. I'd really rather be at work, getting double the usual rate of pay, and go to such places on my days off during the week when there's not as many folk around. Yes, you can have bank holidays. Even when I'm at work I'm not crazy about them. From a policing point of view, they throw up too many surprises. Strange things happen. Unpleasant things. And God help us if it's a full moon as well, because that really can bring out the worst in people.

I've sometimes thought that there's an awful lot of folk out there who are only really happy when they're at work. Perhaps I should say 'men' rather than 'folk'; I mean, what would I know about women? On a bad day – and bank holidays have given me some of my worst experiences as a serving officer – I'd be tempted to say that by the time a Monday comes around there are quite a lot of men who would rather be back at work than stuck at home, given a straight choice. I've seen too much of the bad stuff that kicks off when people are cooped up in the house with folk they'd rather avoid, by which I mean their nearest and dearest. Don't get me wrong; I'm not a cynic. When a family functions as it's supposed to you've got the perfect social unit: loving, supportive, a safe haven from a cruel world. But when it falls apart – well, I'd rather deal with a good old-fashioned punch-up at throwing-out time than what we politely call a 'domestic'.

What surprises a lot of people – including new recruits to the police force – is that incidents involving domestic violence occur right across the social spectrum. Pardon the fancy language: I've been on too many courses about this stuff. Sit there for three days listening to some sociologist rambling on and you soon start talking like one. But the point is that rich or poor, management class or shop floor, council estate or executive village, you get domestic disputes everywhere. Usually, of course, it's a falling-out between a husband and a wife, or I suppose I should say partner these days. Sometimes it involves former partners, occasionally kids. Now and then it'll be a family feud of some sort and the fallout affects an entire neighbourhood. They can happen at any time, but in my experience they're far more likely to occur when people are off work, stuck at home, and skint. You get called out on a Sunday afternoon when the lunchtime drink has got to work. You get called out towards the end of the long Christmas break, when people have been around the house for days on end and are sick of the sight of each other. And you get called out late on a bank holiday.

I was on a late shift. And it was a bank holiday. It was hot, and sunny, and everywhere had been busy. Or so they told me when I went into work. I'd been at Keeper's Cottage all day, well out of the way, cutting logs with Nick, my gamekeeper mate from out Rillington way. One of the great things about Nick is that whatever he's doing and wherever he is, he's always thinking about the wildlife. He was outside with me, first thing, supping the mug of dark, sweet tea without which he could never be expected to start work. 'Hear that?' he said, and before I could answer he was holding up a finger to tell me to keep my mouth shut.

I listened. A blackbird was trilling away in the bushes by the dyke and a fat bumblebee was droning about in a pyracantha that grew up the side of the garage and was just now a mass of creamy white blossom. Then I caught it. Away in the woods was the sound of a woodpecker at work. 'That what you mean?' I started, but he'd strolled across to the beck side and was looking into the water. 'Hmm. Fair few little tiddlers in here,' he said. He had a way of saying things whereby you knew that he approved of what he was seeing. He liked to see nature thriving. He hated pollution, and he couldn't stand waste. 'Wouldn't be surprised if you got a visit from a heron some time. I've seen one down-stream of here a time or two. Not this year, though.' He looked into the field that lay on the other side of the beck. 'Now then,

I wonder where your fox is,' he said. 'You get a rabbit warren like that there'll be a family of foxes in the vicinity. You can bank on it.'

'Funny you should say that,' I said, 'because I have heard some yipping and yowling at night.'

'Aye, you will. I dare say if you kick around in the grass there you'll find a trace or two.' He was pointing towards the dyke that ran down the south side of the clearing. On the other side of it, across a broken fence and a tangle of brambles, was an area of rank grass dotted with shrubby willows and one or two thorn trees. It had probably been pasture once upon a time but it was too boggy for anyone to be bothered with it now.

'Anyway, we have work to do.' He drained his mug and placed it on the kitchen windowsill. 'You fit?'

There was a big old sycamore tree that had come down before I moved in, and he'd been promising me for weeks that he'd bring his chainsaw round, but something had always got in the way. We put in a good morning's work between us, him cutting, and me hauling the big round logs out of the woods or trimming the fallen branches with my bow-saw. By the time we stopped for lunch I had a big stack piled up next to the garage, a tangle of brushwood on the edge of the drive, a huge fat one I'd put aside to make a garden seat, and a nasty little cut on the inside of my left hand where I'd got over-keen. I could also feel a headache brewing up. Nick cast an eye over my pile of logs. 'You'll want to get a tarp over them before the summer's out,' he said. 'Then next year you can split 'em. Reckon you've a good winter's supply there.'

We'd had a productive morning, and a satisfying one, but much as I'd enjoyed it I simply wasn't used to that sort of work.

By the time Nick got into his Land Rover and drove home, I was feeling more like a nap in the chair than an eight-hour shift. My muscles – and my bones – were aching.

I was working from four till midnight. It's a turn we do at weekends and holidays, mainly so that when the night crew come on at ten there are plenty of staff for that first couple of hours, because things are inclined to be hectic. The first person I bumped into when I got to the station was my old mate Jayne. Mate? I suppose sparring partner would be more like it. 'Blimey,' she said, in that grating cockney accent of hers, 'ain't seen you in bleedin' ages. Where you been 'iding?'

I picked up the binder and flipped through the latest briefing notes: who was on the wanted list, what unattended premises we had to keep an eye on, and a sort of digest of what had been happening over the last twenty-four hours. 'I've been where the action is, Jayne. Holding the fort, manning the trenches, keeping this town safe for decent God-fearing people. And do you know what?'

'What?'

'I think it's you who've been hiding. Because every time there was trouble I looked around, and you were nowhere to be seen. I mean, my own fellow officer. Where were you?'

'Come on, Mike, is that fair? I mean, think about it. Is it consistent?'

'What do you mean, consistent?'

'Well, you're always telling me I should stop looking for trouble. Now you're bellyaching cos I managed to avoid it.'

'This is true, but I don't mean avoid trouble as in aggravation on the streets – and you know it. Anyway, Jayne, it looks as though the people of Ryedale will be looking to you and me to keep the peace this evening, so—'

'So you're gonna be really, really nice to me, right?'

'Of course I am, Jayne. Would I ever be anything else?'

It was all good fun. Jayne and I did tend to wind each other up a bit. Neither of us could resist having a go. Call it the north-south divide. But she was turning into a decent enough copper and the odd time I'd been out on the beat with her we'd got along better than I expected. She certainly wouldn't hang back if things turned rough, and you appreciate that in a mate. Trouble is, she was a bit too keen. Always wanting to read the riot act and clap the handcuffs on people, whereas I prefer to find other solutions to achieve the same result. I like to talk the buggers into submission, have a quiet word in their ear, let them know I'm on their case. Apart from anything else, it saves you a lot of paperwork. I prefer to take on those individuals who need squaring up and use my discretion in the case of the minor misdemeanours. But that was me. Jayne was different. As we like to say in our part of the world, she wasn't backward about coming forward.

The first half of my shift was – well, the best word to describe it would be bitty. I was single-manned, as we often are on a late turn, and seemed to spend the first few hours darting back and forth answering calls about trivial matters. Well, they weren't trivial to the people who rang in, but to me, with my headache taking a hold, and the cut on my hand starting to throb, they just seemed like a bloody nuisance. Kids playing football on a green and making too much noise. Really. I was tempted to tell the person who was making all the fuss to close his windows and turn the telly up – but then I remembered that his neighbour had called me out just a year ago because . . . yep, his telly was too loud. And there had been a clutch of petty thefts from cars parked at various tourist spots. First I had to trail out to Nunnington Hall and then all the way back over to Wharram Percy. It was the usual thing: people leaving valuables on display. It's a recurring problem in our beauty spots. Every so often you'll get a spate of it, and it often turns out to be the one gang responsible for it all. Then it'll go quiet for a year or so. If only they would lock their stuff in the boot. But they never learn. On this occasion, at Wharram, it was a holdall left on the back seat. It contained nothing more exciting than the owner's sweaty gym kit, but the thieves wouldn't know that until they unzipped it later. Meanwhile the owner was left with his car full of smashed window glass and a substantial repair bill.

Early in the evening, about seven or so, I made my way back to base for a bite to eat. I was sweating like a pig and my head was hurting, and there was Chris, the desk sergeant, leaning back in his chair, hands behind his head humming a tune to himself. 'By heck,' I said, 'I've seen more life in the chapel of rest.'

'Well, there isn't a lot doing, to tell the truth.'

'That's what I want to hear. With a bit of luck it'll stay that way till the night shift come in.'

Chris pursed his lips and inhaled slowly. 'Long way to go yet, mate. Warm, sticky evening like this, anything can kick off. Very volatile people in this town.'

'Thanks, Chris. Always look on the bright side, eh?'

'All I'm doing, Mike, is alerting you to the simmering undercurrent, the seething tide of discontent that lies beneath the surface of a deceptively peaceful little town.'

'You've been reading those detective books again, haven't you?'

Chris grinned, reached under the desk and pulled out a paper-back book. 'I was just having a crafty dip into this,' he said. 'In me tea break, of course.'

'Of course.' I looked at the cover. 'Inspector Rebus? Hmm, no wonder you're expecting chaos to break out any moment.'

'Mike, we need to be prepared.'

'Chris, I'm ready for anything. But you have to remember, this is rural North Yorkshire, not urban Scotland. They're a different proposition up there. Anyway' – I'd poured myself a mug of tea and needed to take something for my head – 'have we got any paracetemol on the premises?'

After I'd eaten my sandwich I drove out of town and up past the gallops to Leavening. I called on Walt, helped him drain his teapot, and had a quick dip in his biscuit tin. He started telling me about his plans for a pond in the field at the back. 'Are you sure this isn't just wishful thinking?' I said. 'I mean, you've been on about this before. Hell of an undertaking, making a pond.'

'Don't you worry, lad.' He pushed his cap back and tapped a finger against his forehead. 'I'm working up a scheme. Trouble is, I need one of them fancy big diggers. Hydraulic job.'

'They don't come cheap.'

'No, they don't. But I'm working on it.'

'Don't tell me. You know a man who knows a man.'

He grinned. 'I do. Except it's a lady.'

'Walt, if there's a woman involved you've cracked it. You have a way with women. I don't know what your secret is, but they seem to be putty in your hands.'

Walt finished his biscuit, swilled a last drop of tea around his mouth, and reached into his pocket. 'I charm 'em,' he said. 'That's me secret. I'm telling you, you could learn a thing or two from me, m'lad.' And saying that, he popped his dental plate back in.

It was gone half past nine when I came back to town. I was properly tired now, wishing it was a normal late turn and I could be off home in half an hour or so. Still, with a bit of luck I could coast through the next couple of hours. But no, it was going to be one of those nights. I was just turning into Old Maltongate when the call came.

'*Report of a serious domestic incident . . .*' The address was out towards the Castle Howard road.

'1015 to control. Show me en route.'

I got a few more details as I drove back towards the traffic lights. Someone had called in to say she'd heard the sound of breaking glass at her neighbour's house, opened her door to see what it was all about and heard a women shrieking. I'll be honest and say that if I'd heard that reported from some neighbourhoods on my patch I wouldn't have been too concerned. I would've responded, of course I would, but I certainly wouldn't have been as worried as I was now. This call had come from a neighbourhood that was very much at the upmarket end of town. People like that don't start shrieking for no good reason. I didn't like the sound of it at all. It was an instinctive feeling, and I've learned to trust those. I was involved in countless violent incidents during my time in the Met and the shudder I now felt in my lower abdomen was all too familiar. Even as I switched on the lights and two-tones and accelerated away up Yorkersgate, I was asking control to check who lived at this place, and whether any previous incidents had been reported at that address, or whether any firearms were listed as being held there. But no, when Julie in the control room got back to me there was nothing known at that address.

'1015 to control, have we any backup en route?'

'Just on with it now, Mike.'

It was reassuring to hear Julie's voice. She was generally calm, and always efficient. You could count on her.

I was driving fast, foot down in third gear, ready to stamp on the brake. It's a fine line, and you adapt to the circumstances. Back in Battersea you'd almost always have congestion of some sort, the traffic moving at a snail's pace, pedestrians stepping out into the road just to make headway along the crowded pavements, and all complicated by the fact that we were often in unmarked cars. Sometimes, the roads were so busy that we'd mount the pavement, and just for a moment it really was the sort of thing you see on the telly, with the odd wheelie bin getting knocked over. Here in Yorkersgate the street looked clear, so I could give it some welly, but I had one eye on the takeaway shops and pubs just in case. You never know when someone's going to dart out, right across you.

I swung right at the war memorial. The red poppies of last November's wreath were almost glowing in the gathering dusk, and I heard myself say, 'Right then.' Every time I pass that spot, especially if I'm in a hurry, a little voice inside seems to be reminding me, 'Go steady. You don't want to end up dead.'

'Right then.' I repeated the words out loud, and then went through my checks, as if I was a tennis player preparing for a vital match-saving point. 'Remember the family. Don't take risks. Deep breath. Stay calm. Concentrate. Have you got all the information you need? CS gas handy? Body armour?'

We're all issued with body armour, and a lot of officers, particularly the younger ones, will wear it all through their shift, rain or shine. I can see the sense in that, but I just can't stand that feeling of being straitjacketed, weighed down, and hot. So mine lives on the back seat, and, yes, I have been known to worm myself into it while driving to a call, guiding the wheel with my knees. I shouldn't, but I do. We call it body armour, but really it's just a padded, knifeproof sleeveless vest designed to protect your vital organs. So while your heart and lungs and suchlike are safe, your arms, your neck, your head, your crotch, your thighs, are all vulnerable. Still, there's no question that it gives you a lot more confidence when you're going into a dangerous situation, such as this threatened to be.

I was by now within two or three hundred yards of the address I'd been given, driving slowly along a road darkened by the lush early-season foliage of copper beeches and lindens. I switched the lights and two-tones off. It's always as well with this sort of situation. If you're heading towards a street fight, yes, blaze away. You know it'll have some sort of impact. They'll stop and look up. But in a case like this, the silent approach. Always. The last thing you want to do is excite them, and a police car roaring up the street in a blaze of light will just fan the flames, as often as not.

'*Control to 1015. You have backup five minutes away.*'

I was approaching the house now. Five minutes, eh? A hell of a lot can happen in five minutes. I looked at the clock on the dashboard. Half an hour later and we'd have the night shift available. I didn't like the thought of going in alone. If there's one thing that's always on my mind it's that more police officers are hurt when responding to domestic incidents than any other type of call. In London we never took any chances. I've been to more than one false alarm and come away to find six or seven cars pulled up outside and twenty officers ready to pile in and protect me.

The place was a detached bungalow, probably no more than

twenty years old with large picture windows at the front. It was ablaze with light, inside and out, and the curtains were open. As I got out of the car I zipped up the protective vest and folded the velcro'd flaps over it, patted my sides to make sure my Asp was in place, and gave the CS gas a good shake. If you don't do that every so often it'll settle in the canister and just when you need it it'll fail you.

I walked up the gravelled driveway, past a couple of bay trees in terracotta pots. Through a front window I saw a female, mid-fifties, slim, her hair short and dyed blonde. She was wearing a white sun-top and she was standing motionless, breathing heavily, staring at a door that led to another room. Through the adjacent window I saw a man, same sort of age, balding, ruddy face, dark blue sweatshirt. He was looking at the same door from the other side. I saw him lean forward and heard him shout something. I couldn't work it out, but he certainly wasn't asking her what she wanted for her supper. The woman moved towards the door, raised her hand and that's when I saw she was carrying a knife, its blade all of ten inches long, the sort you'd use to carve a Sunday roast. She screamed something, and reached forward to grab the door handle. The man bellowed, backed away, ran across the room and out through another door towards the far side.

'1015 to control. Urgent message.'

'Yes go *ahead, Mike.*'

'I have a female armed with a knife who is threatening a male on the premises. Could you make a request for Armed Response to attend and get me an ETA. Over.' I'd no hesitation asking for an Armed Response Vehicle. When people see one of those pull up and guys leaping out with guns in their hands they think we're going over the top. But ask yourself. How do you get a knife like that out of someone's hands? The simple truth is, you have to be prepared for the worst.

Even as I made the call I saw the woman open the door the man had just disappeared through. If she caught up with him, there was going to be bloodshed. I was in no doubt about that. The hairs on the back of my neck stood up and I could feel the adrenaline pumping through my veins. This was a very nasty situation. It may have been a middle-aged female I was dealing with, but she was armed with a deadly weapon, and was perfectly capable of killing someone. More than that, she really looked as though she meant business.

What were my options? I'd dealt with numerous knife incidents in the Met – especially when I served in the TSG – but I was always in a team, with specialist kit to hand. This was different. It would be foolhardy to burst in alone at this stage, but I was well aware that if things got any worse I might have to. I quietly tried the front door. 'Bugger.' It was locked. And a uPVC door isn't the easiest to smash down.

I hurried across the lawn at the front of the bungalow, past a kitchen window. Nobody there. To the side was a passage that led to the rear. I peered around the corner of the house on to an unlit patio area furnished with a wrought-iron table and chairs, but as soon as I stepped out on came the lights, dazzling me. I shielded my eyes and looked through what appeared to be a bedroom window. Nothing. Next to it was a bathroom, frosted glass. The one beyond that was in darkness. I was now making my way back to the front of the house, past an open side window through which I clearly heard the woman scream a single phrase: 'You've had it coming, you cheating bastard!'

'1015 to control. Better get an ambulance too.'

I was now back to square one. The woman with the knife

was in the front living room; the man was in the dining room and heading for the door that led to the kitchen. There was a tall shrub against the front wall, prickly and dark. Using it as cover, I edged closer. I could see right into the farther room where the man was. He was wearing shorts and was barefoot. He was sweating, and his shoulders were going up and down as he caught his breath. If ever a man had fear in his eyes it was him.

Sometimes in situations like this it's like a combination of an out-of-body experience and watching a movie. As your body reacts to the adrenaline surge, you're suddenly encapsulated in your own sensory world, acutely aware of your heart beating hard in your chest and the pulse reverberating in your ears. You become more aware of your heavy breathing, extra-sensitive to changes in temperature, smells and so on. Any action that kicks off seems remote, as if you're watching that movie. It's separate from you but at the same time it's very real – and very frightening.

I looked back towards the living room, but from where I was standing I could only see part of it. There was no sign of the woman. Where the hell had she got to? Was she behind the curtain, or had she doubled back to attack him from the other side? The man was now opening the door to go through to the kitchen, moving forward warily and looking over his shoulder as he did so. But where was the woman? At that moment I heard the gravel scrunching behind me. As I turned I felt a hand on my back.

'Jesus Christ!'

'Bleedin' hell, it's only me, Mike!'

'Jayne, for God's sake! Nearly stopped my heart.'

'What's the score then?'

'We've got a woman chasing her husband round the house

with a knife. And I mean knife.' Just as I spoke she passed the window, heading towards the door. 'There she is now. See it?'

'Ouch. That is a frigging knife. What's the plan then? Do we go in?'

'We are *not* going in unless we have to. And even then we've got to get through that bloody locked door. Tell you what, though, I may as well let 'em know they've got company. You wait here – hang about.' I reached for my radio. It was an update from the control room. '*Mike, you have two more turning out from Malton and the ARVs are about twenty minutes away.*'

I approached the kitchen window as fast as I could and banged on it with my fist as the woman ran by. She didn't even hear me. 'It's the police!' I shouted. Nothing. No response at all. She had one thing on her mind and that was getting to her man and carving lumps out of him.

I stepped back towards where Jayne was, crouching next to the evergreen to get a better view.

'Oh shit.' Through the window we saw the husband enter the kitchen, pull open a drawer and take out a vicious-looking knife with a black handle and a serrated blade, forked at the end. Jayne was right by my side, breathing heavily, wriggling to get comfortable in her body armour, shaking her gas canister. 'This is like a bloody slasher movie,' she said.

'Aye, but not quite as many laughs.' I was wondering what the hell to do next, but I was determined above all that we were not going to endanger ourselves needlessly.

Jayne had pulled out her Asp. 'Shall I give 'em another tap?'

'Go on then. But back off quick, just in case.' I was remembering Wood coming at me through the window that day last winter. When people are as angry as this woman was they seem to find extra reserves of strength. They forget about fear. And they'll turn on you without any warning.

Jayne went to the window and banged, hard and loud. Still no response from either of them. They were totally absorbed in the business of hunting each other down. 'Now what?' she said. I crept forward to join her, removing my tie as the sweat trickled down my neck. But before I had time to think of an answer the whole thing kicked off. I was at the window, about to whack it one more time, when I saw the door to the kitchen open. In she went, the knife above her head. The man had his knife held out in front of him. He shouted something as he edged backwards, looking nervily over his shoulder, but she wasn't stopping. She advanced on him, stealthy, purposeful, menacing. I felt myself shake, even as my head throbbed with the heat. She was within three or four yards of him. He took another step back and I could see him reaching behind himself, fumbling for the door-knob. One long stride forward and she lunged with the knife, but as he pulled his stomach in and stood on his toes he got the door open and was out, slamming it behind him.

'This way!' I shouted to Jayne as I set off down the side passage once more. We got around the other side in time to see a French door swing open and both of them burst onto the patio, blinking as the lights came on once more. Beyond the paved area was a low hedge, cut so that it looked like a row of birds, and beyond that a lawn, velvety smooth. It was all so perfectly neat, like something out of *Home and Garden*. For a second I stood there, as if hypnotised. Here was this guy, over six feet tall, bulky, broad-shouldered, holding the knife, and facing him was a woman who can't have been more than five two, five three, slightly built, and he was fending her off, holding his own blade in front of him but never looking as dangerous as her. Back he went, one short step at a time, and she kept on coming. We could see what was going to happen. He hit the hedge and stumbled. Somehow, he kept his feet, but she was onto him now, bringing the knife back past her hip and then lunging upwards at his chest.

The first time she missed. God knows how, but she did. By the time she took another swing – and missed again – I actually thought she was about to commit murder in front of us. I dashed forward across the patio with Jayne just behind me. 'Police! Put the knife down!' And as the woman drew her arm back a third time, I leaned back and swung my right leg. It was pure luck. I caught her just as she steadied herself to take aim at his throat. The knife spun away in an arc and clattered against the metal tabletop before hitting the ground and skidding away under a bed of herbs. For a brief moment I stood there, shocked that my foot had connected so perfectly. The woman had turned to look at me, her mouth open, her left hand clutching at her wrist.

'Mike!' Jayne was shouting at me. As I turned I saw her leap across my field of vision towards the woman, catching her in a rugby tackle and rolling to one side as the man dived in. He was roaring like an animal, and there was only one thing on his mind. He wanted her dead.

'You f***ing bitch!' He hit the ground hard, and grunted as the wind was knocked out of him. Even as he turned to pick up the knife he'd dropped I was on him with the gas canister, spraying him in the face for a full two seconds.

'Got her, Mike!' The woman was on her front. Jayne was pressing a knee into her back and locking the cuffs on one arm before reaching out to grasp the other.

The guy was easy. He had his hands to his face, rubbing at

his eyes and spluttering. It was only as I leaned over him to make sure the cuffs were good and tight around his wrists that I caught the alcohol on his breath, through the pungent smell of the gas.

I stood over him, getting my wind back. I was about to wipe the sweat off my eyebrows, but instead just shook my head and watched the droplets fall on the paving stones. My hands were drenched with the CS spray.

'He's the one you want to arrest. He started it.' The woman was on her knees, trying to stand up. The fight seemed to have gone out of her,

'Don't listen to her. You saw her, coming at me, the mad bitch—'

Jayne had sat the woman down on one of the metal chairs. 'Put 'em in the cars, shall we?'

But I was on the radio. '1015 to control, update.'

'*Go ahead Mike.*'

'Two detained in back garden, weapons secure, have had to use CS spray, both in handcuffs, no injuries.'

'*All received Mike, backup should be with you any moment.*'

'Yes.' I was struggling to catch my breath. 'Yes, over.'

Jayne was looking at me. Then she cocked her ear and jerked a thumb towards the driveway. I could hear sirens and see the lights through the trees out the front. Seconds later we were joined by the ARV crew, a young traffic officer I remembered vaguely from an accident we'd attended out towards Thirsk. Chris Cocks was in the van with one of the night-shift officers. As they approached I realised that both the captives were struggling, still trying to get at each other. Chris and I grabbed the man and led him to the front of the house, leaving Jayne and the traffic officer with the woman.

'You're under arrest for affray,' I told the man. He said nothing. He was breathing hard, his fists clenched. I searched him to see whether he had any other weapons concealed, then put him in the back of the van. Jayne put the woman in the back of the traffic car. She'd calmed down and was now in tears.

The ARV lad called across to me. 'You gonna need this?' An ambulance was pulling in behind his car and a paramedic in a green uniform was opening the passenger door.

'Probably not. But we near as hell did. Take a look at the knives they were playing with.'

'Nasty. Any damage to yourselves?'

'No. You hurt, Jayne?' She shook her head, and watched as the paramedic climbed into the back of the police van and helped the man out of his T-shirt to examine him. He had two long red marks on his chest, scratches more than actual cuts, pimpled with blood.

'She do that with the knife?' Jayne said to me, 'or d'you think they were playing rough?'

'Why don't you ask them when they've sobered up?'

'What about you, though?' She was frowning, looking at my hand, which was now oozing blood and stinging like crazy.

'You want to get that seen to, buddy,' the traffic officer said. 'Got you with the knife, did they?'

'No,' I said, 'that was the chainsaw. Or bow-saw. One or the other.'

'Jesus, they had a chainsaw?' When I saw the look on his pale young face, still bearing the scars of acne, I laughed aloud. 'No,' I said, 'I was out in the woods this morning.' I turned to Jayne. 'And I tell you what, that seems a bloody long time ago now.'

I left Chris and the night-duty PC to search the house to

make sure there was no one else on the premises, any kids or anything. He found a set of house keys in the door and locked up before handing them to me. I put the knives into a couple of property bags from the boot of the car. Somewhere I had some special knife-holders – stout plastic tubes – but I couldn't find them, and I wasn't that concerned. We'd come through it with no casualties; that's what mattered.

I don't know about Jayne, but I was shattered. Even so, we drove the happy couple to Scarborough to be taken into custody, one in each vehicle.

The good news for us was that neither of the prisoners was in a fit state to be interviewed that evening, being out of their heads on drink. So a little after midnight I was able to drive back to base with Jayne to write up our notes. On the way back all the 'what if' questions started crowding into my head. Sometimes the horror of what might have happened is worse than the fear you deal with during the actual incident. If you're not careful it'll keep you awake at night.

'Bleedin' hell,' Jayne said as we finally left the station and went across the car park together. 'I've got a doctor's appointment at eight.'

I looked at my watch. Three o'clock. The birds were all chittering and the sky was already a pale blue. There was just the faintest touch of condensation on my windscreen.

'Young lass like you,' I said. 'You should take it in your stride. And think of payday. That's eleven hours at double time. You'll be laughing all the way to the bank.'

As I drove home, gripping the steering wheel, my hand started stinging again and my headache threatened to return, but I took a deep breath and told myself to relax. Yes, it had been a long shift, and a difficult one, but the outcome had been good. We could easily have had a death on our hands, but we hadn't. In the end nobody suffered anything worse than scraped knees and a bruised elbow. We'd done well. We'd resisted the temptation to break in on the feuding couple, which I might well have tried when I was a young copper. Yes, it had crossed my mind to go in, and I knew all along that if the woman had caught up with her husband I would've done so. Maybe we'd just been lucky. That flying kick with which I disarmed the woman, for example. Pure chance that I caught her the way I did.

I would later find out that the couple had been married twenty years or more, that they'd been drinking all day and simply lost control. According to their interviews they couldn't even remember what they were fighting about. Maybe they just didn't want to say. And in the end, as is so often the case in these domestic rows, neither of them wanted to press charges against the other. You hear of people who thrive on conflict. I've never understood it, but I suspected that this was one such couple.

So there we were, four lives in very real danger, both of them within a whisker of meeting a violent and bloody end, and what did we end up with? The pair of them were charged with affray under Section 3 of the Public Order Act, and fined £500 apiece. £500. I won't repeat what Jayne said when we heard the news, but I can remember my words to her, because I'm fond of quoting them. 'An older and wiser man than me once said, "Ours not to reason why; ours but to do and die".'

Two or three weeks after the dust had settled, there was some better news. Jayne and I received letters inviting us to attend North Yorkshire Police HQ at Newby Wiske. We'd had a good write-up for our conduct in this case and the Chief Constable was awarding us a commendation for bravery. We had to clean and press our uniforms, polish our shoes – and buttons – and drive up there. We drank tea out of bone-china cups, grabbed as many cucumber sandwiches as we could eat, and had our citations presented to us by the Chief Constable herself. The press were there, and we were both pictured in the *Gazette* the following Wednesday. Even as we saw our pictures, grinning at the camera, we braced ourselves for the onslaught of mickey-taking that would greet us next time we signed on we were on duty. We knew the form, and Ed didn't let us down. 'They give out awards like bloody confetti these days,' he said. 'Just for doing your job. If you were CID I'd understand it. They're full of themselves. But we're ordinary coppers, Mike. Bloody hell, when you and I started it was understood. No commendations unless you wound up in intensive care.'

'Or dead.'

Ed shook his head. 'We're all getting soft, mate. That's the fact of the matter.'

Chapter 8

A Breath of Fresh Air

'There you are, old boy. All fixed up and ready for the open road.' Algy patted the bonnet of the gleaming red roadster. 'I've had Soapy fill her up for you, there's fresh air in the tyres and he's checked all the fluids. And she's been waxed, by my own fair hand.'

'Oh, perhaps you can do the same for my car while we're gone.' I pointed to it, covered in dust with the wing of a dead pheasant wedged into the radiator grille.

'Don't push it,' Ann said, but Algy just laughed. 'I don't think you can afford our rates, old chap. Oh by the way, I've packed you a little picnic hamper, so you won't need to worry about lunch. All you have to do is pop yourself into the driving seat, fire her up, and it's chocks away.'

The car stood on his gravelled drive, right in front of the pillared main door of the house, framed by the low-hanging foliage of the copper beech. It was like a picture from one of those lifestyle magazines. How the other half lives. 'I'm not often lost for words, Algy, but I have to admit it. I don't know what to say.'

'How about promising me you won't look in the boot just yet, old chap?' He was holding the passenger door open for Ann.

'What about our luggage?' she asked.

'Don't worry about that.' He grabbed our cases. 'This one'll slot in behind you, and this one—' he went to the back of the car and paused. 'In you get, Mike, and face the front, there's a good chap.' I did as I was told, and heard him open the boot. 'Ah yes,' he said. 'Thought so. Just fits in perfectly.' He slammed the lid shut and handed me the keys. 'Now, when you get to the Dales you'll find a little surprise in the back there. So no peeking. Either of you.' He shaded his eyes and looked up at the sky. 'Couldn't be nicer,' he said. 'Perfect day for a picnic. Oh, I nearly forgot. One more thing. Hang on a minute.' He disappeared into the house.

'What's he up to now?'

'Ann, you're dealing with a one-off here. A true British eccentric with enough money to do as he pleases and not care what anyone thinks of him. Whatever he's up to, relax and enjoy it. He's one of a dying breed.'

When Algy re-emerged he was carrying one of his prized possessions, the World War Two Spitfire pilot's jacket I'd seen him wearing that time when he drove his tractor through the floods. 'Here you are, driver.' He paused, and looked at Ann. 'Frightfully sorry, but I've only got the one.'

'Don't worry,' I said. 'She can wear it when she takes a turn at the wheel.'

'I think it might be a touch on the large size,' Ann said. 'It's swallowed you up, Mike.'

'Aye, but it feels right,' I said, as I wriggled in to it. I rubbed my hands. 'Sheepskin-lined as well. Very cosy. Cheers, Algy.'

'Think nothing of it, old boy. Well.' He tapped the bonnet. 'Off you go, then – and I'll see you tomorrow night.'

I took it steady down the drive, checking the various controls as I went. Lights, wipers, horn, indicators. Out on the road I accelerated away towards the village. 'By heck, it's a bumpy old ride,' I shouted above the roar of the engine and the rushing of the wind in my ears.

'It will be.'

'You been in one of these before?'

'Drove down to Devon in one, years ago.'

'Who with?'

'I was on my own.'

'You're a dark horse, aren't you?' I waited, but she wasn't going to tell me anything else. I was learning that that was Ann all over. Her own person.

We were soon through Leavening and heading towards Malton. It was strange, being so low down and close to the road. We could feel every bit of unevenness in the surface, and the verges seemed to crowd in on us. It gave me the impression that we were really motoring, especially on the corners, where the long grass and the cow parsley all but brushed against us. Then Ann nudged me with her elbow. 'C'mon, it won't bite. Give it some welly.' I glanced at the speedo. 'Is that all? Twenty-eight miles an hour? I thought I was doing forty-odd.' I put my foot down and shouted back at her, 'So, which way we going, navigator?'

Ann laughed. 'You mean co-driver.'

'Oh. Yes. Well, just say the word and you can take over. I mean—'

'That's all right. You can do the first bit.' She leaned forward in her seat, and tied her hair back in a ponytail. When I turned to glance at her she had a pair of those big dark glasses on too. She looked every inch the film star. 'I was thinking Sutton Bank,' she said, 'then across to Ripon and Pateley Bridge. It'll be a nicer drive than going through York.'

'Yep. Suits me.'

We were heading for Wharfedale. Grassington, to be precise. I'd been on the phone to my mate Phil, the rural beat officer who covered that neck of the woods, and asked him to recommend a hotel out that way. Somewhere cosy and romantic. And affordable. The plan was, if the sun kept shining, we'd get a bit of hiking in, do a bit of exploring. And if it didn't, well, they aren't short of pubs in the Dales. Anyway, it looked set fair. It was still early, but the sun was already high in an almost cloudless sky. As we drove through town all the lasses were out in their summer clothes, and one or two people stopped and peered into the car as we drove past. I unzipped the jacket. I was too warm, but I was damned if I was going to take it off while there were people watching.

'Funny, this.' We were out on the Hovingham road, heading towards Helmsley. It was hard work making ourselves heard above the noise of the engine, but Ann knew what I was on about right away. She glanced over her shoulder at the line of cars behind us, and nodded. 'When I was a kid if you saw an MG on the road it'd be nipping in and out, overtaking everything in sight,' I said. 'Now we're the ones holding everyone up.'

'They don't mind,' Ann said. 'They think we're quaint.' She was right. Everybody who overtook seemed to cast an envious eye over us, particularly the men.

'They're dead jealous of me,' I said. 'Sunny day, open-top car, leather jacket, and a beautiful woman in the passenger seat. They must think I'm loaded.' Anyway, they could think what they wanted. I was living the dream. I remembered a scene from the film *The Battle of Britain* where one of the Spitfire pilots took off for a couple of days' 'R and R' in a similar car. It somehow made me feel very British. And very proud.

Past Sproxton, when we got out onto the A170, I put my foot down. The engine roared, and the needle shuddered up to fifty-five, then sixty. Above the noise I was aware of Ann shouting at me.

'Try pushing that thing on the gearstick!'

'What, this?'

'Go on, just press it in. It's an electric overdrive.'

I did as she said. The revs, and the noise level, dropped immediately.

'It's like a fifth gear. For cruising.'

'How do you know all this stuff?'

'Boyfriends. First one was motorbike mad. The next one was obsessed with Minis.'

'Ah well, we all liked short skirts.'

'I'll ignore that. The one after him had a Land Rover, and then—'

'Let me guess. You ditched him for a lad with a sports car.'

She grinned. 'I'm a woman with a past.'

'That's all right. I'm a man with a future.' I reached over and squeezed her hand. She didn't say a word, just smiled. I wanted to ask her what she was thinking, but didn't quite dare.

We were at Sutton Bank now, facing that steep, twisting descent onto the Vale of York. 'I wish you were driving right now,' I said.

'Why's that?'

'This is one of my favourite views, but I don't dare take my eyes off the road. It's not easy steering this thing.'

'I know, they're inclined to get away from you if you're not careful.'

I was almost standing on the brakes but they had no real effect until I managed to get down into second gear. 'It's hard work, this.' I wrestled the car round the hairpin.

She nodded. 'Drum brakes. That's the problem with the old MGs. About as much good as a chocolate fireguard on a hill like this.'

'You really know your stuff, don't you?'

'A misspent youth. The other girls were into disco music and make-up; I spent my spare time with a spanner in one hand and a Haynes manual in the other.'

'When you weren't out on that horse, you mean.'

'Oh, I always found time for that.'

By the time we reached Thirsk I needed a break. 'It's a fun ride, but you soon get cramped,' I said, as we pulled up on the cobbled marketplace. Being Saturday, the town centre streets were crowded with people milling around the stalls. We walked around looking in the various knick-knack and book shops before getting a takeaway coffee and sitting at the foot of the clock tower that commemorates the marriage of the future King George V to the lady who would become Queen Mary, back in 1896. Among the many visitors who strolled by as we sat there we heard a fair smattering of American accents. It occurred to me that some of the older ones might well be taking a tour down memory lane. I'd been reading about the thousands of Yanks who were stationed at the various air bases across the area, and how they used to flock into York to dance the night away at Betty's in St Helen's Square. I wondered whether any of them might just recognise the flying jacket.

Back in the car we drove past the racecourse. 'That'd make

a nice day out some time,' Ann said, glancing across at the grandstands. 'You ever been?'

I shook my head. 'Always meant to. Never managed to find the time.'

'It might be fun. Or maybe we could go to York. What's the big day there?'

'There's one or two, aren't there? John Smiths, the Ebor Cup.'

'The Ebor. That's the one. Next month, isn't it?' She was looking up at me and smiling. The sun was sparkling in her eyes.

'Come on,' I said, 'let's get moving, or I'll be forced to embarrass you.'

'How's that?'

'By kissing you in front of all these passersby.'

'Not starting to show our age, are we? I mean, a few years ago neither of us would've given a damn, would we?'

'True. Anyway, I thought you were going to take over the driving?'

'OK then. Pull over.'

'You'll want this then.' I handed her the flying jacket.

'I don't think so, Mike.'

'No, it is a bit on the large side, isn't it?'

'Just a bit. And besides, you want to keep it on really. Admit it.'

It was nice to sit and let Ann do the driving. I could relax and take in the scenery as we headed through Ripon and beyond. Once you get away from the Vale of York the country starts to roll, and there are more trees. You start seeing stone houses. It must have been about noon when we got to Pateley Bridge, and there ahead of us was the dark outline of the moors. 'Not far now,' I said as we swooped down the hill past Stump Cross Caverns. 'Tell you what, I'm about ready for lunch, aren't you?'

'Starving. We need to find a turning.'

We were lucky. We found a beautiful spot, not far off the main road next to Grimwith Reservoir. We had the water in front of us, the sun on our backs, an old stone wall to keep the breeze off, and a great sweep of empty country around us. 'Come on, let's see what your mate's packed for us.' Ann opened the boot and tossed me a rug. 'Hey, it's the real deal. A proper wicker hamper. Leather straps and all.' As I spread the blanket on the ground she went through the contents, 'China plates, silver cutlery, hip flask. Hip flask? There's two of them. Very elegant. I always thought a picnic involved brown paper bags, squashed bananas and Thermos flasks. Hey, Mike, you've got to come and look at this lot.'

'I'm telling you, that man is a star,' I said as Ann lifted a white linen cloth to reveal the feast he'd packed for us. 'Smoked salmon, ham, tomatoes. Look, he's got those bread rolls with seeds on. And olives. And grapes. And hey, what's this?' I unwrapped a white napkin. 'Champers!'

'No expense spared.' Ann touched my arm. 'You weren't thinking of opening that, were you?'

'Course not,' I said, 'it's not properly chilled.' For a moment she looked at me blankly. Then she realised I was joking. 'No,' I said, laying it carefully back in the hamper, 'this is for later, when we get to the hotel.'

We loaded up our plates and sat there in the lee of the stone wall, soaking up the sun. 'Tell you what,' I said, 'that bubbly was still cold. And we've got the perfect insulation for it. I'll wrap it up in the flying jacket. That'll keep it fresh.'

After we'd eaten it didn't take long to complete the drive into Grassington. Our hotel was easy to find, right in the centre and overlooking the little square, which was decorated with bunting for an arts festival that was taking place over the next few days.

'Don't let's check in just yet,' Ann said. 'I've got a little shopping to do.'

'What? Shopping? On a day like this?'

'OK, I'll go on my own. You see to the car and get the bags in. I won't be long.'

By the time she came back I'd checked us in and was exploring our room. It was quaint and traditional. No doubt about that. Plush furniture, a super kingsize bed, tea, coffee, a fruit bowl and a TV standing in the corner. 'Mmm, very Yorkshire,' Ann said when she reappeared. 'And look what I've bought to go with the bubbly.' She produced a paper bag from behind her back.

'Strawberries? Just the job.'

'And see what I found downstairs.' She held up two champagne flutes and a plastic bucket full of ice.

'You're a hero. Let me put the bottle in the ice-bucket while you get unpacked.'

'This is the life, isn't it?' Ann was investigating the toiletries and eyeing up the claw-foot bath. I was arranging a couple of chairs and opening the large sash window that overlooked the square. 'It's like being abroad,' I said.

Ten minutes later we were sitting in the sun tucking into a bowl of strawberries. I'd managed to ease the cork out of the champagne without losing any of the precious contents, and Ann was raising her glass to mine. 'What's the toast then?'

'Two toasts,' I said. 'First, to our good mate Algy, one of nature's gentlemen.'

'To Algy. Mmm.' It was cool and delicious, just on the dry side, the sort of drink you mean to savour but end up drinking too fast if you're not careful. It was that good.

'Go on then, what's the other toast?' Ann asked.

'Can't you guess?'

'No.' She was looking right into my eyes. 'I don't want to guess. I think it'll be more fun if you tell me.'

I held my glass up so that the sun shone through it. Ann chinked hers against it. 'To us,' I said.

'Yes. To us.'

We awoke next day to another bright blue sky. Perfect walking weather, and a good forecast.

'Choice for you,' I said. I'd picked up a few brochures in the hotel foyer and sorted out some local walks to think about while we had breakfast. 'We can go over the top to Kettlewell,' I said. 'It's a bit of a climb, mind. Or we can drive there – it's only a few miles up the road – and then hike along the river.'

Ann pushed her plate away from her. 'That's enough for me,' she said. She'd left a sausage, a piece of bacon and some fried bread, which I immediately grabbed. 'Over the top?' she said. 'That could be thirsty work on a day like this. I think I like the sound of the other walk. Along the – Wharfe, is it?'

'Aye, we're in Wharfedale now so I reckon it must be,' I said, as I bit a lump off the sausage. 'That what you want to do then? Up the river and back?'

'Yes. We've all day, haven't we? What time we leaving for home?'

'Well, I'd say we want to be back before it gets dark.'

'OK then, let's get cracking.'

It only took half an hour or so to drive to Kettlewell. It would've been less, but we had to stop at Kilnsey Crag. Ann wanted to take a picture of the huge block of limestone that hangs over the road there, and I wanted to see what the pub looked like. Ed had been there one time, and spoke of it in glowing terms. 'Pity,' I said, as Ann squatted down to get a good angle on the Crag. 'They're not open yet.'

'A bit early to be thinking about beer, isn't it?'

'I had morning coffee on my mind.'

'But you've just had a pot with your breakfast. Or should I say breakfasts. You cleared my plate as well.'

'Listen, I get an appetite when I'm out in the open air all day.'

'I hope this isn't going to turn into our first row,' she grinned as she snapped the picture.

A few minutes later we'd parked in Kettlewell, crossed the bridge over the river, and were opening the gate that led into a grassy field shaded on one side by a line of sycamores. Our track would follow along the west side of the valley while the river itself meandered along a series of lazy curves to the east. In places you could still see the high-water mark from the previous winter's flood, a trail of straw and twigs and the odd bit of baler twine, almost submerged under the new season's growth. It was good to be striding along, even better to be with Ann. The turmoil of the last few weeks seemed a long, long way away.

We'd been going a mile or two when we paused by a crumbling wall, its stones carpeted with green. 'Enjoying it?' Ann asked, smoothing the thick layer of moss with her hand to make a seat.

'Oh, love it.' I took the top off the water bottle and offered it to her. 'Out in the fresh air, sun on our backs, my favourite woman by my side. It's my idea of what a holiday should be. Only one thing troubling me.'

'And what's that?'

'The fact that we don't do it often enough. We hardly get any time together, do we? Not enough for me, anyway. I'm fed up with all this secrecy.'

She shrugged. 'Not a lot we can do just now, is there? I keep hoping there'll be a vacancy I can apply for somewhere else. Somewhere within reach of home, that is.'

'You mean Scarborough.'

'Yes, that'd do.'

'Or what about York?'

'I wouldn't mind working there.'

'No retirements coming up, are there?'

She shook her head. 'I think we're further up the queue than most of the York coppers I've seen. They're all frighteningly young over there. Mere children, most of them.'

'We could do with someone taking six months' sick leave.'

'That's harsh.'

'Well, time off for stress perhaps. There must be someone who's due a sabbatical.'

A pair of hikers with big packs passed us, going the other way. We nodded and they each raised a hand in greeting. 'What about Harrogate?' I said.

'Harrogate would be OK. Why? Have you heard something?'

'No, just trying to work it out what your boundaries are. Selby?'

She shook her head and slipped down off the wall. 'No, it's too far to travel. I wouldn't mind doing a city beat again. What about you?'

'No way. That's for keen young coppers.'

'Well, I'm keen . . . ' She looked at me, her eyes wrinkled into a smile, daring me to say it.

'You'll have to do better than that, Ann.'

'Worth a try though. And you nearly fell for it. Anyway, that's how things are. Looks as though we're stuck with a secret romance.' She shoved the water bottle into my backpack and handed it to me. 'Which is meant to be exciting, according to all those romantic novels I used to read.'

'But I have got it right, haven't I? That – well, if the

circumstances were right you really would want to spend more time with me?'

She looked me right in the eye, stood up on her toes and kissed me. At that moment I would have trusted her with my life. 'Yes,' she said. 'I think I would.' Then she hitched her pack onto her back. 'Come on, let's hit that dusty trail, shall we?'

We walked on up the valley, through sheep and cow pasture, the wooded slopes to either side of us echoing to the sound of collared doves. High in the sky a buzzard circled on the rising currents of warm air. Below us the river coursed along the far side of the valley, broad and shallow, rippling over stones and glinting in the sunlight before sweeping back towards our path where it took another sharp turn against a shingled beach. It was far too tempting.

'Come on.' I dropped my pack on the ground, ran across the grass and undid my bootlaces.

The water was shallow, and deliciously cool. 'Over here,' I said, as Ann slipped off her boots and walked towards me, dodging the cowpats and thistles near the water's edge. I'd found a patch of still water with a drift of soft sand and was working my feet into it.

'We're not going to get far if we keep stopping to enjoy ourselves, are we?' Ann said as she splashed her way towards me.

'Doesn't matter, does it? We spend every working day battling against the clock. This is our own time. We can do as we please. We should be living for the moment, don't you reckon?'

'You're right,' she said. 'Reminds me of the man who used to fix our bikes when I was a kid. My brother was always working out how far we were going to go and how long it would take to get there. Always in a hurry. And this old fellow used to say, "Don't be in such a rush. My motto is 'smiles before miles'." I've always remembered that.'

We walked on until early in the afternoon, then stopped to picnic under a huge old ash tree. 'Great survivors, these.' I was looking at its gnarled base and the large fire-blackened hollow at its roots. 'One of my favourites, the ash. They're not the most beautiful, they come into leaf way too late, but they're just about indestructible. I mean, look at it. It's been struck by lightning, used as a rubbing post by cattle, and that hole at the bottom – either a badger or a fox had made its home there, and it's still sending out new stems.'

We lay for a while looking up at the sky. One or two big white clouds were starting to puff up to the south of us, but overhead, through the veil of green, the sky remained clear and blue.

'Well, I suppose we'd better think about turning back,' Ann said. 'We don't want to be rushing on the journey home, do we? I was thinking we could stop in at Harrogate and have tea at Betty's. How would that suit you?'

'I'd love it.'

We retraced our steps along the valley, just making one brief detour when we came across some stepping stones in the river. 'Why are we crossing these?' Ann asked. I'd already reached the halfway point. She was still standing on the bank.

'To get to the other side?'

'Yes, but why? We're meant to be going that way.' She pointed along the valley where the path was clearly marked.

'I never could resist these,' I said, balancing on the slick rocks as the water rushed by.

'I think I'll wait here till you come back. I don't trust them when they're wet like that.'

She was right, of course. I was starting to learn that she generally was. I got to the far side OK, but on the way back I got distracted by a pair of swans flying up the valley, and down I went, filling my boots and drenching the bottom half of my trousers. 'Well,' I said, as I stood on the grass wringing my socks out, 'at least I gave you a good laugh.' But Ann was looking at the sky, away to the south and west. 'I can see us both getting a good soaking before the day's out,' she said. The puffy white clouds we'd seen were starting to tower over the hilltops, revealing angry grey underbellies. 'I think that's the direction we're heading, isn't it?'

'More or less.' I put my boots back on, picked up my pack and we set off towards the village. 'Let's stride out, shall we? See if we can beat the weather.'

The sun was still shining when we got to the car, and the storm – because that's what it was, without a doubt – was a long way off, so we still felt in holiday mood. When we passed through Grassington Ann wanted to stop and buy a box of handmade chocolates she'd spotted earlier. I took advantage to nip into a florist and buy her a big bunch of roses, all wrapped up in clear plastic. 'Well, that's a first,' she said, as I presented them to her.

'What, nobody's ever bought you flowers before?'

'Don't be daft. I mean it's the first time you have.' She got back in and lay them across her lap.

Our luck seemed to be holding, at least as we crossed the moors and drove through Pateley Bridge, but all the time the sky ahead was growing darker. A few miles later we started seeing cars coming towards us with their lights on. Ann undid her seatbelt and leaned behind her to pull her waterproof jacket out of the backpack. I'd already put the flying jacket on, and now I zipped it up. 'What do we do?' I asked her. 'Head for

Harrogate as planned or keep on through Knaresborough and hope to get home before we're drowned?'

'How hungry are you?' she asked me, but didn't wait for an answer. 'Stupid question. You're always hungry. How desperate are you, on a scale of one to ten?'

'I'm more worried about this car than my stomach. I've never driven one with no top on. What happens if you get caught in the rain?'

'It gets wet. And so do we.'

'I know that. But does it do any damage? I mean, does everything keep working? We could end up with a paddling pool at our feet.'

'Maybe we should keep going, shortest route possible, and hope we get home before it hits us. And if it really chucks it down there's a sort of waterproof apron in the back that you spread over the seats.'

'You mean we stand there getting drenched?'

'What's more important, our own personal comfort or Algy's vintage car?'

'Aye, fair enough.'

'Anyway, your feet are already soaked.'

'That's true. But they're sort of warm at the moment.'

'Well, if Algy's done his maintenance properly the water shouldn't collect in the bottom in the first place. There's a couple of drainage holes somewhere. I tell you what,' she said, 'you've got yourself a hell of a co-pilot here. I'm remembering things I'd clean forgotten about.'

'Don't think I don't appreciate it.'

We'd just got round York and were on the A64 when the rain started. At first it was no more than a few big drops, and then a few more, with lightning flickering all around us. Instinctively

I slowed down, hunching my shoulders as my head started to get wet, but there was little traffic on the road and Ann was nudging me.

'Speed up!' she shouted.

'What?'

'Kick on.' She had squirmed down in her seat and the rain was just about skimming over her head. 'You'll stay drier that way.'

I put my foot down. 'Hey, you're right.' As our speed increased the rain, which was more steady than heavy, hit the windscreen and bounced over our heads. So long as we could keep up a steady fifty or so we were OK, but it wouldn't be long before we'd be turning off to go through the villages, cross-country to Leavening. As we slowed to take the Howsham road the rain cascaded in. There's only one way to take those narrow lanes, especially in gloomy conditions with the rain pouring down, and that's with great care. And so, after riding our luck all the way from Grassington, we got a thorough soaking in the final few miles. By the time we pulled up in front of Algy's front door we were like a pair of drowned rats, and inside the car, just as Ann had feared, the water was an inch deep.

'What rotten luck,' Algy said as we dragged our cases across his hallway.

'Well,' I said, 'we made it. And up till the last hour we've had a fantastic time.'

'Get your dry things on, and I'll make you a cup of tea.'

Half an hour later dusk had fallen, the rain had stopped and a watery crescent moon was peering out from behind a veil of high cloud.

'Hope you don't catch a chill,' Algy said as we left the house and walked across the gravelled drive towards the garages. 'Still, you'll have those hip flasks I packed for you – or have you already emptied them?'

'Er, no,' Ann said. 'We never touched them. We thought they were just part of the picnic basket.'

Algy was already opening up the boot of the MG. 'No no no,' he said, 'these were for you. They're filled with my finest malt whisky. Dalwhinney. Here, take 'em home and treat your-selves to a nightcap. Ward off the chill and all that.'

'Well, cheers Algy,' I said. 'That's very generous of you. Strewth!'

'Something the matter, Mike?'

'Why, I was only joking when I said about polishing me car up, mate. Look at it.' The old Astra was gleaming. Even the tyres had been cleaned up and smeared with some sort of black stuff to make them look like new.

'Ah well, that was Soapy's doing,' Algy said. 'I think his conscience was troubling him about the – ah, the practical joke. He was rather pleased when you mentioned how dirty your car was. Gave him the opportunity he was looking for.'

'Well, tell him we appreciate it,' I said as I started the engine.

We said goodbye, and drove off. As we turned out of the gate onto the road Ann looked at her watch. 'Eight hours,' she said. 'Eight hours and I'm back on duty. D'you know what I wish?'

'What's that?'

'I wish we had a couple more days of this. It's been good.'

I caught hold of her hand and squeezed it gently. 'It's been very good,' I said.

Chapter 9

Taken for a Ride

Strange how the seasons shift. It's all so gradual, but all so sudden, the way the bright green of early summer fades away. For a few short weeks the fields of wheat and barley, the sloping cow pastures, are all lush and sparkling. Even great swathes of moorland take on an emerald tint as the first growth of bracken and bilberry pokes through the heather. And then, just when you're relaxing and thinking that you've got weeks and weeks of fair weather and easy living ahead of you, you'll be driving along one morning and you'll see the fields have turned the colour of Rich Tea biscuits, and there in the hedgerows is the pale pink of the willow-herb, which I always take to mean that it'll soon be August. And in this neck of the woods, in a bad year, that can mean that autumn is right around the corner.

We like to look on the bright side in Yorkshire. No, I mean it. It's just that we know we're a lot safer if we don't. Someone once told me that pessimism is the best insurance policy against disappointment. Always expect the worst, he said, and that way you might be pleasantly surprised.

However. It was late July, and I had indeed just seen the first of the willow-herb, but a little thing like that wasn't going to spoil my mood. Not this year. I was feeling on top of the world. That weekend away with Ann had given us both such a lift, despite the soaking on the way home. To tell the truth, I was walking on air – and causing a certain amount of mystification among my colleagues. Not Chris, though. He was on my case right away.

'I reckon you've pulled,' he said. We were in the Spotted Cow, at the back of the marketplace. We'd come off a late turn and just had time for a quick pint before we went home.

'Nah,' I said, rolling up my shirt sleeves and exposing my newly tanned forearms. 'You know me: Mr Happy, especially when I've been out in the sun. Look at that colour, you'd think I'd been abroad.'

'Don't be changing the subject, Pannett. Blokes don't go around with a daft look like that on their faces unless there's a woman involved.'

'Or if they've had a bit of good luck,' I said.

'Meaning?'

'Well, you haven't asked me how I got on at Thirsk races last week.'

'I don't need to ask – because I know you never went. You talked about it, but you didn't go. If you had you'd have been flashing your winnings all round the station. We'd never have heard the last of it. No, you're just trying to change the subject. Come on, let's have it – man to man. Tell your uncle Chris all about it and you'll feel a lot better. Just a few basic details, that's all I want.'

'Such as?'

'Ah, so you aren't denying it then.'

'Neither confirming nor denying it.'

'Ha! I knew it.' He was grinning as he asked, 'What's she like then?' but before I could answer he leaned forward across the table, looking concerned, lowering his voice. 'She's not . . . married, is she?'

'Chris, I do not chase after married women.'

'Hey, I know a lot of blokes who don't – but I've also met a lot of married women who make a point of pursuing single men.'

'Well they've never come pestering me, that's all I can say.'

'So, she's single then. That narrows it down.' He had his glass to his mouth, but he paused and looked at me sideways. 'A few months ago my money would've been on Ann, but of course she's Sergeant Barker now. So she's out of the running.'

'Chris . . . '

'What?'

'You have yet to establish that there is a woman in my life. Remember the first commandment in any investigation. Thou shalt have evidence. Or, as a barrister once said to the judge when defending a crook I thought I'd got bang to rights, "I surmise, your honour, that there is no case to answer".'

Chris looked at his watch and drained his pint. 'All right, Mike. Have it your own way for now, but be warned buddy. I am on the case. You can have no secrets from me.'

As I made my way home I turned the whole business over in my mind. Joking aside, the thing between me and Ann was always going to be a bit problematic. Here we were, an item. If word got out among our colleagues it would soon filter through to the higher echelons, and that could well lead to one of us being moved out of Ryedale. For the time being the word was, as I say, discretion, even to the point of being furtive. Our romance hadn't really got off the ground yet, but if it did there was no doubt that one of us would have to move.

However, I had no worries about Chris. He was just being nosy. I was pretty sure he knew what was going on, but he wanted to wind me up – or keep me on my toes in case I got careless and the Super found out. But then there was Ed, who also enjoyed a good wind-up. The trouble was, so long as my mates were in the dark, they would keep on about it. Ed was at it a few days later when I was on the early turn. It was coming up to midday. I'd been out on my rounds and had popped over to see Nick about some poachers he thought he'd spotted that morning. But after an hour circling the estate in his Land Rover, nowt. It probably sounds odd that I would go out in his vehicle, but it was better equipped for off-roading, and a lot less conspicuous.

So anyway, there I was, back at the station tidying up my paperwork, when he kicked off.

'You're all right, Jayne, you can relax now.' He was talking deliberately loud, waiting for me to react.

'Watcher mean?' Jayne was busy photocopying a huge file of papers. You'd have thought she'd just nailed a nationwide drug-running syndicate, not a petty shoplifter in a small country town, but there we go. Some people, higher up the police hierarchy, are impressed by paperwork. They relate it to productivity.

'Why, you won't have to worry about PC Pannett any more.'

'What you on about, Ed? When was I ever worried about Mike?'

'Remember that time when you said he was looking a bit sad?'

'Eh?' Jayne lobbed a ball of screwed-up paper across to where I was sitting. 'You listening to this, Mike?'

But before I could answer Ed carried on. 'Oh no – I remember what it was now. You said he was a sad old git. That was it.'

'Jayne,' I said, 'you have to show a bit of understanding with this lad. He's down for counselling next week.'

'Why, is he feeling stressed or something?'

I shook my head. 'Poor old Ed, he's stir crazy. Needs to get out on the beat and meet some real live people.' Ed was suffering from a recurrence of a knee injury sustained while playing football fifteen years ago. He was on light duties: covering the front desk, dealing with members of the public who came in, fielding phone calls and so on.

'Too many nutters and crooks out there,' he said. 'You meet a nicer class of criminal in the police station. I've earned a few weeks in here. Anyway, Jayne, don't tell me you haven't noticed how Mike's always whistling and smiling these days, like a dog with two—'

'Tails?'

'Aye, tails.'

'Yeah, now that you mention it he has been a bit perkier than usual. I just thought it was spring fever. I know what you blokes are, first bit of sun and you're ogling all the girls in their summer frocks.'

'You're not far off it there, Jayne. There's definitely a woman involved. Thing is, he's suddenly come over all shy. Doesn't want to talk about it, not even with his best buddy.'

'*1015 receiving?*' Thank God for the radio. 'Yeah, go ahead, over.'

'*Mike, the landlord of the Spotted Cow is reporting a till snatch within the last few minutes. Two white males, early twenties, one red top, one blue top, made off on foot towards the marketplace.*'

'Yes, received.'

'Come on, Jayne. Dump the filing. We've got work to do.

In your own time, Ed.' I shoved past him as he hobbled towards the front office to look at the CCTV. We'd be lost without that facility. Eight colour TV monitors displaying images from fifteen or twenty cameras dotted around Malton and Pickering. You can move the cameras up-down and right-left, zoom in or out, and record images to disk for use as evidence. It's a massive help when manpower is stretched, which it generally is.

'They won't be local,' I said as Jayne and I ran across the yard to the vehicles.

'What makes you say that?'

'What? Till-snatching? Not our style, at all. They just don't pull that sort of thing out here.'

As I got into my vehicle and Jayne into hers we heard from control. *'Traffic car on its way from Pickering.'*

'Oh, that's some backup at least.'

I put the blue lights on and shot down to the crossroads. Butcher Corner, as we know it. Over the radio I could hear Ed. *'I think I've got them. Just disappeared round the corner into Wheelgate. Top end.'*

I swung right at the lights. The street was quiet for a summer's day. Very little traffic. Just a few shoppers, mostly female, mostly middle-aged to elderly. No sign of any youths matching the description. It's at moments like this that you have to try and think like the criminal. If they were in a vehicle and away they'd be putting miles between us and them. Not a lot I could do about that. But sometimes they'll play it canny, lying low and waiting for things to quieten down before making a move. If you start cruising around that may be just what they've been waiting for – a chance to slip away un-noticed. So the way I saw it I might as well stay in town for a while and watch the roads. Ed was covering ten times as much ground on the cameras as I could on the move. But supposing they were making for a getaway car, where would they have left it? I knocked the two-tones off and went up to the big car park on Wentworth Street. Nothing there. I got on the radio. 'Jayne, can you go to the scene and find out if there's anyone hurt? And did anyone see any weapons? Aye, and see if you can get any better descriptions, will you?'

'*There they are!*' It was Ed on the radio. '*Two lads, red top blue top, running along Railway Street . . . And they're carrying something. It's them OK.*'

I hit the two-tones and blue light and sped off.

'*1015, they're in Railway Street, right outside Yates's, they've just flagged down a car. Shit, they're in. Both in the back seat. Elderly male driver, Mike. Vauxhall Nova, registration . . . Ah! Bloody bus in the way. Hang on.*'

I swung right at the lights and immediately trod on the brakes. 'Damn it!' The York bus, big blue double-decker thing, was swinging out, right across the road, totally blocking my path. All I could do was wait for him to get out of the way, but his path was now blocked by a builder's delivery lorry coming the other way. I banged my fists on the wheel in frustration. 'Shit.' If that bus hadn't been there I would've been on top of them. 'Where are they, Ed? They hijacked the car, or what?'

'*Looks like it. Elderly driver, white hair, male. Can't believe he was with them.*'

'1015 to control. Did you get all of that? We're gonna to need some more units. Who's the duty inspector?'

'*Mike, we're trying to get hold of the inspector, but he's tied up with an incident in Scarborough.*'

Three minutes earlier the streets had been almost deserted.

Now they were thick with traffic. The crossing gates must've been down before, and now there was a queue all along Castlegate. As the bus got away at last and I turned down Railway Street I was thinking. What if they'd taken the driver hostage? How far would they take him, and what would they do with him when they abandoned the car? Or would they be making off with it?

'I've got a result on the vehicle reg.'

'Go ahead, Ed.'

'It's a John Pointer, lives in Norton. The car is a red, repeat red Vauxhall Nova. I've had a closer look at these images now. He's in his seventies, I'd say. Wearing a dark suit jacket and with a buttonhole – white flower of some sort.'

As I sped up Yorkersgate and out of town I realised I had to make a decision. The runaways had a good two-minute start on me, which would put them out on the main road and halfway to Huttons Ambo if they'd gone that way. But then they could've swung off across country towards Helmsley. Or they could have been real canny and doubled back through the top end of town, and from there they could go anywhere they pleased. The coast, Pickering, up to the A170 and away west . . . Take your pick.

One thing at a time. I got my foot down and made for the A64. What we wanted now was blocks – or surveillance – on all the roads out of town. 'Control? Aye, we could do with a car at Hopgrove roundabout checking anything coming into York. We want an officer up the top end to cover Helmsley. We could do with one to sit by the war memorial, just in case. And we want that camera up at Pickering covering anything from Malton—'

'Mike, we could do with more pay and shorter hours.'

'Right,' I said, as I sped past the Huttons Ambo turn-off. 'You're saying we haven't the available officers.'

'*We're doing our best.*'

As I spoke I was doing seventy, eighty, but I couldn't keep that up for long. That road is a minefield of blind summits, tight bends and restricted visibility. And it's narrow. I've been to too many pile-ups on Golden Hill to be racing along there at high speeds.

Within a few minutes I'd got as far as Whitwell. And I'd seen nothing. Control were now telling me they'd got a car in situ at the Hopgrove on the edge of York, another on the Scarborough road. Extra help was en route from Thirsk and Northallerton. I swung right. If I came back to town along the Castle Howard road, who knows . . . ?

Again, I drew a blank. A lot of things prey on your mind in situations like this is. Are you in completely the wrong place? And what about the poor old man who's been abducted? What's he going through? How dangerous are these youths? Are they on drugs? Are they desperate? Violent? Would they harm him? And what about the old fellow's health? How will he stand up to the shock of what's happening? Then there's his family. Has he got a wife who's sent him out for a prescription, sitting there at home wondering where he's got to?

Time is of the essence. As each minute passes by, the suspects, and the victim, could be getting further and further away. The problem we always have is that the North Yorkshire road network is absolutely vast. Blocking a road here and there – well, it sounds good on paper but in reality it's like trying to catch water in a sieve. In the Met you would have had the helicopter up in minutes for a job like this. A rural force like ours, we can't afford such luxuries. Sod it! I thought.

'Control, can you get on to Humberside and request the helicopter?'

'*We'll need to get authority for that, Mike.*'

'Yes control. This is a potential abduction. As soon as possible, please.' Yes, I thought. You bet you'll need authority for a chopper. I was thinking back to the going-on I had at the rave last year when I called one in, and the dressing down I got over the expense.

It looked as though there was nothing I could do for the moment, not as regards watching the roads at least. It was time to contact the old man's family.

Ten minutes later I was knocking on his door. No answer. There was a bunch of flowers on the front windowsill, all wilted and dry. The upstairs curtains were closed. I knocked again and idly lifted the lid off the dustbin. Empty. I knocked one more time, and that drew his neighbour out from next door.

'You looking for John?'

'John Pointer, aye.'

'We don't see much of him these days. Always out and about in his car. Never says where he's going.'

'Lives alone, does he?'

'Aye, since his wife died – that'd be three or four years since.'

'Do you happen to know if he has any relatives nearby?'

'There's his daughter. You should find her at home.'

She only lived a couple of streets away. As I drove round there I thought about what I'd say. I always prefer to be straight-forward, but to some extent it depends on the person you're dealing with. You don't want them panicking.

'Something happened to him?' she asked me as she dried her hands on a towel and invited me into the back kitchen. 'He's not been in an accident, has he?'

'Look,' I said, 'he's let a couple of lads into his car, and we think they may have been involved in a robbery. He was seen leaving town on the York road.'

'What, you mean he's been hijacked?'

'Let's say they invited themselves into his car.'

'Ooh hell.' She took a step back and leaned against the work surface.

'Trouble is, we haven't managed to track them down yet. Has he got a mobile by any chance?'

She shook her head. 'No. I mean, he's got one – he's got two, in fact but he never switches the blooming thing on. I can try it, I suppose.' She went inside and came back with her phone pressed to her ear. 'Always out and about in that car of his and never says where he's off to. I've told him till I'm blue in the face . . . ' She waited a few more seconds, then held the receiver out towards me with a shrug. '*The person you are calling is not available.*'

'Look,' she said, 'I'll get my car out. We've got to find him before – well . . . '

'I'd rather you didn't, madam. To be honest, the best thing you can do is go round to your dad's house and wait there, in case he shows up. Here, take my mobile number, then you can get straight through to me.'

As I walked back to the car I got an update from the duty inspector. The CID lads were at the pub now, checking the CCTV images, preserving the scene of the crime. Then it was back to waiting, which is always the worst part. Somewhere out there an innocent old man was being forced to drive around with two young tearaways – state of mind unknown – and there wasn't a thing we could do about it.

I retraced my steps back to town, driving along the route we knew they'd taken. I tried to put myself in their shoes. Where would I go if I wanted to get out of the way? But it was pointless. There were just too many options. There was every chance they would've bundled him out of the car by now and gone on their way. But where? Where were they heading? I got back onto control. 'Tell you what, why don't you call Radio York, Minster FM and suchlike, pass out the vehicle details and a description of the suspects?' Anything to give us a fighting chance.

'*Will do. And Mike . . . ?*'

'Go ahead.'

'*The police helicopter from Humberside? Unavailable. They're dealing with a major incident.*'

'Oh well, that'll save us a few quid.'

'*Can you repeat, over?*'

'Nothing.'

I made one more circuit of town before driving back to the station to update the inspector on what I'd done so far. I suggested we search the roads in case the car had been abandoned. The old man could be sitting on a verge in the middle of nowhere, wondering what had hit him.

'Lot of roads out there, Mike,' was all he said. And of course he was right. It was just about pointless, but it had to be done.

I was all set to get back in the car when control came back on. '*The car's been spotted.*'

'Where?'

'*Parked up outside the Malt Shovel in Hovingham.*'

'Who called in?'

'*Couple driving by. Heard the announcement on Minster FM.*'

'I'm on my way. Have they been told "Do Not Approach"? These youths could be dangerous.'

'*They have, Mike.*'

'Right, I'm on my way. Can you get Jayne and the Pickering lad to follow.'

It's only about seven miles to Hovingham, and once I'd got out of town I was there in as many minutes, braking sharply as I entered the village. No lights, no two-tones. I could feel my palms sweating on the wheel as I approached the pub, which sits right on the main street. There were several cars parked on the roadside, and there, sandwiched between a grey Merc and a dark green Range Rover, was the missing Nova. I pulled up alongside it and looked in. Empty. Nothing on the back seat but a tattered old road atlas. So where was Mr Pointer – and his abductors?

'Control, have located the missing vehicle. Parked outside the pub as reported. Driver not with it. I'm going to check inside.'

Before I went in, though, I drove into the car park at the back. It wasn't impossible for the youths to have rendezvous'd with an accomplice, by arrangement – although everything about this job suggested that it was a bit of opportunism, that they'd nicked the till on the spur of the moment and played it by ear from then on. But why would they have driven out here?

The car park was pretty well full, but I couldn't see anybody or anything untoward. I drove back out, left my vehicle on the roadside and went in. No little old man in the bar – nor in the dining room, which was packed. I'd not been in the place before, and was wondering if I'd missed something. I stopped a waitress who was carrying a tray of food through from the kitchen. 'You could try the snug,' she suggested.

And that was where I found him, seated at a corner table, a dapper little fellow in a dark suit wearing the white carnation that Ed had spotted on the CCTV. He wasn't alone. He was with a lady, a seventy-something lady in a flowery dress with permed white hair. In front of them were two empty dessert dishes, and between them the remnants of a bottle of chilled white wine in a bucket of ice

'Mr Pointer?' I said.

'Aye, that's me,' he said, getting up from his seat and dropping his white napkin to the floor. He looked guiltily at the empty bottle. 'I've only had the one glass,' he said. 'I'm ever so strict about that.'

'No, no – I'm not concerned about that,' I said. 'But we've been looking for you.'

'Oh, excuse me,' he said, turning to the lady. 'This is Millicent, Millicent Stoppard. She's a close friend of mine.'

'Listen, Mr Pointer,' I said, 'we've been very concerned about you.'

'Oh really? Why's that then?'

'Those lads who forced their way into your car . . .'

'Oh, they didn't force their way in. No, I gave them a lift. I was just telling Millicent about it. You see, some other youngsters were after them, trying to steal their money. They had it all there in a sort of cash register thing and these other youths had chased them – why, they'd chased them all the way through the marketplace and down Railway Street. They were trying to get to back to the industrial estate where it belonged. I tell you what, they were lucky they found me or those bad 'uns would've had them – and their money.'

'The industrial estate, you say?'

'I believe that's what they said.'

'So you dropped them off down there?'

'No, just by the war memorial. They said they were out of danger and they'd walk the rest of the way.'

'What time was that?'

He tugged back his sleeve and looked at his watch. 'What is it now, a quarter to two . . . why, I should say it were about a quarter past twelve. I told them I wanted to be on the Hovingham road, y'see, and they just said, "This'll do us" and off they went. I do hope they didn't get caught. They looked ever so frightened, poor lads.'

I excused myself for a moment and got on the radio. 'Aye, he's safe and sound,' I said. 'They only went as far as the memorial so they'll be home and dry by now, with their loot. The little sods.'

Back in the snug I explained to our man what had happened, that he'd had a lucky escape. It seemed to trouble him, not so much the thought of what might have happened to him if he hadn't obliged the two runaways, rather the fact that he'd assisted them in their getaway. 'I shan't be in trouble, shall I?' he asked me. 'Aiding and abetting criminals?'

I had to laugh. 'I don't think so,' I said. 'But I'll make a note of your name and contact details. We'll get in touch with you later to arrange for a statement to be taken. You never know, we might pick these lads up, and if we do we'll want you to identify them. Never mind the theft, the most important thing is that you're OK.'

As it happened, we did track the thieves down, thanks to some smart work by the CID boys. The landlord at the Spotted Cow was able to show them exactly where they'd been sitting and even produced their unwashed glasses. Three or four weeks later came the news that the lab had got a direct match between the DNA from one of them and a sample taken from a petty thief in the York area. We hauled him in and under interview he gave us the name of his accomplice.

* * *

There was a nice PS to that case. When Mr Pointer came in for the identification I asked him whether he'd been back to the Malt Shovel recently. 'Oh goodness me no,' he said. 'That were a special occasion.'

'Oh, somebody's birthday, was it?'

'No no, nowt like that. It was my lady friend, see. I popped the question.'

'You did, did you?'

'Aye.'

'And?'

'We're to be wed next April.'

Chapter 10

Getting Married in the Morning

Out in the country the sky was a milky sort of blue. A pale yellow sun was blurred by a late summer haze of dust and moisture. On the land everything had a bit of a weary, end-of-season look to it. One by one the fields had been stripped bare by the harvesters, leaving the bleached stubble of the wheat, the gold of the barley straw. Some had already been ploughed into broad, dusty furrows. Only the fields of sugar beet and the permanent pasture were still green, and the roadside verges, of course, where the grass had been mown by the council gangs and started to come fresh. Around me the trees that had been such a delicate lime green two or three months ago were the colour of overdone broccoli; even the gardens I passed as I turned off the main road and through Scagglethorpe had a shrivelled, careworn look to them. After the hot spell we'd just had the lawns were all parched, the roses infested with greenfly, the bedding plants starting to wither. No, the best thing about August, I was thinking as I drove out of Settrington and on towards Grimston, is the gold and copper I could see as the chestnut trees started to turn. I like to see that. It reminds me that September is just around the corner.

It had been a scorching hot afternoon and I'd been out Rillington way, hoping to get a cup of tea with Nick the game-keeper. But he'd let me down. According to his missus, who was just leaving the house as I pulled into the driveway, he was out releasing some young pheasants in preparation for the new season. For them that would come around on the first of October, a month after the partridges. The Glorious Twelfth, the start of the grouse season up on the moors, was coming up tomorrow, but Nick didn't have much to do with that. 'That's for the real toffs,' he said. 'Continentals and Americans. Big money types.'

A lot of people assume that the pheasants you see in the countryside are wild. They're not, most of them. They're effec-tively raised in captivity. The hen birds are gathered up in late winter and brought into the pens to start laying. Their eggs are removed and put into incubators to hatch, and when the chicks are about six weeks old they go into runs where they're fed for another three months or so. You'll see the wire-fenced enclo-sures, tucked away in sheltered spots on the edge of a wood. By the time July and August come around, when the young birds are about twenty-one weeks old, they're released. And that's when the fun starts.

From Grimston I'd driven through Duggleby and on to Kirby Grindalythe. I was on my way to see a farmer above Foxholes who was interested in joining my Country Watch scheme, and decided to take the scenic route, by Sledmere. There's some lovely country up there, much of it the legacy of the Sykes family who planted thousands of trees on the bare wolds, back in the late 1700s.

I slowed down as I entered a stretch of woodland, but even at thirty-five miles an hour there was no way I could avoid them.

I rounded a tight bend and heard the familiar 'flump!' as I hit a cock-bird, followed by the 'ba-domp ba-domp' as I ran over two more that had already been knocked over and squashed flat. I stopped the car and walked back. They were everywhere, a regular gaggle of cocks and hens, grazing the verge that bordered the wood, pecking at the road where a passing harvester had spilled a few pounds of corn, oblivious to the carnage around them. I bent down and picked up the bird I'd run into. Quite dead. I placed it on the side of the read, in the long grass, and shoo'd the rest of the birds out of the way. But I was wasting my time. They don't have any road sense. In fact, they don't have much instinct for self-preservation at all. It comes from having spent most of their lives in captivity. There must have been a dozen squashed carcasses dotted about the road over the next two hundred yards, but there was nothing to be done about it.

I checked that there was no damage to the car, and drove off. I found myself thinking about Old John, a founding member of Country Watch. He used to tell a tale about how people would deliberately drive at the pheasants on the road outside his farm, then scoop them up and take them home to eat. There was one young fellow, far more money than sense, used to come by regularly, blaring his horn and splattering birds all over the road. He thought it was fun. Old John put up with it for a week or two, had a think, then paid a visit to the blacksmith. Next time matey came by in his souped-up Audi, there was this beautiful cock-bird stood right on the white line. Me-laddo swerved across the road, and went straight at him. He hit him square on with a hideous great prang. When he got out to investigate he found it was three inches thick and made of solid cast iron, which explained why his front end was stoved in and his radiator gushing coolant all over the tarmac. I smiled, thinking about that story – and about Old John, who'd died the previous spring.

I got to the farmer's place, and immediately wondered why I'd bothered. As soon as I drove into the yard I could see his feet sticking out from under a harvester. He had his tools scattered about the concrete apron, and he was cursing his luck. 'Beardy t'engineer can't get to me while tomorrow morning,' he said, 'and when he does it'll cost an arm and a leg.' He slid out from under the machine, sucking a bloody finger, his face covered with sweat, his blue overalls smudged with grease. 'I've another eighty acres to get in and then we're due at my brother's place.' He looked at the sky. 'Just hope the weather holds. They've had hail and lightning down in Lincolnshire, according to the lunchtime news.'

'Look,' I said, 'you've enough on your plate with that old dust-bucket. You sort yourself out and I'll come back in a week or two when things have quietened down a bit, eh?'

I drove back towards town. That was two chances of a cup of tea down the pan. There was only one thing for it. Walter. He'd surely be at home. I hurried back to Grimston, through the Birdsall estate, and up the Brow.

Walt was at home OK. He was standing in his porch, all dressed up in a brown suit with a red tie and a matching rose in his buttonhole. He had his teeth in, he'd had a shave – as indicated by the little cut that was staining the white of his shirt collar – and he'd plastered his hair down with water. He was just running his comb through it before putting his hat on. If I didn't know better I'd have sworn he'd rubbed Vaseline on his bald patch, it looked that shiny.

'Just in time,' he said, as I stood there with my mouth open. 'Here, tek this and come out t'front.' He thrust an old black camera into my hand, a proper antique, one of those where you have to pull the lens out on a set of runners and look through an angled mirror to see the picture you're taking.

'What's going on, Walt?'

'Why, it's a special event, that's what it is. For me—' – he cleared his throat – 'for me young lady and me . . . ' We were round by the back now, and there, on the step, was his lady friend. In all the time I'd known Walt, and lived with him, I'd never met her face to face. She'd generally drive up outside his place, toot her horn and he'd scuttle out to meet her on the roadside. But here she was, in the flesh, a cheery-looking woman, in her late sixties I'd guess, full-figured, wearing a skirt, a lightweight cotton jacket and a pair of very sensible brown leather shoes.

'You'll be Walter's policeman friend then,' she said.

'Aye, the uniform. Bit of a giveaway, isn't it?' I held out my hand. 'Pleased to meet you. Now' – I was trying to work out how to operate the camera – 'what am I doing with this thing?'

'Why, you're taking an anniversary snap,' she beamed. 'Fourteen years today since Walter first asked me out.'

'Fourteen years?' I glanced at Walt, who was pursing his lips and looking at the sky. 'Well, all I can say is, you deserve a medal, putting up with an old rogue like him for that long.'

She leaned forward and touched me on the arm. She was wearing a lavender sort of scent, which reminded me of my grandmother. 'Trouble with young people today,' she said, 'is they're too keen to set up home together. You know the old saying? Absence makes the heart grow fonder?'

'I do.' I was only half listening. I was having trouble with Walt's antique camera. As the lens came out there was like a set of bellows expanding behind it. I'd never seen anything quite like it. It looked like the sort of thing you'd get in a Laurel and Hardy film.

'Well,' she continued, 'that's the secret of a good relationship. We see each other once a week at most. And we never get bored, do we Walter?'

'Never mind the marriage guidance counselling, Muriel. Let him tek t' bloody picture and we can be off.'

'Where's he taking you then?' I'd finally got the upper hand and was lining the happy couple up in the viewfinder. 'Somewhere nice I hope?'

'Same place I took her on our first date,' Walt said. 'T'old Stone Trough at Kirkham.'

'Ve-ry nice. Very upmarket.'

'Oh yes,' said Muriel. 'The food there – well, it's outstanding.'

'Aye, and they do a decent drop of Timmy Taylor's bitter too.'

'Right, Walt, think of that first pint and give us a big smile.' I pressed the shutter release. 'There you go. Have fun. And think of us poor old public servants slaving away while you're eating roast beef and supping beer.'

It was almost eight o'clock by the time I drove through Norton on my way back to the station. A hot Friday afternoon had turned into a steamy Friday night. There were reports of thunderstorms in Hull and Beverley, and the general opinion was that they were moving our way. Town was busy. People were piling into the pubs, or sitting outside drinking long cold glasses of beer and lager. Instinctively, I licked my lips. I could've murdered a pint. Or two. Much as I love my job and enjoy the benefits of working irregular hours, there are times like this when I'm at work and everyone else is unwinding and I feel cheated. We all do at times. There they were, enjoying the warmth of the evening, the weekend stretching ahead of them, safe in the knowledge that we'd sort out the mess later on if things got out of hand. I hurried on, over County Bridge, past a gaggle of young women all dressed up in matching party frocks and bunny ears, teetering along in their high heels and giving me a wave as I drove by. Great, I thought, a bloody hen party. That'll mean fun and games later on.

Back at the station I poured myself a large glass of water, made a mug of tea and went into the CCTV room to have a look at the screens. Sometimes, when we're in the station, early in the evening, waiting to see how the night's going to turn out, I imagine it must be a bit like this for troops about to go into action. You hope your intelligence is good, but you never know quite what to expect; and at the back of your mind is the thought that, yes, you or your mates could get hurt. For some reason long hot days often degenerate into violent nights. Is it the drink or is it the heat? Probably a bit of both.

Ed was drifting in and out, in between writing up a report on an arrest he'd made the day before. His knee was better and he was back on patrol, and all the better for it, as far as I could see. 'Now then buddy,' he greeted me, 'you fit for it?'

'What – that dance at the Milton Rooms?'

'Oh hell, I'd forgotten that. What time does it finish?'

I had it all written down somewhere, and was looking through my notes. 'There's that big do at the rugby club too, somebody's twenty-first . . . Ah, here we are. Milton Rooms. One o'clock.'

'Perfect. Just what we want at the end of the shift.'

On Fridays and Saturdays when we overlapped with the night shift for the first few hours the idea was for all of us to go out around town, four or five off the late shift, a couple of

Specials, and four off nights. That way we can maintain a fair presence. If there's trouble we can respond in numbers and nip it in the bud. There's nothing like waving the flag, letting people know you're there. As a rural officer I would tend to stay in the town on a Friday and Saturday night to be on hand and back up the town officers. As far as we were concerned, on our particular shift, we wanted people to know who was on duty. I'm talking about the regulars in town, hard cases, potential troublemakers, the people who have had dealings with us before. They know well enough that some shifts are a bit of a soft touch. No names, no pack drill, but some coppers aren't as good at dealing with a confrontation as they ought to be. But on the streets of Malton and Norton they knew that our shift wasn't one to be messed with. If things got physical we'd be straight in and we knew how to look after ourselves. Dealing with public order situations was second nature to me having spent a number of years on the riot police in London. The TSG, to give it the proper name. I had total confidence, not only in my own ability but in that of my team. It was no coincidence that we had less bother than some of the other shifts got.

So by about ten fifteen the night lads were in, we'd had our briefing, enjoyed a round of tea and all been paired up. I was with Ed, which suited us both. We understood each other's way of working. And if it happened to be quiet, we always had plenty to talk about, especially as it was early August, the time of year when we football fans look ahead to the season in prospect. It's a time when everything is possible. You can look at the league tables and there you are, even steven with all the fancied teams on zero points, the whole season a blank sheet laid out in front of you. 'Mind you,' Ed pointed out as we drove down to the traffic lights, 'our lot aren't like other teams. We're unique.'

'How d'you mean?'

'Well, have you looked at the pre-season tables on the internet sites? All arranged in alphabetical order? I mean, they say it's an even playing field, right? But York City start every season bottom of the pile with a mountain to climb. Us and Wrexham and suchlike.'

'Hey, don't you worry about York City. This is the year.'

'Right. I'll make a note of that in my diary. And remind you about it next April. Like I do every year.'

We did the usual tour around town, past the potential trouble spots, then crossed the river into Norton. We slowed down and had a few words here and there with groups of people gathered on the streets. Now then, how's it going? That sort of thing. We didn't get involved, just made sure that people knew we were there. As ever I got the odd shout of 'Dirty Harry!' as we drove down Commercial Street.

'I love it,' Ed laughed, as we drove away from the Derwent Arms and back over the railway crossing. 'Dirty Harry. I bet you wish you'd never said that. How long ago was it?'

'Year. Maybe two. But Ed,' I said, 'did you get a good look at the lads as they shouted it out?'

'Can't say I did, buddy.'

'Ah well, you wouldn't have seen what I saw.'

'Go on, let's have it.'

'No, I'm serious . . .'

'And I'm listening.'

'Next time, Ed, look into their eyes. Look deep into their eyes.'

'Not sure I want to do that, Mike. It can be disturbing.'

'Ah well, if you did . . . If you did, you'd see what's lurking behind the bravado. Sheer naked dread. It's Dirty Harry. He's coming to get me . . .'

'Mike, you do talk a load of bollocks at times. You know that, don't you?'

'Aye, but you ride out with me, mate and you get what no other copper gets on this beat. In-flight entertainment. It's a laugh a minute on a Friday night when you're riding shotgun with me, laddie.'

'Laddie? You sound like Thommo.'

'Aye well, I was out with him again last week. It rubs off on you. Hoots mon and all that.'

Night had fallen, but it was still too early for trouble. When it gets to about half past eleven, that's when things are likely to kick off. It's when people move from the pubs to the late licensed bars and clubs. 'Maybe we'll get that storm they've had on Humberside,' I said, 'and our old mate PC Rain will drive 'em all inside.'

Back at the station we went into the CCTV room. Phil the operator was sitting there in front of a bank of screens, ten or a dozen showing pictures from around town, another handful from Pickering. He was twiddling the knobs and panning the cameras this way and that, leaning forward in his swivel chair to close in on anything that looked interesting – which at that moment appeared to be a group of lasses on a night out.

'Hey,' I said, 'we don't pay you to watch the local talent. I saw you – zooming in on them.'

'Tell you what,' he said, 'one of them was a bit of a looker.'

'So long as I'm in uniform I'm only interested in villains,' I said.

'Well, you would be.'

'Meaning?'

'From what I'm hearing you're already spoken for.'

'Ah well, you want to be careful who you listen to. Now then, what's that on camera eight?'

'Don't be changing the subject.'

'No, have a look. Zoom in.'

He reached out and twiddled the control. 'Bloody hell, aye. See what you mean.'

I was looking at a view from outside the Gate pub, barely a hundred yards from the crossroads in Yorkersgate. It was dark now, and we saw a huge man, big broad shoulders, six foot five or six, shaven head, standing outside, legs apart, unsteady on his feet, pointing towards the doorway as three or four lads shoved him back against the wall.

'Zoom her in, Phil.'

'Christ!'

Another man stumbled out from the pub and waved his arm at the first guy, shouting something. The first guy ripped off his jacket, exposing a barrel chest with a bandolier full of spent shotgun cartridges looped across it. He sported a pair of upper arms about the size of your average guy's thighs. 'He looks just like that bloke off the TV ads,' I said. 'Whadda they call him?'

'Tango Man?'

'Aye, that's it. It's bloody Tango Man – and he's about to explode,' I said, as his bald head glinted in the lamplight and he lurched towards the doorway.

'Aye, and some bugger's gonna be tango'd if we don't get there sharpish.' Ed was out the door and I was following. Even as we ran to the car I was on the radio.

'1015 to control, active message.'

'*Go ahead, Mike.*'

'We're on our way to the Gate public house. There's a man mountain. Looks like he may need to come in. Can you get some backup? CCTV are monitoring from Malton.'

We raced out of the car park and onto Old Maltongate. It would only take us a minute or two to get down there, but once people start shoving and shouting the odds – especially where drink is involved – anything can happen. As we drove past the Old Lodge a blaze of light flickered across the sky. 'Eh up, here's that storm,' I said. Ed got on the radio and asked Phil to keep us updated on what was happening. '*There's a little guy with spiky hair keeps popping his head out of the pub and shouting at your Tango Man,*' came the reply.

'Stirring it,' Ed said. 'Always has to be the little fellers, doesn't it?'

'*OK Mike, you've got a couple of units responding. On their way. Two or three minutes. The other van's on its way from Norton with the specials – if he gets over the level crossing. There's a train due.*'

By the time we'd got across the lights and arrived at the pub we could see we were going to need all the help we could get. Tango Man was shouting and bawling and trying to get back into the pub and there were now eight or ten other guys holding him back against the wall. At the door of the pub three bouncers in black suits were standing watching it all. They weren't going to get involved, although to be fair they had their hands full trying to stop another lot of youths from getting out. And in among them all the little fellow with the spiky hair was bobbing up and down.

We approached the melee up against the wall where Tango Man was still struggling to break free. 'Well, whose bloody side are that lot on?' I said, as the gang around him pushed and shoved. I stopped the car, half on the pavement, half off. I left the blue lights on, partly to guide the backup teams in, partly to calm some of the people down. At the very least it would let them know we were there.

'They're with Tango Man. Trying to calm him down,' Ed said. We piled out of the car. Somewhere over by the door a glass hit the pavement and smashed into a thousand pieces. At the same time we heard the first crack of thunder. 'They've a bloody job on, though. Look at the size of him.'

The guy was an absolute monster. There was no way I was going to wade in. In any case, Ed was right about what was happening: his mates were trying to restrain him, take the heat out of the situation. The only danger was if he managed to break free, but it didn't help when a carload of youths went by shaking their fists and mouthing off at everyone, and it didn't help when the same little fellow kept darting in and out of the pub entrance. 'Where's Johnno?' he was shouting. 'Where the f*** is Johnno?'

'What the hell's he keep yapping about?' Ed said, as I stood there shaking my CS gas. I was wondering whether it would have any effect at all on Tango Man. He was roaring now. 'They touch him and I'll bloody 'ave 'em – and their mates too!' he shouted. He was properly wound up, all but foaming at the mouth.

I was still deliberating about when – and how – to get involved when the little fellow came out one more time. 'Hey lads!' he shouted. 'He's inside. Johnno's in here.'

The lads who were holding Tango Man back let go of him and looked at the little fellow. He was facing into the bar. Suddenly he turned around and beckoned the others in. 'Come on, them other twats have started on him,' he shouted.

That did it. The whole lot, Tango Man too, moved towards the door en masse. Ed and I still couldn't work out what the hell was happening or why. But I knew if that lot got inside it was going to be an almighty ruck. I immediately went up the few short steps at the entrance to the pub. With the bouncers behind me I shouted at them, 'Get back, and calm down.' It made one or two of them stop shoving and try to calm the others, but Tango Man still kept moving forward with a hard-core of mates following him. I drew my Asp into the ready position and raised my CS gas. Crack! went the lightning, and I felt the first few drops of rain on my face.

'Ed!' I shouted. But I'd lost sight of him. I was right in their path as Tango Man moved closer again, shouting, 'I'll sort the buggers out!' I stood my ground and tried to make myself look at big as possible. I shouted in my deepest and most authoritative voice, 'Get back!' But as I looked him in the eyes I could tell he just wasn't listening. He took another step forward and let out some sort of war cry. It was ugly, bestial, and terrifying. In that split second and with no time to spare I sprayed him full in the face with CS. Next moment my left arm was trapped behind me as I backed into the bouncers with Tango Man bearing down on me. He wasn't going to stop, and I wasn't going to ease my finger off the button. Not bloody likely. The droplets mingled with the sweat on his forehead, and ran down into his nose. It seemed he was going to keep coming, like the lad Wood did when he came at me with that samurai sword. And if he did, I was in trouble. The closer he got, the bigger he was.

I tried to back off but the bouncer kept pushing against the small of my back. I could feel his breath on my neck, hot and stinking of tobacco smoke. As I shoved my way back trying to create some space in which to swing my Asp I trod on his feet and he yelped. Then, just when I thought Tango Man was going to reach out and grab me he stopped dead, roared like an animal, and doubled over, his hands clasped to his face. Down he went, like a sack of spuds, right at my feet. His mates were straight in. For a moment it looked as if they were coming for me, but instead they clustered around their man, stunned.

'Hey, Joey!' they shouted, shaking him. The little fellow who'd been doing all the shouting turned to me. 'You ain't poisoned him, have you? He never started this. It was them daft pillocks in there.' He pointed to the bar, then looked at Tango Man again. 'Christ,' he said.

Tango Man was on his hands and knees, spitting onto the pavement. He looked up at me, his eyes red and streaming, his mouth twisted. I waited for it, the abuse I knew was coming. There was another rumble of thunder, and a few more fat raindrops landed on us. Come on, I thought. A good old-fashioned downpour. That'll calm 'em down. Tango Man opened his mouth, drew a breath and half stood up. I had the canister in my hand, ready. I was quite prepared to give him another dose if he needed it. He looked me right in the eye. 'You've been CS gassed,' I said. 'Don't go rubbing your face or you'll make it worse. Just calm down. You're under arrest for public order offences.'

I was surprised at what happened next. I was expecting an eruption. Instead I got a mumbled 'Sorry officer, I just lost it. I thought my mate was getting beat up.'

'That's OK, buddy,' I said, hoping nobody would see the huge relief on my face.

He nodded, and slumped back onto the pavement, propping himself on one hand, his legs splayed out in front of him. All

I had to do now was get the cuffs on. He had massive shoulders, and despite his apology he'd made his mind up that he didn't want to be cuffed. He didn't want to fight with us but he certainly wasn't helping matters. Due to his sheer size I knew it was going to need three sets of cuffs to do the job. When you get someone who has shoulders and arms the size of his it's physically impossible to do the job with a single set. They've so much muscle that their wrists won't meet at the back. I got one on his left, but I hadn't the strength to pull his other arm across and complete the job. The rain had started in earnest and he was slippery as an eel. Looking up I saw that the Specials had arrived, Keith Nicholson the forester, big burly lad, and another fellow I didn't know. 'Thank God you're here,' I gasped. 'Give us your cuffs, will you?' I had my knee in the small of Tango Man's back and was struggling to hold him still. At the same time I heard someone shout, 'Johnno mate!' and another fellow appeared, bursting out from the pub, a tall slim guy with neat dark hair. He too had a bandolier around his chest. Tango Man was still squirming around. I looked up. The newcomer was shouting the odds at the bouncers. Ed had grabbed hold of his bandolier and was trying to drag him back, away from them. The bouncers had got the pub doors shut. Tango Man's mates were standing there, uncertain as to what to do. While they hesitated, Keith got his cuffs on Tango Man's right wrist. All it needed now was for me to link the two sets of cuffs with a third. I finally managed it, just as a flash of lightning illuminated the street, followed by an earsplitting scream and a clatter of high heels, and there along the road from the lights came the posse of eight or ten females I'd seen earlier in the short pink dresses and bunny ears, except that now, instead of laughing and joking, they were all spitting feathers.

'Gerroff him you!'

The girls marched towards us, led by a large lass with a big silver wand in her hand.

'Hey, steady on Ellie.' One of the lads was walking down the road to meet them. 'It's all right, everything's under control.' But he was no match for her. He bounced off her, slipped on the wet pavement and fell, smack against a shop window. 'You can't arrest him,' she said, brandishing her wand in my face and pointing at Tango Man. 'He's getting married in t'morning.'

'Oh aye,' I said, 'and who's the lucky lass?'

She didn't answer. She'd spotted Ed as he pinned the tall thin fellow to the ground. She ran forward, took off, seemed to hurtle through space for several yards with her little glittery handbag raised above her head. Reaching Ed she swung the bag in what can only be described as a tenpin-bowling action, smacking him in the face and sending his glasses flying. 'And he's the best man,' she shouted. 'So you can leave him alone an' all.'

Between us, Keith and I grabbed her wrists. By hell, she struggled. 'I don't know what they feed you lasses these days,' I said as Keith held one arm, and a night-duty PC held the other while I snapped the cuffs into place, 'but I reckon I need some of it.'

'You're nowt but a bloody big bully!' she shouted, her hair all matted by the rain, the mascara running down her cheeks. 'And a killjoy. Picking on a lass on her hen night.'

'I'm sorry, love, but I've no choice,' I said, tucking my shirt back in and trying to look calm and dignified. We had a fair old crowd now, mostly from the pub, but one or two passersby had stopped to watch the fun. Another car went by and another load of abuse was shouted at us. 'Now then,' I said, nice and loud so that everyone could hear. 'I want you all to calm down. I don't want to arrest anyone else, so don't make me do it.'

'You don't need to arrest no other bugger.' It was the mouthy little fellow, giving Keith's mate a hard time as he marched them to the back of the van. 'You've got t'bride, t'groom and t'best man. You want me to go and fetch the vicar for you?'

'Ed,' I said, as I helped Tango Man to his feet, 'I'm going to take this gentleman, Keith can take the young lady. We'll see you back at the station, OK?'

What we needed to do now was get the troublemakers out of the way, fast. The sooner they were removed the sooner things would calm down. Of course the lads outside the pub wanted to argue the toss about what had happened, but I wasn't going to get engaged in any banter with them. Go in, grab the ring-leaders and remove. ASAP. That's my policy. Anyway, my prayers had been answered. The rain was sheeting down, driving them back inside.

By the time I'd got the big fellow in the back of my car and driven him to the station he was less Tango Man and more Milky Bar Kid. I brought him a drink of water and put him in front of the duty sergeant. I repeated what I'd told him earlier, that he was under arrest under Section 4 of the Public Order Act, for making threats of violence. He started shivering. He was thoroughly soaked, bare-chested, and still had his bandolier around his torso. 'What's this in aid of anyway?' I asked him.

He shrugged. 'Just a bit of fun, like. The lasses were going out as rabbits. We decided we'd go out as Mexican bandits. I had a sombrero when we started out. God knows what happened to that.'

I fetched a blanket for him to put around his shoulders, while we got his details down. He lived out Hovingham way, worked as a forester, he said. This was his stag night. Then we took him down to the cells. They're actually on the ground floor, but we still use the old term. There are only three at Malton nick, plus a juvenile detention room, so we were going to have a full house tonight. Tango Man was still unsteady on his feet. He actually stopped and shuddered when he saw the big heavy metal doors. 'Chrisst,' he slurred, 'into t'bloody dungeons, is it? Then he started apologising. 'Oh shit, I've really blown it, haven't I? Look, I'm sorry mate. I never meant to kick off. But that was my mate in the pub, me best man, and them lads were giving him grief. You have to stand up for your mates, don't you?'

'I s'pose you do,' I said as I turned the key in the lock.

Ed was at the desk with the bride-to-be. Twenty minutes earlier she'd been an Amazon on the rampage, storming in to protect her man and putting the fear of God into us. Now she was a hunched, tearful figure. She'd lost her bunny ears, and was sitting there wrapped in a blanket with her silver wand, her hands cuffed in front of her, blinking back tears as she was processed for assault on a policeman. Ed stood in front of her trying to bend his glasses back into shape. She told us she was a chef at a pub. She'd never been in trouble before, and now here she was, due to get married in the morning. With her big panda eyes – well, I have to say I could only feel sorry for her. 'See, I saw me man on the floor,' she sniffed. 'In handcuffs. Then I saw that policeman fighting with the best man. I just had to wade in. Lost the bloody plot.'

'It's OK,' Ed said. 'You didn't hurt me.'

I couldn't help grinning at Ed. He knew he'd never live this down. Floored by the bride-to-be. Was he going to cop some stick next time we went out to the pub! We finally got the bride booked in, and then turned to the tall thin fellow, the best man. He hadn't really done much damage, but he'd been arrested in order to prevent a breach of the peace. He told us he worked for a financial services firm and was studying to take his professional exams. 'Well,' I said, as I took him to his cell, 'that's a first for me, locking up an accountant.'

At that Phil poked his head around the door to the custody suite. 'Mike, that little fella is back outside the Gate causing problems with the bouncers again, I've got him on CCTV.'

'Him? Right Ed, come on. I knew there was one we'd forgotten.'

We drove back down and sure enough there he was, on his own now, mouthing off to the bouncers. He was very unsteady on his feet, and now that there was no crowd around him he simply looked ridiculous, strutting about shouting the odds. I'm sure the bouncers would've swatted him if we hadn't shown up when we did. As Ed and I walked over I said, 'There's always one, isn't there.'

'Tell me about it,' one of the bouncers said. 'There's no way he's coming back in here.'

But matey wasn't listening. I don't think he'd even noticed us. He stood there on his toes, teetering, his chin jutting out, threatening them with destruction. If he'd tried really hard he might just have reached the bouncers' collars.

'He has to come in,' Ed said. 'We can't have him on the loose in this state.'

Thank goodness he came quietly. Within minutes of arriving at the station and being booked in as drunk and disorderly, he was sleeping like a baby on the cell bench in the juvenile detention room.

Chris was at the desk when I got back to the parade room, and Ed was standing beside him. 'That kettle on?' I asked.

'Ed's just mashed. Should be ready to drink by now.'

'Chris,' I said, 'take a good look at that man beside you.

What you have there is a modern policing hero. There he was, lying on the pavement, poleaxed by the amazing runaway bride – spreadeagled he was, with fourteen stone of female flesh lying in top of him, felled by a single blow from her silver handbag. But does he go crying to the first-aid box, writing it all down in the injury-on-duty book? No. Selfless to the last, all he cares about when he gets back to the station is the well-being of his fellow officers. Priorities, Chris. That's what we're talking about. Gets the tea mashed. Then goes and patches his wounds up.'

'Mike.'

'What is it Ed?'

'Go and pour the tea.'

'Right, Ed.'

Normally we would have sat down and written up our notes at this point, but we'd no sooner got our tea than we were called out to another incident, at the rugby club right across the road from the police station. We got a proper soaking this time, rounding up two suspects in the car park, chasing another one up to the road. They'd crashed a birthday party in the club and assaulted one of the guests. This was an ambulance job, just what we needed after the going-on at the Gate. Three more arrests, drowned rats all of them and nowhere to lock them up. It was a right bloody nuisance, but that's Friday night for you. I was all for holding them in the cars, handcuffed of course, but in the end we had to take them to Scarborough to be locked up there. So now it was fingers crossed that there was no more aggravation in town, because we were going to be short of two double-crewed cars for the next hour and a half.

Still, that wasn't a problem Ed or I needed to concern ourselves

with. We were due off. And the good news was that the Milton
Rooms had turned out with no trouble at all, everyone scuttling home as fast as they could with PC Rain lashing down.
We got our notes written up, then went to see how our prisoners were doing. The little fellow was still out of it, dead to
the world, but the bride, the groom and the best man were wide
awake, and grateful for the cup of tea we took them. I spoke
to the bride through the wicket, the metal shutter in the cell
door through which you pass food and drinks. She was beside
herself. 'We're supposed to be getting married tomorrow,' she
said, her eyes filling with tears. 'What's going to happen? What
we going to do?'

'Where's the wedding, love?' I asked her.

'Hovingham church. Then we've a reception over at t'Lodge.'

'What, across the road there?'

'Yes.'

'When are you due in church?'

'Two o'clock.'

I sighed. I was at the end of my rope. I wanted to go home.
I wanted to have a long soak in the bath, a little nip from that
hip flask Algy had given me, and about nine hours' kip. But I
was concerned for these people. They weren't criminals as such.
They'd just got completely carried away. Too much drink
combined with the excitement of the wedding coming up.

'Why didn't you have your hen night and stag night a week
ago?' I asked her. 'Why tonight?'

'It was Joey. He knew he'd be tied up until the Twelfth.
He works on the estate up at—' I knew the place she meant.
'He takes his work seriously. They've a big party of Yanks
flying in.'

'Well, you're lucky,' I said. 'There's a lot of coppers – one or two in this station, I can tell you – who'd have you waiting for a court appearance some time next week.'

'Court?' She was looking at the floor and shaking her head. 'But we're booked on a flight to Corfu Sunday morning.'

'You know what I'm going to say, don't you?'

She looked up. 'That we should've thought about that before we . . . We never meant to start a fight. Really.'

As I shut the wicket I said, 'Leave it with me. I'll be back in a few minutes. And you keep your fingers crossed.'

It was all down to Chris, the custody sergeant. He was the one who would make the decision, but I knew he would want my opinion, so I told him what I thought. Two basically decent people. Screwed it up, full of remorse, and no real harm done, if we overlooked the blow to Ed's self-esteem. I wanted to tell Chris about what we used to do in the Met, but he'd heard it before. Down there we were encouraged to take the common-sense approach, to think about 'What would twelve ordinary people off the Clapham omnibus say?'

Chris knew where I was coming from anyway. He was as level-headed as any desk sergeant I'd worked with. 'OK,' he said. 'You've checked for previous form, I take it?' I had. The good news was that none of the wedding party had any convictions or cautions against their name. They weren't any entries on any of our intelligence systems. As for the little fellow, we still didn't have a name for him. He was dead to the world.

It was getting on for three o'clock now and, much as I wanted to get home, I couldn't allow our guests to think we were rushing this through. We still had to show them that they were in trouble, and that it was a serious business. After some deliberation the decision was made that we could caution them, and that required the presence of an inspector. This being night-time, there was only one inspector covering the whole area from Scarborough and Whitby through Ryedale to Northallerton and the Hambleton area. Sally Cordley was a well respected farmer's wife as well as a police inspector. She ran Vale Watch over at Easingwold, the equivalent of my Country Watch. She agreed to drive over and administer the caution, giving all three of our prisoners a stern talking-to. Then we fingerprinted them, did the mouth swabs for DNA, and photographed them.

I finally saw them off the premises a little after four o'clock on the morning of the Glorious Twelfth, when the bride's father collected them in his car. By the time I got back to Keeper's Cottage the rain had stopped but the leaves were dripping and a pair of pheasants were poking about in the flattened grass beside the wood. 'Good luck,' I murmured to them as I got out of the car. Fifteen minutes later I'd collapsed into bed to sleep like a dead man until mid-morning.

As I came in to work a little before four, I could see the cars all arriving at the Lodge. It's a lovely old building dating back to Tudor times. I've often wondered what the owners' main house was like, because this place, built as a hunting lodge, looks like a mansion in its own right, set as it is in its own grounds and encircled by a lovely old stone wall. I couldn't resist pulling up and watching the people arrive, and I'm glad I did, because what I saw is still fresh in my memory. There was the bride and groom, standing on the lawn in front of the entrance, greeting their guests. He had a black eye, she had a fat lip, and there was the best man helping the aged relatives out of their cars with his wrist all bandaged up. I got away quickly, before they spotted me, and went to tell the lads what I'd seen. As Ed said, thank God we have our CS gas. If we'd had to fight with that lot we would of all been in a much worse state and the offences could have been far more serious. The days when a cop could wade in with his truncheon swinging and get into hand-to-hand fighting have long gone, and I for one am not sorry. As to Ed's ignominious defeat at the hands of the bride, I didn't think it was wise to mention that.

Three weeks later I was sitting in the Jolly Farmers having a quiet pint with Ann. We weren't in the bar as such, but in the next room, where they have the fire in winter, right under the clock that Soapy had altered that time. Walt had joined us, and when the door opened I looked around the chimneybreast, expecting to see Algy and Soapy, who'd said they'd be popping in later.

Instead I saw Tango Man entering with a couple of his mates, big blokes, although nowhere near his size. He looked tanned and fit, but his brow was furrowed. I couldn't help noticing his hands. They were huge. He looked around, and went to the bar. I heard him say to the landlord, 'Now then, mate, they tell me PC Pannett drinks in here, that right?' I nudged Walt. 'If owt kicks off here, mate, you take off. Ann and me can deal with this.'

Before Walt could react, Tango Man was walking through the bar and over to our table. I stood up, pushed my pint to one side, and took a step towards him. Even so, he loomed over me as he reached out a big bronzed fist. 'You,' he said. 'It is you, isn't it?'

'What is it you want?' Ann asked, getting out of her seat.

'He's PC Pannett, right?'

'I am, mate. Now, what can I do for you? If you've something to say we'll deal with it outside.'

He still had his hand extended in front of him. 'I came out

here to thank you. In person. I nearly managed to screw up my wedding day but thanks to you, well, it all came right. Put it there. If you will.'

I shook his hand – or rather he shook mine. 'Now,' he said, motioning to my glass, 'looks like you and your good lady could do with a refill.'

'Why, that's very decent of you,' I said, draining the rest of the pint and passing him the empty. And before I could say another word Walt piped up. 'Aye, and how about one for the old man as taught him all he knows?'

Tango Man leaned across the table and offered Walt that giant paw of his. 'A privilege to meet you, sir. You've raised a fine lad there, Mr Pannett. Pint, is it?'

Chapter 11

A Storm on the Moors

It's funny how you get to know people – I mean really know who they are and what makes them tick. I have some friends I've known for years but still don't know a great deal about them beyond the things we have in common. People that I maybe see in the Jolly Farmers, or play darts with, mates I go to watch York City with. There's one lot I meet up with every year and go fly-fishing with in the Outer Hebrides, a group of people I was introduced to through an old contact from my time at Battersea nick. We have a fantastic time up there, but we never really talk about where we come from and what else we do. They just seem to belong in that particular place, that part of my life. And when we're together we mostly talk about the job in hand. We don't get into our personal histories: where we lived when we were kids, what our parents did and so on. But when Ann and I got together we really wanted to know everything about each other. There was quite a bit to tell, on both sides, except that we never really saw enough of each other, what with working shifts and having to keep our romance under wraps. So even after eight or nine months each of us only had a sketchy sort of knowledge of where the other came from. I was chuffed to bits to find out how much we had in common: both growing up in the Vale of York, and barely three miles apart; both serving in the Met, and at the same time; both patrolling Battersea Bridge for several years, me on the south side of the river, her on the north. I still marvelled that we'd never managed to meet up but, as she said one time, it was probably for the best. We each of us had our respective journeys to make. If we hadn't got all that growing up out of the way we probably wouldn't have got along so well when the time came.

Even though we saw so little of each other those first few months, I'd told her plenty about my childhood, my teenage years and some of the later stuff – joining the TA, for example, when I found that country life wasn't giving the teenaged me enough excitement. She laughed when I told her how I'd failed to get into the North Yorkshire police because of my eyesight. It turned out that she couldn't get in either: she was too short. It makes you think – well, it made us think. If it hadn't been for the Met, who were less fussy about you wearing glasses, or being vertically challenged, as they say, we might never have met.

But there was one thing I'd never mentioned. And that was a part of my childhood, a part that really moulded the person I was to grow up to become, instilled into me my love of the North Yorkshire countryside, and fostered my interest in wildlife too, I suppose. I don't know why, but I'd just never talked about it. When it did come up it was as a result of us having a rare day working together. In all the time she'd been at Malton I could've counted the number of times we'd been out on patrol together on one hand, and now that she was acting sergeant I didn't expect it to happen again. But that's the beauty of our job: you never know what the next shift's going to throw at you.

It had started off as a really beautiful September day. Sunny, warm, still. Under a pale blue sky the woods around me were still green. The only brown leaves to be seen were on the single chestnut tree that grew at the edge of the wood along the driveway. Around mid-morning I walked down to the village to pick up a couple of things at the shop. Everywhere seemed especially peaceful. The kids were back at school, of course, and out in the country the harvest was in – all apart from the taties and sugar beet, that is. The rest of the fields had been ploughed, harrowed and drilled, and the winter wheat was already poking through the moist earth. As I strolled back up the hill towards the narrow lane that led to Keeper's Cottage I found myself thinking about how satisfying it must be for a farmer at this time of year, to have the corn gathered in and the next year's crop already in the ground. Mind you, knowing farmers, they'd most likely be fretting about what they were going to get when they took their grain to market, or the price of fertiliser, and they'd be watching the weather as they prepared to get the spuds in. I could see their point on that one: the day that had started so brightly was already on the turn. The early sunshine was fading behind a veil of high clouds, and when Walter called by to bring me a couple of rabbits he'd killed that morning he had no doubts about what was in store. 'It'll be raining cats and dogs come teatime,' he said. 'You just see if it isn't.'

The old fellow was right, of course. By the time I left for work, about half past one, the wind had got up and the moors were obscured by low clouds. You didn't need to be a genius to see what lay in store. It wasn't a day to be out and about. So I was well chuffed when I got to the station and Chris on the desk told me he had a full crew on duty, plus a couple of probationers. 'Does that mean I can stay here in the dry and let some other bugger patrol the wilds of North Yorkshire?' I said.

'It does, mate, but only on certain conditions.'

'There had to be a catch, didn't there?'

'I want you to stick to your paperwork. I don't want you hanging around here annoying me with your daft jokes . . .'

'Who, me?'

'Or any more stories about your glory days in the Met.'

'But you haven't heard the best ones yet, Chris.'

'Or another tirade about York City.'

'What you saying? You like a good moan about the Minstermen as much as I do.'

'Yeah, but the difference between you and me, Mike, is that I've got past the point where I find it funny. Don't get me wrong. I can accept the ups and downs of life as a supporter. I took relegation on the chin and got on with my life, but I tell you what, if we don't pick up soon the trapdoor to the Conference will be yawning. And as far as I'm concerned that'll be the end of a twenty-year romance. If I want to support a non-league team I'll pop across to Harrogate Railway. It's a bloody sight cheaper. So – as long as I'm on duty I am hereby banning all talk of York City within earshot of this desk. Got that?'

'He's got it.'

'Oh, hi Ann. Didn't know you were on this turn.'

'Very convincing,' she murmured when we were out of Chris's earshot. 'Nobody would ever think the last words you said to me last night were "see you tomorrow, Sarge".'

'Aye well, I did warn you: I'm a slippery customer. Cunning as a fox. And who knows – maybe something'll come up that'll take us out on patrol together.'

'You know the old saying, Mike: be careful what you wish for.

Anyway I'm taking the parade with Chris in a few minutes. Can you get everyone together and warn them. It seems we're getting a visit from the superintendent.'

'I don't like the sound of that,' I said.

A few minutes later we were sat around the table in the parade room. A couple of the night crew had joined us. They were due at court the next morning and had been dropped back to a late shift.

Ann and Chris ran through the posting and the latest intelligence briefing. They had just finished and Ed was arguing with Fordy about who was having the last biscuit when Superintendent Grey entered the room with Birdie, the inspector.

'Parade', Chris said, and everyone stood up. It's the done thing when a senior officer enters the room.

'Thank you, please sit down,' the Super said. 'Now, I expect you're all wondering – perhaps even worrying – what this is all about. Well, I've come to tell you about some exciting new developments.' But first we had to sit through the usual spiel about how well we were doing, but how there's always room for improvement. How many times had we sat through that, I thought. A bit of praise and then a spot of fault-finding. Then he went on to tell us how the new chief constable had been in post long enough to have made up her mind on what improvements could be made. First off, we were going to get a chief superintendent for our area. A totally new command and control computer system with the latest software was to be installed. Eh oop, I thought: more courses for the likes of Thommo. We were also going to get a revamped shift pattern in the new year, one that would provide more overlaps of staff at peak times. But before we could enjoy that bit of good news, came the bad. Were we aware, he asked us, that the present shift system was killing us off, that the average life expectancy after retirement was five years? That made a few of us sit up and take notice. You could hear people shuffling in their seats. Five years. It's not long.

As he droned on, my mind began to wander again. The fact is that once you've got a few years under your belt you've heard all these pep talks before. Or you think you have. But this one was now venturing into new territory.

'So, ladies and gentlemen,' I heard him say, 'very exciting times ahead. The way I look at it, we're on the platform waiting for the train. It's a brand new, streamlined train. High-speed job. Fast track. Give you the ride of a lifetime. And I ask you the question: do you want to join me on my train for that exciting journey to a new future? Do you want to go all the way? Because I want people who are on board with me.'

Before we had the chance to chew it over, the Super was looking at his watch, and Birdie was assuring him that Ryedale would be 'all aboard!' At that the Super left the room, with Birdie scuttling behind him.

For a few moments the whole parade room was in silence. Stunned, we were. Then Ed spoke up. 'Christ,' he said, 'my mate at Scarborough retires next year. I'd better call him. Tell him he's only got six years to live.'

I looked across at Ann, who raised an eyebrow. 'Well,' she said, 'I've heard some management pep talks in my time, but what the hell was that lot about?'

'You heard him,' Ed said. 'He wants us to get on a train with him. Reading between the lines, like. Unless I was picking up the wrong signals.'

'Gawd 'elp 'em at York,' Jayne said. 'They're a hundred-mile-an-hour jobs there. They won't know what's hit 'em.'

'Well, he'll need to slow down when he comes out Malton

way,' I said. 'Start flying up and down the branch line at that speed and they'll soon be off the rails.'

'Sod it,' Ed said. 'I think he's jumped the track already. Anyway, I'm a steam man myself. If he wants me on board he can pick me up at Pickering and take a run out Goathland way. Now that's what *I* call a train journey.'

'That's the spirit,' Ann said. 'Bags of enthusiasm.' She looked at her watch. 'Tell you what, though. Off the record, are we sure we want to go where he's taking us?'

'No,' Ed said. 'So take my tip: make sure you've got a return ticket.'

An hour later I was preparing my Country Watch newsletter when Ann came and threw my hat onto the desk. 'What are you, bloody psychic?' she said.

'What d'you mean?'

'Chris has just asked me to go out on the moors – and take you with me.'

'Oh – off for a picnic, are we?'

'If I were you I think I would bring a sandwich, yes. Some woman's got herself lost. Went out with a party of hikers, got separated, and nobody noticed she was missing.'

'Oh, right.' I shoved my papers back into a folder. 'And where was this?'

'Somewhere above Rosedale. Come on, let's get on the road. I'll fill you in on the way.'

It was now a comprehensively lousy afternoon. The wind was gusting up to gale force, and the rain was lashing against the windscreen. As we drove down towards the bypass in the trusty four-wheel drive we had to stop and drag a fallen branch off the road.

'Not a good day to be stranded on the moors,' Ann said as she took us across the roundabout and onto the Pickering road. 'I wonder if she's properly equipped.'

'If she was with a group she probably was.'

'Yes, but you know as well as I do you get some right idiots.'

She was right. I've found people wading through a foot of snow in denim jackets and jeans. I've found them in midsummer without so much as a bottle of water. Stuck out in the middle of nowhere with no grub, complaining because the pub's shut. Going off into the wilds without a map and then phoning for help when they get lost. I've seen them limping back into Farndale on a Sunday afternoon carrying high-heeled shoes and nursing blisters on the soles of their feet.

'Still,' I said, as we headed west from Pickering and took the road up to Cropton, 'at least we've plenty of daylight left.'

We caught up with the hikers, huddling under the abandoned stone arches on top of Rosedale Chimney Bank. As you approach the arches they look like an old railway viaduct; in fact, they're what's left of the kilns where they used to fire up the ovens and process the iron ore. Looking around Rosedale today, it's hard to imagine what it must have been like a century ago: an industrial boom town, with mines and railways and steam-powered machinery everywhere you looked. They employed thousands, right up to the 1920s. Yorkshire's own Klondyke.

'Now then.' There were ten of them all told, retired by the look of them, all dressed for the weather in waterproof coats and hats, with stout boots, gaiters, gloves, poles, the lot. A couple of them were sharing the contents of a Thermos flask, blowing the steam from plastic mugs. They all looked pretty glum. 'So you've lost one, have you?' Ann said.

'We didn't realise she was missing till we got into Rosedale village. And we've no idea which path she took.'

'Why, which way did you come?' Ann asked.

'We were going to take the track past Ana Cross – the one that runs up from Lastingham village.'

'That where you started from?'

'No, we started at Cropton. Left the cars there and set out along the road. We were making for Lastingham church. We were going to look at the old cross in the crypt there. Then the rain started so we decided to take the shorter route. I mean, she could've gone missing there. Anywhere. I knew we should've had a head count, but . . .'

'So when did you realise you'd lost her?'

'Not for a while. It didn't sink in till we met up here. She was with us when we started out on that little lane that leads on to the moor. We got to where it forks and decided to split up. Some of us took the lower path along the moor side, the others went on the main track to Ana Cross. We said we'd meet up here at the arches. Then we could take the road back to Lastingham together.'

'Well, which party was she with?'

'That's the whole point. We don't know. When we realised she wasn't with us we assumed she was on the upper path. And the other lot assumed she was with us.'

One of the men chipped in. 'I remember her saying she had a stone in her shoe. I'm wondering whether she stopped to fix it and just lost sight of us. You can see what it's like out there. Once we got fifty yards ahead of her we'd have been out of sight.'

'Out of earshot too. It was really blowing by then.'

'Well, it's easily done,' Ann said. 'Listen, I'm going to need a description. What colour coat did she have on?'

'Bright orange. Really easy to spot.'

'Have you been back to look for her?' I asked.

'Well, no.' The woman nodded toward a couple of the men behind her. 'They were going to go back to Ana Cross, but we thought if she's on that path she'll surely find her way here. It's plenty wide enough. Unless she's hurt herself, of course. We just decided it would be sensible to get help.'

'You did right,' Ann said. 'You'd be surprised how many people get into trouble going out to look for their mates. Next thing you know you've two search parties on the go.'

'We thought of turning back and searching the lower path, but we didn't want to risk it.'

'You mean the one that runs parallel to the beck?' I said. She nodded.

'You know it?' Ann glanced at me.

'Well aye, as well as you can know it.'

'Meaning?'

'Why, it goes where it wants to go. It's barely a footpath, more like a little sheep trail through the heather. Bad enough to follow even in clear weather. And I tell you what, this time of year there's whole stretches that are overgrown with bracken. You're fighting your way through the stuff.'

'He's right,' one of the men said. 'We all ended up taking a different line. You're on the slope, you're wading through it and in the end all you can do is just follow the lie of the hillside. Sometimes there's a track and sometimes there isn't. That's why half of us decided to take the upper route.'

'Well, let's hope your friend didn't get lost on that path,' I said, 'or she could be anywhere by now. She got a compass with her?'

'Yes.'

'Whistle?'

'Should have. And I know she has a torch. We try to make sure we're properly equipped.'

'Mobile?'

'Ah.'

'You mean she didn't?'

'She never brings one. Reckons she hardly ever gets a signal up here.'

Ann had gone to look at the big two-and-half-inch map of the National Park area. I stood there for a minute with the hikers, looking out to the south through the drips that were falling steadily from the stone arches. All we could see was the verge of cropped grass that bordered the road and a couple of bedraggled sheep buffeted by the wind. Beyond them there was nothing but thick mist – low cloud, more like it – billowing in from the west. Our four-wheel drive was barely visible.

I walked over to see what Ann's plan was. Right at that moment I was scratching my head over this one. There was clearly a limit to what we could achieve in the conditions.

'What I reckon,' she was saying, 'is that we need help. The weather's appalling, it's not going to get any better, and we've a big area to cover. Can you get on to control, give them an update and ask for authority for search and rescue to be called out.'

'Will do.' Ann was right. In a situation like this there would have been little point in requesting further police units. We needed the experts, properly equipped and trained for these conditions and terrain.

I spoke to Birdie, and he authorised the control room to call out the team. 'They say we can expect them within an hour,' I said, as Ann struggled to fold the map with the wind threatening to rip it to shreds.

'Good job you had this laminated,' she said as she put it back in the glove compartment.

'I learned the hard way,' I said. 'My original set got pulped, first time out.'

'Right, Mike, looking at the track, what do you reckon? Can we make it down there in the vehicle?'

'Towards Ana Cross, you mean?'

'Yes.'

'Yeah. It's rough, but we should be OK. You thinking what I'm thinking? That she might have started out on the sheep trail, then taken a bearing to cut across to the main track?'

'Well, that's what I'd do if the clouds came down like this. According to the map they're barely half a mile apart at the most.'

'That's a long way through wet heather though.'

'True. What I was thinking was, we could cover the actual path while we're waiting for search and rescue. Let them go into the heather.'

'Yep, sounds like a plan.'

I knew plenty about the search and rescue team. I'd had dealings with them before. They may be a volunteer outfit, but they're very well equipped and they have dozens of people they can call on. Doctors, nurses, paramedics, farmers, police, ex-Army, all sorts of people from all walks of life. They started out in the 1960s as a genuinely amateur organisation to help the National Park wardens when hikers got into difficulties. Back then they had little more than their foul-weather clothing, a whistle apiece and bags of enthusiasm. Every time they were called out to an incident they'd just grab their flasks and sandwiches, pile into someone's car – a Land Rover if they were lucky – and set off. Then as they started to grow they attracted funding, and now they're seriously well equipped. In our area they operate from two centres with a small fleet of vehicles.

They have such a fantastic reputation that they actually run training courses for mountain rescue personnel.

So we had a plan, but what about the rest of the hikers? A couple of them had come across to ask us what they should do while we went in search of the missing woman. 'It's up to you,' Ann said, 'but if you want my advice I'd say a couple of you should stay put in case she shows up here – making sure you have a flask and some food with you – and the rest of you start back to your cars at Cropton. You don't want to be on the road when it gets dark. And at least you'll keep warm. No point all of you sitting here shivering. Mike and I are going to drive as far down the path as we can. We'll come back here, whatever the result, to rendezvous with search and rescue. Meanwhile put my mobile number in one of your phones. We'll do our best to stay in touch. Mike, can you grab one of the blankets from the car and leave it with them just in case anybody needs it.'

'Will do.'

Just as we were leaving I had a thought. 'What if she battles through on the lower path and comes up the road way? Wouldn't take five minutes to check, would it?'

'Fair point.' Ann turned the Puddle Hopper around, put it into second gear, engaged four-wheel drive and set off down the bank.

'Never liked this hill,' I said as I watched the narrow tarmac strip fall away in front of us. 'First time I ever came down here I was driving a beat-up Mini with dodgy brakes. I was just eighteen, my first car. Never thought I'd make it to the bottom in one piece.'

'Why am I not surprised by that?'

'They reckon it's one in three on the bend. There aren't many this steep in the entire country.'

'I know. They used to do hill climbs up here. In the old days, I mean. Came from all over the country in their open-top road-sters. My dad used to come and watch them. My grandad competed one time, or so he said. It wasn't even a paved road in those days. Just crushed rock and the odd sheep.' She braked hard as we approached the steepest part of the hill where it turns sharply to the right. 'This is what used to do them,' she said. 'According to Grandad they'd come belting up the hill in a cloud of dust, and if they didn't get their gear-change spot on they'd stall and slither back down.'

We were on our way to the bottom now, and not a soul to be seen. 'Hardly any wonder on a day like this,' I said.

'They still come out here, you know.'

'Who?'

'Vintage car enthusiasts. They'll get together and tour the area. It's not a competition any more, just a rally. You'll see baby Austins, old MGs, bull-nosed Morrises, those little three-wheelers. They set up camp for the weekend at Castle Howard or over here. Then they drive around various routes, and have treasure hunts and so on. They always have daft names.'

'What do you mean, daft names?'

'Like the MG Flat Cap and Whippet Weekend. Things like that.'

'You're full of surprises, you are.'

'I'm a woman of mystery, Mike.'

'All women are a mystery to us blokes, Ann.'

We'd reached the bottom and she was turning the car around. 'Right,' she said, 'back to the top.' By this time we were in mobile-phone contact with the search and rescue team who'd come out from Scarborough. The signals up on the moors aren't always reliable, especially when the clouds have come down. But the good news was that they'd managed to get a full complement together and were en route with a team of twenty. The arches would be our RVP, or rendezvous point. The search would be co-ordinated from there.

When they showed up you could have been forgiven for thinking they were about to tackle the north face of Everest. Their equipment was – well, let's say it was comprehensive. Ann and I spoke with the team leader, Andy. He'd studied the area we were likely to be searching and divided it into grids. I gave him a spare police radio so that we could keep in touch. We agreed on a thirty-minute ground search first. 'If that fails,' Ann said, 'we'll see if we can get the police helicopter in from Cleveland.'

The teams set off on their given routes. One was to drive out as far as the farm track would take them and work its way along the side of Spaunton Moor in a southerly direction; the other would fan out from the other end of the moor and work northwards. Ann and I would check out the track to Ana Cross.

'Well, between us we've surely got a chance,' I said, as we left the paved road, bumped along the broad, rutted track and splashed our way through the brown rivulets of water. To either side of us the wiry dark roots of heather poked through the peaty banks. A wave of mucky water splashed against the wind-screen as we lunged into a puddle. 'Shows you how easily this sort of land gets eroded,' I said. 'It's all very well hiking and biking along these paths. But soon as you break the skin, the rain gets to work and next thing you've got a horrible great scar.'

We made slow progress, each of us peering into the gloom. We had the headlights on and the blue light flashing. We hardly saw a living thing, just a couple of grouse skulking under the embankments. Even the hardy upland sheep had sought shelter as the rain lashed down and the wind tugged at the heather.

A few weeks ago it had been in full bloom, a beautiful pinky purple; now it was looking dark and lifeless. The Puddle Hopper bucked and lurched over the exposed rocks and gravel where the water had scoured away at the bed of what was in places a proper stream. Now and then the wheels spun as Ann swung us away from ridges of gluey, black mud.

'Here we are,' I said, as the tall stone obelisk came into sight. Every time I see it it strikes me as slightly disproportionate, the main stem rising ten feet or so from its base to a short, stumpy crosspiece. But I suppose it was built to last. The original top was already centuries old and badly weathered when they took it away, years ago, and put it in the crypt at Lastingham. I opened the passenger door and stepped out into the wind. Maybe the woman would be sheltering on the lee side of the cross. But no: I had a quick look around, hunched against the weather, and scuttled back to the comfort of the cab. 'Nowt,' I said. 'No sign of her.'

'Maybe it's worth waiting here for a while.' Ann got on the radio and called search and rescue. Neither of the teams had found anything. 'If they're not finding her, the chances are she's on this path or making her way towards it across the moor.'

'Seems a fair assumption. Unless she turned around and made her way back to the village.'

'Where she'd maybe get a signal – if she had her bloody mobile with her. Beats me why people leave them at home.'

We sat there in silence for a few moments. Well, I say silence: the vehicle creaked as it was buffeted by the wind, the rain lashed against the driver's side window, and every couple of seconds there was the swish of the wiper blades.

'Wild.' One thing I was learning about Ann was that she rarely used two words where one would do.

'Aye,' I said. 'The wilder the better for me.'

'So long as you're inside.'

'No, I don't mind being out in it. I spent a lot of time on the moors – well, the edge of the moors – when I was a kid. Every summer.'

'But you said you lived near me – around Huby.'

'I did, but we had an aunt out towards the coast. Lived right on the clifftops. Staintondale.'

She frowned. 'Where's that?'

'I'll have to take you there some time. Fabulous place. It's out – well, it's a few miles south of Robin Hood's Bay. Maybe five or six miles north of Scarborough. If you've ever walked the coast path, there's a little beck comes out at a place called Hayburn Wyke.'

'I've done the coast path. Done the whole Cleveland Way, in fact. Helmsley to Scarborough.'

'Well, you'll have crossed the beck. There's a little pool halfway down it, and then a waterfall where it hits the beach. Super spot for kids. We spent all day there if the weather was right. And if you climb right up to the top you come to a farmstead and a couple of houses. Completely isolated, they are. That's where my auntie lived. We used to get taken there in the holidays, and every weekend just about in the summer.'

'And what did you do there?'

'Do? We ran wild. I don't mean getting into mischief, like – well, not much – but you know, larking about in the woods, picking blueberries, brambling on the clifftops. Sometimes Mum would send us off to the beach for the day with an old frying pan, a loaf and a bag of sausages and we'd build a huge great campfire. We loved it. Sort of thing all kids should have the chance to do if you want my opinion.'

'Oh, I agree with you. A hundred per cent.'

'The beach down there's fantastic. All rocks, just a tiny bit of sand. Loads of pools as well. I learned the art of sea fishing there. Used to climb out on the rocks and catch codling when the tide was right. Loved it when the big waves were coming in. So' – I wiped the condensation off the window beside me and looked out at the windswept moor – 'wild landscapes, wild weather. I can't get enough of it.'

Ann looked at her watch. 'I'm wondering how long to give it,' she said. 'Before we think about the helicopter.'

'Well, we need the search and rescue teams to meet up first, don't we?'

'Yes. Then maybe we should think about searching further along this path. I mean one of us. The other to stay with the vehicle in case she shows up. And I think you just volunteered your services, didn't you? All that stuff about liking wild weather.'

'It's a fair cop, as they say.'

We sat for a few more minutes before she got on the radio to the team leaders again. They were now within half a mile of each other.

'Found anything?'

'*Negative.*'

'OK then, we'll have a look further down this top path.'

'Right,' I said, 'shall I make a start?'

'May as well. Another hour or so and it'll be getting dark. Then we will have a problem.'

'I'll stick to the track. Give me a blast on the two-tones every so often.'

'OK, and not too far, I could do without losing you.'

I opened the door and zipped up my coat, put my woolly hat on, checked that I'd got my torch. The wind nearly took me off my feet. In fact, as I stepped out from the shelter of the passenger side it knocked me sideways and I stumbled right into a stream of water that was gouging a rut alongside the vehicle.

I made my way steadily down the track. I'd barely gone a hundred yards when I turned back. There was no sign of the Puddle Hopper. The light was poor, the visibility worse. I hoped to goodness that the woman wasn't hurt, wherever she was, although I realised there was every chance she would be. She could simply be exhausted, or if she'd crossed the moor on her own she could easily have turned an ankle. The last thing you'd want in conditions such as these is to become immobilised. Because then you're talking hypothermia.

I carried on, staggering as the wind kept shoving me to the side of the path. Every so often I heard Ann giving it a blast on the two-tones. That did feel weird, almost ghostly. As I walked I shouted out as best I could. I started to wonder how much further I should go. If the woman was on the path either she'd be heading up to the cross or back towards the village. Unless, of course, she was lame. Or confused. Once the clouds come down on those moors you can soon become disoriented. At least I was still in radio contact with Ann. She had nothing to report, neither had the two hikers who were waiting up at the kilns.

I was now feeling the effects of the weather myself. However good your clothing, the rain always manages to find a way in, especially when the wind comes into the equation. It was the usual sequence of events. You get warm and loosen your collar. The rain runs down your neck. Your collar soaks it up, and before you know it you're all clammy around your shoulders. It's OK so long as you keep walking; it's when you stop that the cold starts to get through, rapidly, and that was what was worrying me about this woman – that she might have sat down to rest and caught a chill.

I decided I'd give it another half a mile or so, maybe ten or fifteen minutes, before turning back. If none of us had got a result by then we'd have to rethink our strategy. I'd just stopped to look at my watch and time myself when I looked up and thought that maybe, just maybe, I'd spotted a flash of colour through the gloom. I strained my eyes and stared ahead along the track, but it was no good. The harder I looked, the more the wind made my eyes water, blurring my vision. No, there was nothing there. The mist seemed thicker than ever, and yet, as I looked away to one side I thought I saw it again, a faint flicker of orange to one side of my line of vision. I hurried on a few paces, then stopped and shouted at the top of my voice. 'Ha-llo-o-o-o! Anyone there?'

You can feel pretty daft, standing in the middle of nowhere, shouting to no one. The only sound was the wind whistling past my ears. I hurried on, stepping from rock to rock, then stopped to take another look, rubbing the water from my glasses. This time I knew my eyes weren't deceiving me. There was a definite patch of colour, an almost luminous orange.

As I came closer I could see that it too was moving, making its way purposefully towards me. Surely it was her.

She was within just a few feet of me when she looked up, startled. 'Oh, my goodness!' she said. 'Are you – is it . . . ?'

'North Yorkshire Police, madam. We've been looking for you.'

'But I'm not lost.' She looked genuinely bewildered, standing there with the wind on her back, blinking at me.

'Maybe not, but you've put the fear of God into your mates,' I said. 'They were all gathered at the top of the Chimney Bank a couple of hours ago. We've got Scarborough Search and Rescue out combing the moor from end to end.'

'Oh dear. Well, I did get left, a few miles back. I stopped to take a stone out of my boot, and by the time I got started again they were out of sight. But I was never lost, as such. I tried the lower path, but it was all overgrown so I tried to work my way down to the beck side. That was no good, so I doubled back and . . .'

'And time flies when you're having fun, eh? They were worried you'd maybe twisted an ankle or something. And in weather like this . . .'

'Yes yes, I quite understand. But I'm fine, really I am – I just lost such a lot of time floundering about in the bracken, and of course I had this wretched wind blowing me about.'

'Are you OK for food and drink, cos I've got supplies with me.'

'No, I packed plenty of flapjacks and trail mix. I'm fine, really I am. Thank you.'

I got on the radio to Ann and Andy. 'I've found our lost sheep. Yep. A bit wet, but safe and well. No, no need for an ambulance. We'll be making our way back to the four-wheel drive, and then to the RVP. Maybe half an hour, forty minutes.'

The woman may have been fine – she certainly looked a real determined sort – but she was no spring chicken, and the walk back to Ana Cross seemed to take us twice as long as it had taken on the way out. We really struggled against the wind and rain. But finally, exhausted, we met up with Ann and clambered into the Puddle Hopper. Within fifteen minutes or so we were back at the arches to pick up the two hikers, who had been waiting patiently. The two search and rescue teams wouldn't catch up with us for a while yet, and the weather was so foul at the arches that we arranged to meet them at the New Inn at Cropton for our debriefing.

'Wonder when we'll overtake your friends,' I said as we drove along the road towards Hutton le Hole, our lights picking out the staring eyes of an occasional sheep on the grass verge.

'They'll be striding out, you can be sure of that.'

'To get there before dark, you mean?'

They laughed. 'Well aye, that's one factor. But we'd planned a dinner at the New Inn, booked a table for seven o'clock. They won't want to be late for that.'

We caught up with them at Lastingham, just as they were trooping past the Blacksmith's Arms. We told them to wait there while we ferried them in groups back to their vehicles.

'All right for some,' Ann said an hour later as we left the debrief at the New Inn.

'Aye, I could just murder a pint and one of their evening specials.'

'Some other time, eh?'

'Sounds like a date to me.'

In fact, our next date wasn't to Cropton. It was out to Staintondale, where I had the pleasure of showing her the old house where I used to stay all those years ago, and walked her down to the beach at Hayburn Wyke. We took some burgers with us, some salads, and a couple of bottles of beer. We lit a fire of driftwood and sat there watching the daylight fade. It was like the old days, except that this time we didn't have to scurry back up the gorge at sunset. Instead, we unrolled our bags and had a few hours' sleep at the top of the beach, then walked back to the car at first light.

'Thank you,' Ann said as we prepared to drive home. 'I think I understand you a bit better now.'

'You mean where I come from?'

She nodded, and kissed me. 'Come on. Breakfast.'

Chapter 12

A Dark Day

Someone once said that other countries have climates, whereas the British just have weather. I wonder whether he'd been on holiday in North Yorkshire. After the autumnal storms that caught those hikers on the hop, we had several more days of heavy rain and wind followed by a couple of really chilly nights at the end of the month. 'Nowt wrong with an early frost,' was Walt's verdict when I called by on the first day of October, rubbing my hands together as my breath hung in a cloud in the bright, still morning air. 'Puts a bit of flavour into t'parsnips. Kills off them garden bugs as well.'

'It'll see me off if you don't let me inside and get that kettle on,' I said. Walt laughed. 'Ee, once the sun gets above them trees it'll warm up nicely. You see if it doesn't. We'll most likely have an Indian summer now we've got them gales out of t'way.' He was right, of course. He generally was. When I went back to my car half an hour later, fortified with a cup of tea and one of his sister's mince pies, the shadows of the old sycamores had retreated across the garden and it felt more like an August morning. I drove down through the village, took the bottom road along to Grimston, and headed north towards the A64. The potato harvesters were out and about and the roads were splattered with mud and clods of earth. I remembered my youthful days picking taties, and was suddenly very grateful that I now spent much of my working life in a nice warm car with clean clothes and dry feet.

I was on my to Westdale to see the Colonel. He hadn't been to any of the Country Watch meetings in several months, having had trouble with his knees. He suffered from arthritis, although he rarely mentioned the fact. He was of the old school: 'grin and bear it'. Of course, I frequently drove by his place, and every time I did I found myself smiling when I saw the nice new stone 'orbs', as he called them, on top of the pillars that guarded the entrance to his driveway. The originals had gone missing the previous year, and I'd never found the culprit. But I hadn't clapped eyes on the old boy in quite a while, so when Jayne told me he'd rung the station I presumed he just wanted to have a natter and a bit of a catch-up. 'I hope he ain't mislaid them balls of his again,' she laughed as she handed me the message. She never tired of telling people that story – and of reminding me that it happened on my patch.

'Now then, Colonel.' He was standing outside his front door, his faithful bulldog Winnie at his heels, an empty milkbottle in his hand.

'Ah, the crime-busting Czar of North Yorkshire. That's what they call you chappies these days, I understand.'

'You're reading the wrong sort of newspapers,' I said. 'I'm just a humble beat bobby doing my best for the community.'

'Well, I'm afraid I have to report an outbreak of petty crime in the village. Schoolchildren, I shouldn't be surprised. The sort of thing we used to get up to in prep school.'

'What have they been doing? Scrumping?'

'Ha! Scrumping. Now, that's not a word you hear these days. Did my share of that when I was a little whippersnapper in short bags. By Jove yes. And did we run when the gardener came after us! Or anyone else for that matter. Used to whack us round the rear end with whatever came to hand. I've taken a few beatings in my time, I can tell you. All manner of lethal weapons.' He paused and gave a little chortle. 'A rolled umbrella, a walking stick, a dog leash . . . But the most painful blow I ever received – d'you know what that was?'

'I shudder to think.'

'Got chased by a painter fellow. I mean a landscape artist, not a decorator. Wasn't even his orchard we were raiding, but he was out there with his canvas and easel – and in those days, you know, little boys with pockets full of stolen apples were fair game. A grown-up's word was law, and we simply accepted it. That was our version of "community policing", you might say. Anyway, this fellow dropped his brushes and came galloping after us. Caught me right across the rear end with his mahlstick.'

'Mahlstick? What's one of them?'

'Slender thing, two or three feet long. Wrapped in leather. They use it to support the wrist when they're dabbing away with the oils. Saves them from smudging their handiwork, I believe. Or getting arm-ache. By jingo did it sting. Carried the mark for weeks afterwards.'

His smile faded and he looked at the bottle in his hand. 'Anyway, more to the point, what are we going to do about this?'

'What do you want me to do?'

'Ah, you diverted me there. Down memory lane. This empty bottle is all that's left of my morning delivery. Twice this week I've gone down to the gate to collect it and what do I find?' He waggled the bottle in my face again. 'I'll bet some little blighters who can't find an orchard to raid are stealing my milk instead.'

'And you suspect the children from the village?'

'Well, I can't see an adult stooping to this sort of thing, can you?'

'Probably not, but we mustn't be jumping to conclusions. To tell you the truth, there's not a lot I can do, other than put out the word and ask people to keep their eyes and ears open. And I'll make a note for the briefing so that the other officers are made aware. In the meantime, can't you ask your man to bring the milk up to the house?'

'Hmph – out of the question. Fellow's in far too much of a hurry. He has two other jobs, y'know. That's why he drops it off at such an unearthly hour.'

'What time's that then?'

'Four o'clock, they tell me. Not that I can verify it by empirical means, you understand. I'm generally tucked up in bed at that hour.'

I made a note to raise the matter at the next Country Watch meeting, and left the Colonel to it. The sun was blazing down as I drove back towards town, and the countryside looked a picture. Hard to believe it really was autumn. I turned off the main road at Scampston and paid a call at the little village bakery they have there, picking up a pork pie and a homemade cake for my lunch. I was thinking I'd maybe pull over by the river and grab a quiet twenty minutes.

Thinking about it was as far as I got.

'*Control to 1015.*'

'Go ahead, over.'

'*Mike, we've had a call from a farmer's wife out towards Butterwick. Worried about her husband's safety. He's gone missing and she's found a note suggesting he might take his own life. Can you take it?*'

'Will do.' I got directions, turned the car around and headed back through Sherburn.

There's no way to prepare yourself for this sort of thing. You're in a hurry, your heart is thumping, and a thousand things are racing through your mind. Foremost is that question, that hope, that maybe it's a false alarm. We get plenty of those – not malicious ones, just cases where people genuinely fear the worst but turn out to be wrong. People are always going missing. It might be for an hour or two, and it might be longer. Sometimes they've stormed out in a temper and the last thing they've said has set the alarm bells ringing. Jostling with that question is the other one, the one you can't help asking yourself but don't want to know the answer to. What will I find? No, you don't want to dwell on that because it immediately brings back all the things you've managed to suppress, those ugly images lurking in the recesses of your memory.

So it's back to question one. 'Is this genuine?' Something told me it was. The guy had disappeared, he'd left a note, and he was a farmer. You soon learn that when it comes to taking their own lives, farmers are up there with doctors and dentists, and vets, of course. I'm talking about statistics. It's nothing to do with them being more depressive than the rest of us, or anything like that. They're no more likely than anyone else to find that life is getting on top of them. But there's one big difference. They have the means at their disposal. With the medical professionals it's drugs. With farmers, guns.

'Control, can you just check if there are any firearms registered at that address please.'

'*Received Mike, just checking now.*'

A few minutes later I got the response. '*1015, two shotguns held at that address.*' Bloody hell, I muttered to myself. This was not good. Sometimes you have a bad feeling about what you are going to find, and this was one of those times.

* * *

242

I knew the location I was heading for. It was a small farm, a one-man operation, out on the top of the wolds. Five minutes after turning off the main road I was there. It was more of a smallholding than a farm, I suppose, a hundred acres, maybe two. The house was detached and a bit ramshackle, over-shadowed by a stand of ragged sycamores and a rusting Dutch barn with gaps in the corrugated asbestos roof. Lying around the yard were bits and pieces of abandoned farm machinery, a couple of cars with no wheels, and a big mound of something – silage, most likely – covered in black plastic sheeting that was held down by a scattering of old tyres.

I went to the back door, knocked and walked in. You don't generally wait for an answer in our part of the world, not in these country places anyway. 'Anyone at home?' I called out as I entered the little back lobby and stepped over a pair of muddy wellington boots.

She was in the kitchen, sitting at the table with the breakfast things all around her. A cereal packet, a couple of dirty bowls, a teapot, a plastic bottle of milk. In her hand she had a telephone. She looked up at me, reached inside her pinafore and pulled out a crumpled sheet of paper. I recognised her face. I'd seen her at the Tuesday livestock market in Malton. She was probably only in her mid-fifties.

'He left this,' she said, handing me the piece of paper.

The room was quite dark. I took the note over to the window. Even there I had a job deciphering it. It was handwritten, in pencil. Scrawled would be more like it. There was something about how much he loved her, how she was to tell the children he was sorry, that he couldn't go on. Then the last sentence, in a much firmer hand, the one phrase that sticks in my memory. 'It'll be done when you read this.'

My heart sank, but I knew I had to act positive. 'C'mon,' I said, 'have you had a good look for him?'

'I've been out in the yard. Shouted his name.'

'Well, perhaps if I go and have a scout around. He's maybe not wanting to answer you.' Even as I said that I wished I hadn't. 'You're quite sure he's not in the house?'

'Course I'm sure.' She stood up, scraping her chair on the quarry-tiled floor. 'He's gone – and so's his gun.'

'Where does he keep that?'

'In there.' She pointed towards the hallway.

There was a tall sort of wardrobe, antique, dark wood, carved, the door half open. I walked through and looked inside. There was a four-gun steel shotgun cabinet with the door left ajar. One gun was still in situ; the other was missing. Below it on the floor was a pair of old leather lace-up boots, covered in dust, and a scrunched-up waterproof jacket. Underneath it I found a box of shotgun cartridges, half empty. As I turned I saw one on the floor, right at my feet.

'You see? What did I tell you?' She was standing there, her arm raised towards the rack, her eyes narrowed. I've seen many a grieving wife or mother, but never before one so angry as she was at that moment, not in the face of potential tragedy. 'He's bloody taken it,' she said. 'He's sloped off somewhere and shot himself, the cowardly bastard. Left me to find him and sort out the mess. That's what he's done.' She turned and walked back to the kitchen. 'How can he do it, eh? It's craven, that's what it is.'

'C'mon,' I said, 'sit yourself down. Have you called anyone? Is there anyone who can come and be with you?'

'Me daughter. I've left her a message. I warned her this would happen. I just had this sick feeling in here.' She had her hand against her stomach. 'Way back in the spring. And she told me not to exaggerate. God knows when she'll get me message. She's out and about all day, hairdressing. Filey way today, she said.'

'Is there a friend or anyone else you can ring?'

She looked at the phone in her hand. 'That's what I was doing when you walked in.' She sounded very weary all of a sudden. She keyed in a number. 'My neighbour Julie. She's only across the fields. She'll come round.'

'Right,' I said, 'I'm going to pop outside for a moment. I need to make a call myself.'

I kept it as short as I could. You don't like to leave someone on their own in these situations. '1015 to control. Aye, I'm at the scene. There's a shotgun gone missing – and he's left a note. It doesn't look good. I might need some assistance to help me search. I'll let you know how it goes. If there's anyone else in the area that can pop down that would be helpful.'

'*Yes, received Mike.*'

Back in the kitchen the woman was standing at the window looking out into the yard. It was half in shade, but where the sun was on the concrete it almost hurt your eyes it was so bright. 'What's going to happen?' she said, to herself as much as to me. 'We're only tenants. But it was our life. Twenty-eight years we put into this place and every time we got our noses in front sommat happened.' She turned to face me. I could see she'd been crying. 'There's no money in it, livestock farming. That's at t'root of it all. God knows you pay enough for your meat at the supermarket, but what do we see?' She took a tissue out of her pinafore pocket and dabbed at her eyes. 'It's all we ever wanted, a place with animals.'

'Look,' I said, 'I need to go and check around outside.'

'Have I to come with you?'

'No, no – you can sit here and wait for your friend. Get the kettle on. I don't know about you but I could do with a cuppa.' It was the last thing I wanted right then, but it would give her something to do and keep her occupied while I looked around.

I went out into the yard. The Dutch barn was empty as far as I could see, just a hay-rake and a muckspreader, with a stack of old roof timbers and builders' rubble at the far end.

I walked beyond it, past some old straw bales sprouting green at the top. I called his name. 'Derek. Are you there mate? Where've you got to?' My gut feeling was that I was about to find a dead body, but I hoped against hope that maybe I might be in time to talk him out of it. As much as anything I was calling his name out of instinct. They train you to do that when you're searching for someone, in the hope that if they're just lost or perhaps hurt they'll respond and make it easier to locate them. Somehow, shouting his name made me feel slightly less apprehensive. Maybe it was just that it uses up some of the adrenaline that pumps through my body in these situations. I've never liked death or dealing with dead bodies and I was beginning to feel the blood draining from me. I thought of the wife back in the house and told myself to get a grip. This wasn't about me. It was about her. She was expecting me – needing me – to get this sorted out. It was my job, as far as she was concerned.

Beyond the yard was a big old garden. There were fruit trees, raspberry canes, a couple of rows of leeks, a patch of taties half dug up. It was tidy, well cared for. There was a lovely stack of well-rotted manure at one end with a spade stuck in the ground beside it. The exposed face of the muck was moist and black like Christmas pudding. Right next to it was an empty chicken house. Beyond that was a potting shed cum greenhouse, a proper old wooden-framed structure built on a brick base.

I approached it slowly, my heart thumping, and called his name again. For God's sake, answer. 'You there? Just shout out, mate. I only want to talk to you.'

There was a brick path that led to the potting shed, shaded and damp, covered in green algae. Through the open doorway I could see several strings of onions hanging from a beam, and below it, partly obscured by a work bench of some kind, a man in dark green overalls sitting against the wall. I stepped forward, my shoulders relaxing. 'Thank God for that—' I started. Then I saw the blood, all over the wall behind him, and the gun, lying between his legs with the barrel tilted against his neck.

'Oh Christ.' I braced myself, took a deep breath of clean air and walked slowly towards him.

There was no doubt he was dead. The blood was that deep dark red colour, and it was all over the place: clothes, floor, wall. His face looked fairly normal. That was the odd thing. You could have thought he was having a nap. But as I leaned forward I saw a huge exit wound where the back of his head should have been. I turned away, quickly. He'd put the barrel in his mouth and pulled the trigger.

Back outside I stumbled on the brick path and almost fell. I knew I was going into shock. I could feel my strength drain away. Even as I pulled out my radio my hands had gone cold, and all the strength seemed to have gone out of me. I fumbled for the switch and had to squeeze twice to get it on. Thank God I'd no need to feel for a pulse. They don't come much deader than that.

What you try to do in these situations is compose yourself. You're reeling with it, you want to sit down, blank it out, get away – but you have to take charge. Every bugger's going to be looking to you to sort it out. There's no one else. Whatever your mind wants to do it'll have to wait till later. You have a procedure to follow, a job to do. As soon as you put your uniform on for the first time you accept that there will be days like this, when you feel you've woken up in the middle of a horror movie. And when you have to deal with such events the uniform acts as a type of body armour. You're not you any longer. You're a policeman; on duty; coping; dealing with it. That's when your training kicks in, all those daft mnemonics they hammered into you day after day at police college.

CCD . . . CCD . . . I'd actually sat down on an old galvanised metal tank. It was half full of stagnant water. CCD? No, that's not it. I remember now. CDCD. C – inform CID. D – inform the duty officer. C again – inform the coroner. D – call the doctor. He had to come and pronounce life extinct even though it was obvious that the man was dead as a doornail, way beyond any hope of resuscitation. Now that I had it clear in my mind what I had to do I started to feel calmer.

'1015 to control.'

'*Go ahead Mike.*'

'I've found the male with what looks like fatal gunshot wounds. It looks like a suicide. Can you inform the duty inspector, CID. And I'm going to need a doctor.'

'*All received Mike.*'

After that I had things to do. Procedure again. You cling to it. It keeps your mind occupied and your hands busy. Preservation of the scene: that was next, because as obvious as it seemed, on the face of it, that the man had put the gun to his own head, you can never, ever jump to conclusions. Until the cause, and the means, were established, it would remain a suspicious death.

It would be a while before anybody came out to me. I had

all the time I needed to go back into the house and talk to the wife. That's another thing you hate to do. So you prepare yourself, walk in, and get it over as quickly as you can, with as much compassion as possible. At least, that's how I do it. And in this case the woman was prepared. She'd already told me her worst fears, was already in reaction to it. But even so, you never know.

She had her hands on the table, ready to stand up. Perhaps she thought there was hope. 'Well? Have you found him?'

I sat down at the table opposite her and looked her in the eye. 'Yes,' I said.

She knew, right away. 'He's dead, isn't he?'

'I'm afraid so.' There was no point beating about the bush. It had to be done, and now I'd done it. To think that ten minutes ago she'd been angry, calling him a coward. And now here she was, her head on her hands, sobbing uncontrollably.

'How's he done it?' she asked through the tears.

'I'm afraid it looks like he's used the shotgun.'

She went to pieces then. But as I said, you never know how people will react. She had been expecting the worst but hanging on to a thread of hope. We often have to call on people and inform them that a loved one has died, in a car crash, for example. They all react differently and it doesn't matter how many times you have to do it, I always feel a great sense of compassion for their individual loss. I reached across the table and put my hand on hers. 'I'm sorry,' I said. 'I really am sorry.'

What does it mean when you say that? What good does it do? But I felt it, so I said it. What else can you do?

Thank God her friend arrived then. Her neighbour. 'What's happened?' she asked as she walked in, taking off a pair of sunglasses and tucking them into her hair. She wore a hacking jacket and a pair of jodhpurs, and she was followed in by a retriever who went up to the distraught woman and nuzzled her leg. She put her hand on the dog's head and looked up at her friend.

'He's bloody gone and shot himself.' She blurted the words out. Anger again. 'That's what he's done, the bastard. Just blown his brains out and left me to it.'

I felt myself relax a little now that I had the help of the friend. I wanted to get on with what I had to do: firstly fetch that roll of blue and white police tape and seal off the scene. It suddenly seemed very important. I got up to go to the car. Julie was putting the kettle on to make some tea. I heard another car pull up and went to see who it was. I was expecting the CID, but as I stepped into the sunlit yard I saw it was a uniformed PC. Not one of ours. A lad from Scarborough Traffic. James. I knew him vaguely. He'd been dealing with a broken-down lorry on the A64 and had come to help with the search.

I went back and closed the kitchen door. 'Down the green-house, mate,' I said, when I was sure I was out of earshot. 'I'll show you.' I got the tape from my car, then walked him past the Dutch barn towards the garden. 'Watch your footing,' I said as we came to the brick path. 'Shot his bloody head off, near enough,' I heard myself say as we came towards the greenhouse door.

We taped off the scene and I left James on the cordon while I went back into the house to see how things were going. Just then the inspector showed up with the CID. I excused myself and went outside where we could talk. I was suddenly aware how warm it had become. A few minutes ago I'd been cold, my fingers stiff; now I was sweating. I briefed the inspector. Strange, that. As I relayed the full details of what had happened my mouth went dry and the words would hardly come.

'Right,' the inspector was saying, 'you'd better show us.' I didn't want to go back. I really didn't want to see the sight again. I led the way to the greenhouse once more, and stopped short. What he was about to see was now classed as a crime scene, and in theory as few officers as possible were allowed to enter. 'Through there, sir,' I said. But even as I ducked out of that one I knew that what I'd seen would be there in my mind for the rest of my life in that little chamber of horrors. Most of the time you can forget about it, but every time you creak the door open to stick another memory in there you're reminded how they're mounting up. Even when you're retired and your uniform has been hung up for good, the memories live on.

Back at the house the daughter had arrived. She was just getting out of her car. The Scarborough lad was on the ball. He realised I'd had enough. He took her to one side and told her. I watched it all over again as she came out with the same mixture of pain and anger as her mother. She was saying, 'We knew he was suffering but he wouldn't talk about it. Wouldn't admit to it.' Her mother was just shaking her head and looking out through the window. I picked my moment and asked the neighbour, Julie, whether there was any other family member I should be contacting.

'There's their son,' she said. 'He works in town.' She gave me the name of the place and I set off. Another job I could've done without, but in the circumstances my goodness I was relieved to take it. I didn't want to be around that house any longer than I had to.

The lad – well, he was thirtyish – worked for one of the car dealerships near the industrial estate, just out of Malton. I was there within twenty minutes. Found the manager out on the forecourt and asked him to fetch Adrian over. 'And if you don't mind, can I use your office for a few minutes? I've got some bad news to tell him. He's not in trouble.'

He fetched the lad over. He was a charmer. Handsome,

confident-looking, well turned out in a sharp suit, all smiles and a firm handshake. He never suspected a thing, just nodded at the patrol car and said, 'Now then, officer? You're wanting to trade it in, are you?'

'I'm sorry,' I said, 'but I've got some bad news for you. Can we just go inside and just sit down for a moment?'

Poor lad. He didn't say a great deal at first. Didn't react the way his sister had. He agreed that he'd better get to his mum's place right away. 'Probably better if you didn't drive,' I said. 'I'll take you there in my car. I have to go back anyway.'

On the way he told me about his dad. 'He's worked that farm all his life. And that's all he ever did do. Work. Seven days a week with livestock. You're always on duty. And he never made a bean out of it. Always had the bank manager on his back.' We were driving along the bypass, speeding towards Rillington. The country-side can rarely have looked better in the bright autumn sun.

'Don't get me wrong,' he said. 'We were well fed and looked after. No holidays, owt like that, but we liked the farm when we were little. Feeding the calves, pet lambs . . . Then you get older and . . . ' He tailed off and was silent for a few minutes. 'Dad expected me to take it over one day, but . . . Nah. Me and me sister, we wanted other things.' He shook his head and blinked at the emerald green fields, the winter wheat shimmering in the light as we climbed out of Sherburn. 'We knew it was getting to him, so did Mum. I still help him out as and when, weekends and that. Do the milking if they want a night out. Not that they've had one of them in a while now.' He shook his head. 'Christ, I never expected this though.'

When we got to the house I took him as far as the kitchen door and left him to it. Out the back the CID had organised a scene of crimes officer to take photos. What a job that must be.

What kind of memories do they have at the back of their heads? The gun and the note had been seized as evidence. The statements could wait for now. You can't put people through that when they're still in shock.

The undertakers arrived to remove the body. They were good. I mean quick, efficient. The PC from Scarborough followed them in his car. He had to witness it, make sure they did as required. They put the body into a zip-up bag, then took it out to their van. The Scarborough lad had seen the body; his responsibility now was to ensure continuity of evidence – making sure that the body that arrived at the mortuary was the same one that had left the greenhouse. So he had to follow the undertakers to the mortuary, book the body in and tag it. Then when he was all cleaned up we'd call the son in to ID him.

I went back to the house. Someone brought me a cup of tea. They'd sugared it without asking me, but I was glad of it. I felt better once I'd got that down.

You'd think that it would be a relief to see the body go off. It isn't. There's a kind of vacuum. While it's still there you have so much to do and think about. You have an objective, even if it's only to keep people from seeing it, not that I expected these folk to want that. I knew what I had to do now, and I didn't want to face it. The thing is, in these situations there is no provision for any cleaning up. Imagine it. Someone's blown their head off in your greenhouse and you're left to scrub it clean next time you're down the garden. How could I leave that poor women to do that?

I slipped out, closed the door behind me and popped my head into a sort of utility room by the back door. I found a yard brush and bucket, and took a bottle of Fairy Liquid off the shelf, plus some disinfectant. I used the water out of the old tank, and went into the greenhouse, or potting shed or whatever it was. I threw the soapy water all over the floor and wall and started scrubbing with the brush. The red turned a muddy brown as bits of algae and potting compost got mixed in. By the time I'd chased the suds down the drain the place looked pretty reasonable. I rinsed the whole area with fresh water and disinfectant, then got away, leaving the door open to dry it out.

By the time I was done my shift was up. More than that. I was on overtime. I drove back to the station. The place was almost deserted, just Chris on the desk, the inspector in the Wendy House. I felt as if I wanted to talk to someone, tell them about what I'd just been through, but you soon learn in our job that the only people who really understand are the ones who've been through it with you. The Scarborough lad had gone a long time since. I made as few notes as I could get away with, then packed up and left. I could sort that out in the morning.

On the way home I did what I've so often done with an experience like that. Put it in the box and shoved it into that dark place at the back of my mind. To be dealt with later. By the time I got to Keeper's Cottage I was shattered. I looked at the pork pie I'd bought all those hours ago, and the bun, and binned them both. They'd been sitting in the sun on my back seat all afternoon. I stripped off all my clothes and put them in the wash. There may have been blood on them, but I wasn't going to look for it. I didn't have the stomach. Then I showered, got into some fresh things and gave Ann a ring on the mobile. She would understand. She would help me get it out of my system. Then I walked down to the Jolly Farmers. I was in need of a beer with friends and a return to normality as soon as possible.

Chapter 13

The Big Bang

Every year it's the same. September comes and people think it's the end of the world. Well, the end of the decent weather, the slippery slope that leads to winter. And to tell the truth I've tended to be that way myself. When I was a youngster September always meant 'back to school', and for that reason I've always thought of it as the first month of autumn. But if you look at the records you'll find that it's really a summer month: warm, with plenty of daylight, the garden full of flowers, the trees full of greenery, and the weekend air full of the sound of lawn-mowers. Because in my experience the grass grows faster in September than it does in August. And nowadays, now that I haven't got to go back to school, I love it, and I want everyone to know how great it is. You can't beat this time of year, I'll say – until a few weeks have passed and I've just had a walk in the woods above Hovingham where the trees are a blaze of yellows, reds and browns. Then I change my tune again and suddenly there's no better time than October. For a lover of trees – and now that I was settled into Keeper's Cottage I spent a long time looking out onto the woods that surrounded me, watching the colours change – even November isn't as depressing as some people say it is. It all depends on your outlook.

I was sitting outside on that big old sycamore log I'd put there way back in the spring when Nick had come over with his chainsaw. It was basically a section of the trunk, about four feet long and three feet thick, and between us we'd set it up outside my back door, towards the beck. I still hadn't got around to carving a seat out of it, but to tell the truth it was just about the right height, it had stopped wobbling as it settled into the grass, and it caught the morning sun, so it suited me fine the way it was. There was even a little flat spot where Nick had shaved a piece of bark off, on which I rested my mug of tea. It was a beautiful morning, a Saturday. I sat there finishing off a piece of toast, watching the golden-yellow needles drift down from the larch trees as a gentle breeze blew along the lane. Through the bare branches of the mixed wood I could see the outline of a big old oak tree, another of my favourites. I remember my old grandad telling we when I was a nipper that they grow three hundred years, stay the same three hundred years and then take three hundred years to die. I've no idea whether he was right, but I always liked the idea. As I sat there staring at the woods I thought about how he sometimes walked me to primary school. One day the teacher asked us to draw a tree and we all did the same thing. We took out a chocolate brown crayon to do the trunk and the branches, then scrabbled around for a nice green one and do the leaves. Simple. I put my hand up and said, 'Done it, Miss, what next?' and she came and ticked it. But later on when I showed it to Grandad he said to me, 'Now then, lad, you take a walk with me some day and see if you can find a brown tree.'

He was right, of course. And sitting there that morning,

remembering, I was surprised yet again at how many of the tree trunks were shades of grey or green, almost lime green where the sun caught them right. There was that solitary Scots pine of course, across the field behind the rabbit warren; that had a red-brown tint towards the top. And there were the larches. They were a dark sort of colour. Brownish, I suppose. But otherwise everything was grey or green. All except the silver birch that stood at the junction of my driveway and the track that came up from the road. That was a dazzling white. Magic.

I drained my mug and went back indoors. I had a few bits and pieces to see to around the house before I sat down to watch the midday football preview. Then it would be off to work.

As I tidied the place up, brought in a few logs and laid a fire ready for the next time I had an evening at home, it occurred to me that if you're lucky enough to live somewhere as remote as my place you'll find something to enjoy in every month of the year. Out in the country things are happening all the time, and if you live there you have time to see them. Even in the depths of winter you can find signs of life in sheltered spots in the woods, where spring bulbs will start pushing up through the leaf litter before the solstice. And the bare trees make it far easier to watch the birds at work. The first time I caught sight of the woodpecker was one morning after the leaves had fallen, when it was hammering away at the top of a linden tree. But people who live in towns and cities seem to think that once summer's over they may as well stop indoors and hang in there till the following spring. Not kids, though. Kids are different. They don't really care what time of year it is. Or we didn't when I was young. We found exciting things to do in every season, especially autumn. Splashing through puddles in the rain and building dams in the little rivulets that ran down the lanes, hurling lumps of wood up into the trees as the autumn winds tugged at the clusters of ripe brown conkers. And all through October, as the days shortened and the first frosts nipped at our bare legs, we counted the days, because soon it would be November, and November would bring just about the best fun we had all year. Bonfire night. Guy Fawkes. Bangers. Rockets. And, in our part of the world, the excitement of the fourth of November, Mischief Night.

I was brought up to believe that Mischief Night was peculiar to our part of Yorkshire. I've since heard that something like it takes place in many parts of the north and Scotland. Later I was told that it stemmed from Guy Fawkes, who was a native of York and was educated at St Peters School, which is why they still don't put a guy on their annual bonfire to this day. I mean, burning an effigy of an old boy? Not quite the done thing!

Thank goodness, Mischief Night was unheard of in the Met. But in our part of the world it's a tradition, beloved of children, a pain in the neck for adults. The idea is that it's the one night of the year when kids are allowed to play practical jokes or create a bit of mischief and go unpunished. Knocking on doors and running away, throwing eggs and flour, swapping people's dustbins around, unhinging folks' gates, that sort of thing. Harmless pranks, as they're called, although I suppose it depends whether you're dishing it out or on the receiving end. These days, unfortunately, it tends to get out of hand as older kids get involved, and some serious vandalism takes place. Some of the youngsters seem to think they can run riot and not have to pay the price. The run-up to Mischief and Bonfire Night has community bobbies on their toes, in town or country alike. We get roped in to the schools with the Fire Brigade to give talks on safety, and warnings about the dangers of misusing fireworks. Then there are visits to the shopkeepers to warn them about selling fireworks to underage kids – or eggs and flour for that matter. We even get the local councils on board, encouraging them to make sure the litter bins around town are empty – and less easily ignited. So, Mischief Night: much as I loved it as a kid, I had learned to dread it now. And it was only twenty-four hours away, as I was reminded the minute I walked into the station.

'You spawny bugger, Pannett!'

'Ed, d'you think it's acceptable to abuse a man who's visually impaired?' It had turned cloudy and a lot colder since the morning, and my glasses had steamed in the heated building.

'But you deserve it. I've just seen tomorrow's roster.'

'Well, ain't you a lucky fellow? I can't see a bloody thing.' I took off the specs, polished them on my handkerchief and put them back on. 'Now, what's the problem? You sound right tetchy, and that's not like you. You're normally such a mild-mannered, cheery sort of bloke.'

'Why, slithering your way out of Mischief Night like that.'

'Now come on, Ed, have you ever known me slither? Do I look like the slithering type? Have I suddenly got scales and a forked tongue?'

Ed held his hands up. 'OK, OK. But you have to admit you got lucky there.'

I had. Jayne had asked me to do her a big favour and swap rest days with her. She got the day off she needed but in return had copped for my Mischief Night. So it would be down to Ed, Jayne and whoever else was on duty to cope with the youth of Ryedale as they ran amok. But, as I told him, they could do it. I had every faith in them. 'I know it'll be difficult without me on board,' I said, 'but dig deep and think of yourself as the A-Team – but ravaged by injuries.'

As it happened, I'd no sooner set off on my rounds that afternoon than I ran into a couple of rapscallions myself. The weather had properly spoiled itself now, and a cold wind had got up from the north-west. I was out on the flat lands that lie between the Hovingham road and the A170 alongside the Rye, the river that meanders across the Vale of Pickering and gives our district its name. When you're out there on a grey autumn day such as this, with the fields stripped bare, the scattered ash trees clawing at the sky, the farm buildings huddled against the wind, you become very aware of the sky. It seems absolutely vast. Even the distant outlines of the wold tops to the south and the moors to the north seem somehow reduced, as if the clouds are weighing heavy on them. I was somewhere between Great Habton and Brawby, near the point where the river Seven comes in from the north. About a couple of hundred yards ahead of me was a little copse, maybe an acre or two of mixed woodland. What had caught my attention was a flock of seagulls showing flashes of white as they wheeled against the metallic grey of the sky. And there below them, of course, a plough was at work. Despite the cold I wound down the window just to smell the freshly turned earth. It always reminds me of my younger days when we used to help out with the potato picking. Now, if you want to know what cold is, try taty-picking. I shivered at the memory, and was about to wind the window back up when I thought I heard a shout. I pulled over into a gate-hole and sat for a moment or two. Nothing. The tractor had reached the headland, turned around and was making its way to the far end of the field where a line of willows marked the river's course. Then, as the sound of its engine faded, I heard a high-pitched laugh and, looking across to the woods, I spotted a couple of young lads casting anxious glances over their shoulders before slipping in among the trees. They had matching blue jackets and green wellies. They looked about eleven or twelve. They'd no sooner disappeared from sight than a plume of smoke billowed out from the undergrowth before being caught by the wind and torn to shreds.

I drove as close as I could, then left the vehicle, put on my new police-issue high visibility woolly hat, and set off on foot towards the copse. I had come to loathe that new hat. Yes, it kept the cold out, no doubt about that; but otherwise it was as much use as a chocolate fireguard, glowing like a beacon, which is not what you want when you're trying to approach someone with stealth. Yes, maintaining a visible presence is part of effective policing – but not always. Sometimes we need to creep up or blend in, to lie in wait and observe, unobtrusively. That's why, despite management objections, I always carried my plain black hat and jacket; to give me options, especially on nights when the bosses were tucked up in bed. Up here we like to say what you don't see can't hurt you.

'Now then, lads.' They were on their knees, huddled together with their backs to me. They didn't half jump. One had a box of matches in his hand, and on the ground, among a pile of leaves and twigs, was a brown paper bag. I could see straight away what was inside it. The younger one of the two pushed his hair back off his forehead and looked at the older one. He was the spokesman, and he seemed very sure of himself. 'It's all right,' he said, 'we're not doing any harm.'

'How old are you?'

'I'm twelve. Me brother's ten.'

'But I'm eleven in three weeks.'

I had my notebook out, and my pen. 'Twelve,' I said, scribbling away, dragging it out to impress them. 'And near-ly e-le-ven.' They looked honest enough lads, and the way they'd stood up and faced me suggested that they'd been brought up to respect an adult. If this had been Battersea I'd most likely be chasing them by now. 'So, what are you up to?'

'We're allowed in the woods. We aren't trespassing.'

'Whose woods are they then?'

The older boy pointed towards where the plough was at work and gave me the name of the farmer who owned the field. I knew him OK. I'd met him on one of Algy's shoots. 'We help him muck out his hen houses. He says we can play here any time we like. We have a swing – look.' He pointed to where a length of blue nylon rope hung down from a branch.

'Well,' I said, closing my notebook, 'you may not be doing any harm, and you may have his permission. But you know you're breaking the law, don't you?'

The younger boy cast a guilty look at the pile of leaves. 'What d'you mean?'

'Well, what's in that bag?'

'Just some fireworks,' the older lad said, lowering his voice.

'Let's have a look.'

There was a bunch of bangers, and a few other odds and ends. 'You do know it's against the law to buy these at your age, don't you?' I said.

'We didn't buy 'em. Our brother gave 'em to us.'

'Another brother, eh? How many lads in your family then?'

'There's us two, him, and we've a little sister.'

'How old's big brother?'

'Eighteen.'

'And he gave you these?'

The little lad looked at the ground. 'We – we sort of borrowed 'em like.'

'I see. And what was that puff of smoke I saw just now? You weren't planning to have a bonfire, were you?'

'No, honest.' The older boy was looking at the pile of leaves. He saw me watching him and pointed at the bag in my hands. 'We were just letting a couple of them off.'

'Any good?'

'Eh?'

'Were they any good? I bet they aren't as good as the ones we had when I was a lad. They didn't half go bang.'

'What? Were you allowed bangers and that? In t'olden days, like?'

'Steady on, lad, it wasn't that long ago.' I walked forward and stirred the leaves with my boot, where they'd been crouching. 'Ah, thought so.' They'd dug a little hole in the ground and put a bundle of bangers in, all tied up with an elastic band. There must have been about a dozen. 'What was the plan, then?'

'We were gonna let 'em all off at once,' the little lad said, 'and—' His brother interrupted. 'We was gonna stand back though. We aren't daft.'

But the little lad had the bit between his teeth now. 'See, if you light the blue touch paper and bury them in a bit of soil and leaves and that '

'I know. You get a nice big bang and a cloud of dirt in your face.'

'Aye, like a bomb.'

'Look, we've all done stupid things this time of year,' I started. And then I stopped myself. I was on the point of telling them about the time my mates and I cut some sticks and made little floats, tied our bangers to them, lined them up and raced them across the pond over at . . . But on reflection I decided it might be better not to plant an idea like that in their heads.

'Tell you what,' I said, 'give me the matches.' The little lad handed them over. 'Where'd you get these, anyway?'

'Out of our dad's shed.'

'And where's that? Where'd you live?'

'Brawby.'

'What, and you've legged it all the way across there?'

'We come across the little bridge there.' The older lad was pointing up the river. 'Only takes ten minutes.'

'Well, I tell you what. Your mum and dad in this afternoon?'

'Mum's gone shopping. Dad'll be watching t'racing.'

'Right. Well, I want to have a word with him.'

'Oh no. Do you have to?'

I could see the alarm on their faces. 'Now don't worry, I shan't dob you in it. Just want to tell them – aye, and that big brother of yours – to make sure they keep any fireworks under lock and key in future.'

'What about them?' The older lad was pointing at the bundle of bangers I'd uncovered.

'That's a point. I tell you what.' I was remembering the fun we'd had, years ago, slitting them open, piling up all the gunpowder and setting it off. 'What you need,' I said, 'is adult supervision. Like it says on the packet. I was trained in the TA how to use explosives so it's your lucky day, lads. Come on, stand back.' They backed off several yards. I knelt down, put a lighted match to the blue touch paper, then kicked the pile of leaves over the whole bundle. There was a bit of hissing, a few wisps of smoke, a pause, and then a rather satisfying *Bang!* as the leaves flew up in the air and a cloud of blue smoke drifted into our faces.

The boys whooped. 'Mint!'

'Hmm,' I said, shaking my head, 'nowhere near as good as them old tuppenny cannons my dad used to bring home. Now look,' I went on, 'you two walk home. I'll be along in a few minutes.'

'Can't we ride with you?'

I looked at them. They really were kids. Proper kids who were still capable of being thrilled by the idea of riding in a police car. Not world-weary and scornful like so many are at their age.

'C'mon then. If you're going to behave like baddies I may as well treat you like baddies.'

We got to the house just as Mum was arriving back from town. She was shocked to see her boys climbing out of a police car, but she realised straight away there was no need to panic: they were grinning from ear to ear. I sat with her and their father and talked them through the rules about fireworks. Big brother was out somewhere, so I pointed out to them that he could have been held responsible if things had gone wrong. Fireworks are dangerous. That's why we have these restrictions. Both the parents thanked me for being lenient, as they put it. 'Look,' I said, 'we've all been there, haven't we? Larking around with matches and fireworks. As far as I'm concerned I want these lads of yours – well, I'd like to think they'll grow up remembering that the police are OK. Reasonable. At the end of the day, we want them on our side, don't we? We don't want them thinking of us as the enemy.'

When I left, the boys followed me to the car. 'So,' I said, 'what you going to tell your mates about the police on Monday morning?'

The little one was going to tell everyone I was 'way cool'. As for his brother, 'I'm gonna tell 'em what happened,' he said. 'Some of the kids at school are always slagging you lot off.'

'Aye, but don't make me out to be too nice. Cos I'm telling you, if I get any reports of any bad stuff going off on Mischief Night, I'll be coming down hard.'

I was pleased with the way it had all worked out. It's so easy to get kids wrong, wade in and start throwing your weight about. To me, a part of a policeman's job is to be something of an ambassador and educator, to show the public that we really are there to help. Youngsters are bound to experiment. How else will they learn? As I see it, our job is to steer them towards behaving more sensibly rather than trying to catch them out.

I drove back through Malton and headed up towards Leavening. I was disappointed not to have been offered a cup of tea at Brawby, and I was gagging for one. I called in at Walt's, and found him at the gate, leaning into the wind and clasping his hat to his head. The old sycamores were swaying about and the fallen leaves were being whipped this way and that.

'I was hoping you'd call by,' he said, as I stepped out of the car. 'Got time for one?'

In the kitchen I hung my coat on the back of the door, and sat at the old wooden table. The kettle was, as ever, simmering on the stove. Walt gave it the usual tweak and twist so that it sat nice and flat on the cast-iron hotplate, then placed the brown teapot nearby to warm up. As he measured three spoons of tea into it the door creaked open and Tess, the black Lab, waddled across to greet me. 'I see he's still looking after you, old girl.' I stroked her head and patted her ample rear end.

'Aye well, she's past working for a living,' Walt said. 'And she won't walk as far as she used to.' He filled the teapot, replaced the kettle and slipped her a ginger biscuit before offering me the packet.

'I were hoping you'd come by,' he said. 'I need a hand with sommat.'

'Fire away.'

'I've made a big decision.'

'Oh heck, you're not getting spliced, are you?'

'At my age? Don't be daft, lad. No, it's about me pond.'

'Oh.' I grabbed another biscuit. 'You've decided it's a stupid idea and you'll leave the field as it is, right?'

Walt tapped his head with a forefinger. 'Mike lad, have you ever known me give up when I get a notion up here?'

'Go on, then. What's the plan?'

'Why, I've had a good look at t'site, and I've paced her out. I can see it all in my head. It just needs a gang of willing hands.'

'I don't like the sound of this, Walt.'

'Don't you worry. I've had a word with Cyril, and he's sending his two lads. That'll make four of us. We're in a dip already. We just need to go down a couple more feet, then puddle in some clay to line her.'

'Couldn't you just hire one of them mechanical diggers?'

Walt pursed his slips and shook his head. 'Why, they want a bloomin' fortune. I can have Cyril's lads for a tenner an hour between 'em. Besides, them machines, they chew t'ground up. It's all hell and no notion with them buggers. We want to go at it right. Skim t'top off before we get started.'

'How d'you mean, skim t'top off?'

'Why, remove topsoil. Can't be wasting that. That's what's wrong with them mechanical jobs; they turn everything upside down. No, we'll barrow the good stuff back here for t'garden.'

'Hell, Walt, it sounds a lot of work to me. When you planning to start?'

'When are you free, Mike? That's the question.'

'Well, if the weather's owt like I can come tomorrow. I've got the day off.'

'Right, I'll get on to Cyril and see about getting them lads over.'

'But I don't want to spend all day at it, mind. It sounds like donkey work to me. We'll be better off putting in a few hours as and when, rather than tearing into it.'

It was wild that evening. I was going to go down to the Jolly Farmers for a drink. It had been a few weeks since I'd been down there, but when it came to eight o'clock and I found myself sitting by a blazing fire and listening to the rain lash against the windows, I decided I was better off where I was. I thought about putting the telly on, then decided that no, November's edition of *Salmon and Trout* magazine was entertainment enough. By ten o'clock I found myself drifting off, dreaming of catching huge salmon and sea trout in North Uist.

When I got up next morning the wind had died down, and the sky had cleared. It looked as though Walt was going to be lucky. I had a quick breakfast, put on an old shooting jacket and a pair of steel-capped work boots, and walked up the hill to his place just as the sun appeared over the top of Leavening Brow.

'Are we fit?' He was already loading up his wheelbarrow with a couple of spades, a mattock, and a pair of old leather gloves. 'Come and have a look,' he said, and led the way into the field where he'd marked out the proposed site by sticking canes into the ground.

'Bloody hell!'

'What's the matter, lad?'

'Why, it's plenty big enough, isn't it? What you going to do, take up waterskiing?'

He laughed. 'Wants to be a bit bigger really. You need plenty room if them wildfowl are going to come in to land. And a bit round t'edges to grow a few rushes and suchlike. Encourage 'em to breed.' He was rubbing his hands. 'I can see it now. This time next year I'll have a big fat mallard in my roasting tin. Home grown. Come on, Mike, let's not be idling.' He grabbed the handles of his barrow and set off across the garden with me following behind.

'Aye, we may as well make a start,' I said, 'before them other lads show up.' I still didn't feel that keen, but I thought I'd better show willing.

'Oh.' He stopped the barrow and gave me an apologetic look. 'You mean me nephews?'

'Aye, you said they were coming to help.'

'They've cancelled.'

'What?'

'They reckon they've a job on in York.'

'It doesn't involve propping a bar up, does it?'

'Could do. They're a rum pair of lads, them two. Anyway, the way you and me work, we'd only shame them. Besides, we couldn't agree terms.'

'I see, and my terms are acceptable, I suppose.' But he wasn't listening – and I was only joking. I owed him enough favours, the way he'd treated me over the past year or so. I looked at the rank grass, sodden and windblown, raised my spade to shoulder height and whacked it into the ground. It was going to be a long old morning. We stuck at it for a full three quarters of an hour before I cracked. 'Thirsty work, Walt.' I stepped back to assess our progress. I suddenly felt very reluctant.

'Aye.' He carried on digging.

'Why don't I have a word with Algy and see if Soapy could bring the tractor and trailer down to help?'

'Soapy? I don't want that daft bugger down here. He'd probably dig it in next door's field. He's all hell and no notion, is t'lad.'

I took off my coat and wiped my forehead. 'You can soon get dehydrated if you aren't careful, y'know.'

'We'll just finish the circuit, shall we?' he said. I'd been digging one way along his line of canes and he'd been going the other, just taking out a single sod so that we'd at least mark the outline of his pond. We still had a few yards to make before we met up.

'At least you can see where we've been,' Walt said half an hour later when he came back from the house with two mugs of steaming tea and a couple of eccles cakes.

'So all we have to do now is strip the rest of the turf, dig down a couple of feet, and line it with clay,' I added.

'Aye, then paddle it and fill her up with water.'

'Gonna be a long old job.'

'Not if we stick at her, lad.'

We drank our tea and got back to work, digging in from opposite ends and stacking the rough turves as we went. Plod, plod, plod.

By lunchtime we'd got the area stripped, and I was starting to look at the sky, hoping for rain. My back was aching, and my hands were sore. But the low autumn sun was still shining from a cloudless sky.

'Here, get that down you.' Walt may have worked me hard, but my reward was a nice wedge of the game pie that he was pulling out of the oven.

'This is all right,' I said. 'I was expecting a cheese and pickle sandwich and a bag of crisps.'

'Aye well, I reckon to make sure me workers are well stoked up with fuel, keep 'em going all afternoon.'

We didn't break for long. I'd just wiped up the gravy with a piece of bread and was looking for a second helping when Walt had me back outside. 'You fetch them turves into t'garden, Mike, while I start digging out from the middle yonder.'

I loaded up the barrow and set off across the field. What the hell am I doing, I thought, on me day off and all? The barrow bumped across the uneven grass, all but wrenching my arms out of their sockets. There was no way I could keep this up all afternoon. I began wondering whether I had any chance of making off with the leftovers when we stopped work. Walt's game pies were out of this world. It'd just do me nicely for supper. I was just imagining a few sprouts and some roast spuds when from behind me I heard a shrill yelp.

'What you done, mate?'

His spade was on the deck and he was hopping about, shaking his right hand. 'Ooh,' he said, 'I've just clouted a rock or sommat. Jarred me bloomin' wrist.'

I walked over to where he'd been digging, bent down and scraped away the soil with my own spade. 'Whoa, stand back, mate.'

'Why, what you found?'

I knew right away what I'd found. We used to have a collection of them in our TA hut, for training purposes. 'That,' I said, as he came close and squinted at the rusty casing I'd exposed, 'that is an incendiary device, probably from the war. And by looking at it, it's a big 'un.'

'Why, what the hell's that doing there?' He reached for the mattock. 'We want to get that bugger out.'

'Steady on, Walt.' I took the mattock from him and laid it to one side. 'I reckon it's a live 'un.'

'How can you tell? Looks rusted to buggery.'

'Well, if I just clear away a little more soil . . . Grab us a little scraper, will you?'

He went and fetched a small branch that had come down in the gale, and snapped a stick off it. I took it from him and very carefully teased away a bit more soil. 'Look at that,' I said. You could see the fin now, almost rusted through, but clearly visible. 'Now, if this had exploded I don't think that fin would be intact, would it now?'

'Reckon you're right there, Mike.'

'So we have to assume it's live.' I stood up. 'I'm afraid we're going to have to down tools, Walt. We need to get the professionals in.'

'Why, couldn't I just kick-start it?' he said. 'You know,' he shaped his arms and cocked his head as if he was looking down the barrel of his shotgun.

'Walt, you ever seen one of these buggers go up?'

'Can't say as I have, lad. No. But I'd like to. Wouldn't you?'

'Trust me, Walt, they pack a punch. You wouldn't want to be standing this close. You'd want to be behind that shed of yours with a sack over your head. Come on, back in the house while I phone the station.'

I got hold of control. It wasn't the first time they'd had a call from me off duty. I explained that we'd uncovered what I suspected to be an unexploded second-world-war bomb of some sort. 'Right,' they said, 'we'll get onto the bomb disposal team at Catterick. Meantime we'll send you a PC over.'

Walt wasn't happy. 'I've been plotting and scheming over this pond all year,' he said, 'and now look. Nice dry afternoon, willing worker, and we shan't get a thing done.'

'Aye, and all that fuel you've just pumped into him, eh? Looks like you may have to make your peace with Cyril's lads and pay them to finish the job off. Or hire that digger.'

Walt didn't answer. He started clearing up our lunch dishes. I was casting longing glances at the remains of the game pie when there was a knock and there was Ed sticking his head around the back door.

'Anyone home?'

'No, clear off. It's Mischief Night. Go and find out what the bad lads are up to.' He was inside now. 'You know Walter, don't you?' I said.

'We've met in the Farmers.'

'Aye, we have,' Walt said. 'And tek no notice of this youth.'

We all went outside and from the safety of Walter's back garden I pointed to where we had made the discovery. Ed and I agreed that it could be some time before the bomb disposal team – the Expo as we call them – were likely to arrive. The best thing was to put a quick 100-metre cordon in place just in case any farmer or stray rambler came along. We grabbed some blue and white tape from the boot of Ed's car and tied it in place, using Walt's canes. Technically Ed should have stayed with the cordon – and later on I was to wish he had – but realistically we couldn't see anyone coming along on a weekday in November. 'I reckon we can keep an eye on this just as well from the kitchen,' I said, which was mistake number two.

We'd no sooner got back inside than Walter picked up the pie dish and said to Ed, 'Get yourself sat down and clean this lot up, will you.'

'Steady on, Walt,' I said. 'That was for the workers, remember? Fuel, to keep us going.'

Too late. Ed had drawn a chair up and already had a fork in his hand. I had to sit there and watch him polish it off with a mug of tea. And then, to add insult to injury, Walt gave him the last of the eccles cakes. I was about to tear into him when the phone went and I heard Walt say, 'Aye, I'll fetch him over.'

It was the bomb disposal team, which had Walt all excited. 'What they want?' he said when I'd put the phone down.

'They say they'll call by to find out from the horse's mouth what we've found and where it is. And they want to make sure we aren't doing anything stupid.'

Walt didn't like that. 'Such as what?' he said.

'How about popping off your shotgun at it?' I said.

'Oh, that.'

'Aye, that.'

'They should be here in thirty minutes or so. Just time for you to tell us how you're preparing for Mischief Night, Ed.'

'It's early days yet, buddy. Just don't expect to use the female cell for a couple of days, though.'

'How come?'

'Bloody kids, that's what. We've already seized enough fireworks to put Castle Howard to shame. Best one is a massive hundred-round repeater.'

'A hundred-rounder? Strewth.'

'Aye, we got that down the industrial estate. Jayne came across some lads, went to investigate and they legged it, leaving this big bugger behind. She brought it in and Chris decided the safest place for it was the female cell. Good job we don't use that one too often.'

'Bloody hell,' I said. 'Mind, d'you remember that farmer who found a hand grenade that time, put it in his Land Rover and drove it to the nick?'

Ed laughed. 'I do, mate.'

I turned to Walt, who was all ears. 'Aye, popped it down on the front counter. Scared the hell out of the civvies in reception. We had to evacuate the whole building for an hour until Expo turned up and got rid of the damned thing. What a carry on that was. Course,' I added, 'in the Met we were always expecting to find explosives. There was a time when every station had its own bomb bin in the back yard. When the IRA were active.'

'What the hell's a bomb bin look like?'

'Oh, a big thick rubber tub with a lid. If someone handed in a suspect package or an abandoned briefcase or some such you had to stick it in there till the Expo showed up.'

'But who was responsible for carting it over there in the first place?'

'That's what we said. Then someone came and risk-assessed it and decided that it wasn't such a good idea after all. Hey, I tell you, it's a good job we have so many bright sparks in the corridors of power, mate. Who said all that graduate recruitment was waste of money? Ee, happy days.'

At that the bomb squad pulled up. 'This'll be fun,' I said to Walt.

'So long as they don't bugger up me pond,' he said, as he danced about from the Rayburn to the window, out into the yard and back to the stove again.

Ed and I explained what had happened and where the mystery object was. The experts got themselves kitted up and went into the field to weigh up the job. 'Rather them than me,' I said as we watched them approach the site. 'Imagine telling your family, "Oh by the way, I'm putting in for Bomb Disposal".'

They didn't take long to identify the find. 'It's a one kilo-gram German incendiary bomb,' they said. 'World War Two.' They went on to explain that they were going to conduct a controlled explosion and we'd best get inside.

'What about my bloody field?' Walt said as I almost dragged him back through the door.

'Your field'll survive,' I said. 'Now, let's just sit here, away from the window, and enjoy the show. Nowt like watching a nice explosion.' Walt brought Tess in from the hallway and got her settled in her basket by the stove.

'On Mischief Night too,' Ed laughed. 'This'll probably be the loudest noise we hear all evening. I bet they'll get a few calls down town when this bugger goes up.'

They did. It was one hell of a bang. As soon as they heard it in Malton the phones started ringing, according to what we heard next day. I was partway through telling them about my escapade with the lads in the wood the day before when it went off. Ed nearly jumped out of his chair, and Walt was straight to the door with us behind him.

The smoke had cleared and the disposal lads were peering into a very substantial crater. The main man walked over to us, removing his hard hat and gloves. 'Now that explains why we didn't want to move it off site,' he said, as Walt edged towards the fence, craning his neck. His mood had changed. He was sniffing the air and grinning. The Expo man continued, 'And I'm sorry about the hole in your field, sir. Do you want to come and take a look?'

'He-heh, don't you worry about that, lad.' Walt was over the fence and on his way, with us following. 'You've saved me a lot of time and quite a few bob, lad.' He stood there for a moment, looking into the hole, which very nearly filled the area he'd marked out before we started, all but a few square yards in one corner. 'Tell you what,' Walt said, 'you don't keep any explosives in the wagon yonder, do you?'

'As a matter of fact we do carry a bit, yes.'

Walt put his hand in his back pocket. I knew what was coming, and I moved forward to try to stop him, but I was too late. He had his wallet out and was in full flow. 'You don't fancy just blasting that corner away, do you? Only I jarred me wrist on yon bugger and I'm not fit to wield a spade. Be nice to get t'job done before winter sets in.'

'Walt,' I said, grabbing his arm. 'In the house, mate.'

Chapter 14

Moving On, Moving In

'Ann,' I said, 'it's not good enough.'

'What's up with it?' We were at my place, eating a dinner she'd cooked. Roast spuds, a joint of beef, a bottle of red, all the trimmings. I'd been away a few days on an informant-handling course and – well, what a pleasure to come home and find a nice fire on the go and all that lovely food on the table.

'No, don't get me wrong. This is fantastic,' I said, spearing the last piece of parsnip out of the roasting tray. 'But I'm not talking about the food. This is about us.'

'You're not happy with us? That what you're trying to say?'

I have to admit it, I'm not one for bottling things up. If I have something on my mind then I have to get it off my chest. I come from a very open Yorkshire family, where if you've got sommat to say, you say it. Throughout my life I have always worn my heart on my sleeve. Most of the time it's worked well, but sometimes it can get you into a bit of bother. So as far as Ann was concerned I had tried to tread a bit more warily. But enough was enough and I needed to let her know how I felt. I'm a determined person, and when I want something in life,

I give it my all to get it. I was starting to get frustrated and was having a struggle containing myself. So out it came.

'Well, we simply never see each other. That's what I'm saying.'

'The price we pay for working shifts, isn't it?'

'Aye, but are you happy with it?'

She put down her knife, took a sip of red wine and thought for a moment. 'No. Course I'm not.'

'I mean when was the last time we had a day out together?'

'Good question.' She frowned, trying to remember.

'Got you thinking, hasn't it?'

'No, it's coming back to me. It's that day you took me up to Staintondale, back in October. After we rescued that woman off the moors.'

I wagged my fork at her. 'Wrong.'

'Hey, don't be pointing your fork at me, young man.'

'OK, I'm sorry. Thing is, you're right: it was the day we hiked up there.' I pushed my plate away and topped up our glasses. 'But I checked my diary last night. It was September. The fifteenth.'

'Really?'

'Really. I mean, here we are, supposedly an item, and the last proper day out we had was – hell, that's getting on for three months ago.'

'Well, it's the hours we work, isn't it? I mean, we're always clashing. You on days and me on nights. One of us knackered after a week of earlies, the other tied up on lates.'

'There is that, yes. But there's also this stupid daft business of keeping our heads down – I mean because of you being a sergeant and so on. Don't you ever think how nice it would be once in a while just to pop out for a quiet pint after a late shift? To go out in town and not be looking around to see if there's anyone we know?'

She didn't say anything at first. I think she was digesting the fact that we hadn't had a trip out since the summer. Then she said, 'Maybe we ought to congratulate ourselves. At least we've kept it under wraps.'

'Well, apart from Ed. Mind, you could trust him with your life.'

She looked doubtful. 'Yes, but what about Chris – because he suspects something. I'm sure he does.'

'Oh, he knows. I'm sure he does. But if he was going to stir things up you'd have heard about it by now.'

Ann had gone to sit by the fire. She was staring into the flames. I went over and put my arm around her. 'Look,' I said, 'we'll work it out.'

She took a deep breath. I wondered what was coming. 'I wanted to tell you this later,' she said, 'if it comes off.'

'What? Has something happened?'

'It's not in the bag, but I've applied for a posting.'

'Where? You're not – you're not going to be moving away, are you?'

'Hey, relax. Think back to what we said that day we were hiking along the river.'

'You mean when we stayed at Grassington?'

'Yes. One of our other days out. We talked about me looking for a job away from Malton.'

'I remember. And we said it would have to be Scarborough or York.'

'Hey.' She reached up and tapped the side of my head. 'The old grey matter's still functioning after one of my dinners and half a bottle of supermarket plonk.'

'Never mind that. Just tell me.'

'York. I've put in for a custody sergeant's job in York.'

'Permanent?'

'Well, as permanent as any job is.'

'And have you heard owt?'

She grinned and drained her glass. 'Got a board. Friday week. And I have a good feeling about this one. How many ordinary sergeants ever volunteer for custody jobs?'

'Can't remember any in my time.'

'There you go – but I did it for a spell in the Met.'

'What time?'

'What time's what?'

'Your board.'

'Does it matter?'

'It does, aye. You got your diary with you?'

'Yep. In my bag over there.'

I passed it to her.

'Right,' I said when she'd riffled through the pages, 'how you fixed for a night out?'

'When?'

'Friday week.'

'It's my day off. And the interview's at two thirty. What have you got in mind?'

'Dinner for two. Somewhere really nice.'

'I'll write it down. She delved in her bag for a pen. 'Mike buying me posh dinner.' There you go. And who knows – maybe we'll be celebrating.'

I was on an early shift the next day – and when I went outside to lock up a little after eleven I wished I wasn't. It was freezing hard, but as I looked up into the night sky I could see a big halo around the moon, which in my experience means one thing only. Sure enough I awoke to the sound of drip drip dripping from the gutter outside the bedroom window, and when I poked my head outside there was about an inch of slush over everything. It had snowed, and now it was raining. As I drove in to work the roads were a mess, with great slicks of icy stuff covered in standing water. It was going to be a busy morning for the traffic lads. They'd be tied up with the inevitable spate of accidents; then it would fall to the rest of us to muck in and sort things out.

But when I got to the station things were quiet. Very quiet indeed. Just for a few days it seemed that Ryedale's criminals had gone into hibernation. 'What's up with all these villains?' I asked Chris. 'There's only sixteen shoplifting days left to Christmas. They lying low, or what?'

'Mike, the idea is to prevent crime. If it's gone quiet, you're doing your job. Yes?'

'Aye, but I don't like it. Where are they? What they planning? You can't tell me they've all gone into early retirement. I want 'em up and about where I can see 'em.'

'They've gone to ground, that's all. And you know why? Your average criminal is just like you and me: they don't like getting cold and wet.'

'They still need to make a living.'

'Don't you worry, they'll be holed up in their comfy houses, looking at next year's diaries and planning their holidays. Come Christmas and the New Year you'll have plenty on your plate. Meanwhile . . . ' He pulled out a report sheet with a flourish. 'You ready for this?'

'What now?'

'More bad news, I'm afraid.'

'Hey, I can take it. I follow York City, remember?'

'Milk. Person or persons unknown are nicking milk off doorsteps.'

'You what?'

'Aye, I've had three of these while you've been off on that course. Hovingham, Sheriff Hutton and somewhere else.' He rummaged through a pile of papers. 'Ah, there you go. Terrington.'

'D'you know, I'd forgotten about it, but we had a milk snatcher out Rillington way a few weeks ago. Never got anywhere with it.'

'Well, the disease is spreading. You've a major outbreak now, sunshine. Maybe you can apply what you learned on that informant-handling course you skived off on and – as you Met boys like to say, find a snout. Show the inspector it was time well spent. He'd like that.'

They say there's no time like the present. And I knew just the man to talk to, if I could catch him before he finished for the day. I got my gear in order and set off on my rounds, heading along the Hovingham road. Although I'd seen him around I hadn't spoken much to John since – hell, it must've been close to two years now since he put me on to the Barnsley Three. I caught up with him in Slingsby. He wasn't hard to spot in the gloom of a December morning, his bright red felt hat standing out like beacon.

He laughed when I asked if it was the same one he'd got for Christmas the year before last. 'No,' he said, 'that went ages ago. Wore it out. Then the missus bought me a replacement and everybody started complaining. Said it didn't suit me. I was "John with the red hat" – and there I was wearing a green one. Next thing I knew they'd had a whip-round and bought me this.'

'Now that's what you call a loyal customer base, mate. You must be coining it.'

'If only. I'm competing with the bloody supermarkets, don't forget. And once milk starts going missing off the doorstep . . . '

'That's what I wanted to talk about. Was it you who called in?'

'No. I was going to, but you know me – always on the go. One of me customers must've beaten me to it.'

'Four at the last count.'

'Four eh? I'm not surprised. I must've had half a dozen complaints this past couple of weeks. Separate incidents, like. I thought it'd be some kid on the way to school, but it's happening all over. I mean, what's going on? You don't have gangs of milk-snatchers, for God's sake.'

'I can't fathom it,' I said. 'Nope, it's a bloody head-scratcher, mate. That's what it is.'

'I tell you what Mike, I could really do with you sorting this one for me. It's hard enough making a living as it is.'

A case like that can annoy the hell out of me. It's petty, you might even say it's insignificant, but it causes grief to ordinary, law-abiding people – and someone, somewhere is getting away with it. It gnaws at me. I can just see the perpetrator, glugging all that milk down, lobbing the bottle over a hedge and going on his way, with a big slick of white around his lips. And I really want to wipe that daft grin off his face, whoever he is. Trouble is, you can't dedicate huge chunks of time to the theft of the odd pinta when there are far more serious offences being committed on a daily basis. Still, I always say that a rural bobby is there to serve a community – and that you ought to regard yourself as a part of that community, which I do. If they were being ripped off, so was I. Yes, I suppose you could say I take it personally. But if you did, I'd accept that as a compliment.

* * *

After I'd said goodbye to John I drove on through Hovingham and into the woods. I had a visit to make in the Easingwold area about a wildlife job – deer poaching – but I had a bit of time in hand and fancied making the long sweep along the crest of the Howardian Hills and onto Yearsley Moor. It was just about light by now. Most of the snow had long gone, the rain had eased, and the visibility was improving slightly. The woods up there are beautiful, and well managed. In fact, there was a bit of felling going on – a dark brown scar where the earth had been stripped bare, and maybe twenty yards off the road a large stack of felled beeches, the smooth grey bark covered with a thin layer of slush. I pulled up and wound the window down to take in that wet woodland smell. I was just thinking how many logs you could make out of a felled beech, and how beautifully they would burn, when my attention was caught by the sound of an engine revving up. Vroom vrooom vroom! For a moment I thought it must be one of the wood-cutters' vehicles, but it was too high-pitched, and whoever was working the throttle was doing so in anger and frustration. Somebody was stuck – and probably getting more stuck by the second.

I edged the car forward a few yards and peered around the pile of beechwood. A Vauxhall Astra pick-up, piled to the gunwales with logs, its rear wheels well and truly bogged down in the mud and spinning like crazy, was rocking to and fro and getting nowhere. I stepped out of the car, walked over and peered through the grimy windscreen. The revs dropped immediately as the driver took his foot off the pedal. He switched off the motor and the forest was suddenly silent. A jay darted down from a tree and landed on the stack of cut timber.

'Ronnie bloody Leach,' I said, as he wound his window down.

'Aye, morning Mike. Don't fancy giving us a hand, do you mate?'

'If you think I'm gonna stand in that pile of cack while you spin the wheels, forget it.'

'No, you can drive her,' he said, opening the door and stepping out. 'I'll push.'

'Now then, hang about a bit,' I said. 'Whose logs are these?'

He grinned with pride. 'Oh, they're kosher, mate.'

'What, you're in the logging business now, are you?'

'Aye well, ducking and weaving. Y'know how it is.'

'No, you tell me how it is.'

'Why, I drop a few loads off around the villages for my mate. He has a licence to cut up here.'

He knew I wanted more than that. 'No, honest. Here, I'll fetch t'list he gave me.' He dived into the glove compartment and pulled out a crumpled sheet of paper with his mate's name crudely printed on the top.

'OK, so maybe you're clean . . . ' Ronnie Leach, I thought to myself, a legit job? You must be joking. That would be too good to be true. He's a gambler and a seasoned criminal. He has to be up to something – or know about something. Maybe this was a chance to apply some pressure, like they'd taught us on the course. A chance to see what I could glean.

'I don't like the look of that windscreen, Ronny.'

'Aye, mucky as hell up here, Mike.'

'Which is why we have windscreen washers. Switch her on and show me.'

'Oh, you wouldn't ticket me, would you? I only ran out this morning on t'way up.'

'Press the button.'

He did as I said, turned the ignition on and flicked the washer lever. The motor hummed, but nothing came out. 'You do realise it's an offence . . . ' I started. As I spoke I walked around the truck, checking out the tyres. 'Why, you've barely any tread, lad. No wonder you're stuck. You've a few offences here, Mr Leach. What are we going to do about this?'

'Oh, bloody hell!'

'Don't worry, I'm not going to ticket you. I'm not a lover of paperwork. But I do take this seriously. And I'm telling you. Get them tyres sorted and that bottle filled up.' I was leaning over the windscreen, rubbing at the accumulated grit and salt with my finger. 'What if the sun comes out? You won't see a bloody thing. You haven't got a water bottle, have you?'

He brightened considerably. 'Aye, matter of fact I have.' I followed him round to the passenger side. He opened the door and reached in, and I took the opportunity to look over his shoulder. 'What's all that then?'

On the floor were half a dozen empty milk bottles, and three or four screwed-up foil caps.

'Oh, just empties.' He grabbed a plastic container of water and slammed the door again.

'No, open her up again, Ronnie, I want to have a look. Drink a lot of milk, do you?'

'Why, y'know how it is. Thirsty work, this.'

'I'm sure it is. So where d'you buy it?'

'Er . . . ' It's remarkable how the slightest hesitation gives people away. Everything about the way he'd carried himself up to that point had suggested he really was doing deliveries for his mate. He'd been almost swaggering with pride, as if it was a new feeling and he was still getting used to it. He may have been legit on one front, but he was in deep water on this. He really wished I hadn't set eyes on those bottles, because he'd somehow forgotten where he got them from. So I reminded him.

'Where've you been delivering recently, Ronnie?'

'Oh, round and about. Can't remember half the places.'

'Shall I make a stab for you? Terrington? Sheriff Hutton? Hovingham?'

He didn't put up much of a fight. He knew he'd given himself away. Yes, he said, he came up here early, before daylight. He needed to get a good start because he was doing a few hours in the bookies in town, and what with winter racing starting at midday he hadn't time for breakfast before he left home and you know how thirsty you get after a night on the beer . . .

'How long you been doing stuff like this, Ronnie?'

'What, logging?'

'No, nicking milk.'

'Never done it before – well, not since I was a lad. I tell you what – I'll replace it, every pint of it.'

'Ever had any from a gateway over Rillington way? Big country house? Stone pillars?'

'Er . . .'

'C'mon, mate, spit it out. We may as well clear 'em all up while we're at it.'

He didn't resist any further. He knew there was no point. I noted down what he'd said, then came to the point. 'Right Ronnie, I'm not happy with you driving this vehicle in this condition.'

'Oh hell. I'm due back in town at eleven thirty.'

'Well, I tell you what,' I said. 'I'll give you a lift back to town.' His mouth almost broke into a smile before I followed it up with, 'Because you're under arrest on suspicion of stealing milk on my beat.'

* * *

It was gone one o'clock before I'd got Ronnie interviewed, charged and out of the station. Even though he declined the services of a solicitor and 'coughed' the lot, it still took me the thick end of five hours to process him. Such is the amount of procedure attached to modern-day policing.

Outside the gloom had descended again and a fine drizzle had set in. Another hour or so and it'd start getting dark. Everywhere you went the lights were on. I only had a few loose ends to tidy up, and if nothing came up in the next half hour or so, I was thinking, I could be on my way. I was just walking past the CCTV room when Jayne came in for her late turn. There was no avoiding her in that narrow corridor.

''Ere he is,' she said. 'The man 'imself.'

'Oh aye?' I was still a little wary where Jayne was concerned. She'd never done me any harm as such, and she'd been with us well over a year now, but her manner – as well as her accent – still grated.

'Yeah,' she said, 'I got you on me list. For the old night out.'

'First I've heard of it.'

'Well, me, Chris, Ed, couple of the WPCs from Scarborough – we fancied a bit of a knees-up. Few drinks, bite to eat.'

There was no way I wanted to get involved in that and I couldn't believe that she'd got Ed on board. 'Are funny hats involved?' I asked.

'Whatcher got against funny hats? You wear one every bleedin' day.'

'Aye well, I'm not dressing up, I'll tell you that right now. Anyway, when is this do?'

'Friday week – after our early turn.'

'Ah.'

'Wass the problem?' she said.

'I'm otherwise engaged, Jayne. I've got something planned.'

'What, with yer girlfriend?'

'What girlfriend would that be?'

'Come on, Mike. It's bleedin' obvious. The way you come in to work every day, whistling like a little bird. It's like Chris said. That whistle is the sound of a man in love.'

'Yeah, all right Jayne. I'll come clean. She's a Super from the Midlands. Married woman. We meet up Manchester way, at a Travelodge on the M60. And we're booked in again on Friday week. OK?'

Jayne laughed. That was the thing about her: she could get on your nerves OK, but she was basically good-humoured. 'Oh well, your loss,' she said as she edged by me.

Just then Phil called through from the CCTV room. 'Hey, check this out will you?'

We both went over to where he was zooming in one of the cameras.

'Bit early to be tanked up like that, innit?' Jayne said.

There was a man on the bridge on Railway Street, one foot on the pavement, one on the road, waving his arms at the passing traffic. Cars were slowing down, swerving around him as he staggered towards them.

He was shaven headed, dressed in jeans and a shirt. Powerful build. 'He wants sorting out before he causes an accident,' I said. 'Who've we got?'

'There's nobody in town,' Phil said. 'Scattered to the four winds. Fordy's up at Pickering dealing with an accident, Ed was last seen heading out to Claxton to take a statement . . . '

'Right,' I said. 'I'll go down there. Jayne?'

'Gimme two ticks to grab me stuff.' That's another thing I liked about Jayne. Keen as mustard. As she shot off down the corridor I peered at the screen. 'Oh hell . . . you know who that is, don't you?'

'Can't say I do.'

'Have a closer look, Phil. You'll remember him. With that sodding great sword, last winter?'

'Oh God aye. What do they call him? Woodcock or something?'

'Wood.'

'That's the boy. Didn't they put him away?'

I snorted. 'A slap on the wrists and a community service order. Even his wife went straight back to him. Well,' I said, 'the bugger's in play this time. Keep the cameras on him, Phil, we don't want his brief twisting events and getting him off scot-free again.'

'What did yer mean back then, "in play"?' Jayne was back, and ready to go.

'It's that bloke Wood, that idiot that had the sword and base-ball bat last winter. Remember?'

'Hell yes. Right bleedin' nutter.'

'In play – I suppose I mean he's fair game,' I said as we walked across the car park. 'As opposed to the situation we had last time. You know, a woman and a child in jeopardy, so we had to tread cautiously.' I pulled my radio out.

'Oh, right.'

'1015 to control.'

'*Go ahead Mike.*' Julie's voice came over the radio.

'It's déjà vu all over again.' She'd been the operator on my last encounter with Wood. 'Julie, we've got that man Wood again. Looks much the worse for drink. He's in Railway Street. I've got Jayne with me, but can you organise another unit just in case he kicks off.'

'*Oh, deep joy, Mike, I'm on to it.*'

I eased the car out onto Old Maltongate and sped off past the Roman Camp. 'This time it's just him and us, so if things do get rough . . . '

'We can get stuck in.'

'Well Jayne, just bear in mind that he can be a right handful, and the worst-case scenario is that he might be tooled up. You got your CS gas?'

'Yep.'

'If he does turn nasty don't be afraid to use it. And at least it'll all be on CCTV'.

'OK, Mike. No worries.'

She tried to sound relaxed, but I could hear the nervousness in her voice, and I recognised it. I felt it myself. It's the old adrenaline again, preparing you for that familiar 'fight or flight' situation.

'Asp?'

'Mike, I've done this before.'

Julie was on the radio. '*Yeah, Mike, we've had Wood's wife on the phone. Claims he assaulted her. Cut her mouth. Backup on the way and I've got a late turn WPC from Pickering to go to her place.*'

'Well, that helps,' I said, as we approached the lights. 'We can arrest him right away on suspicion of assault.'

The traffic was heavy, and I was tempted to put the two-tones on. But from this distance Wood would hear us, and we didn't want that. 'We wanna keep this low-key,' I said. 'This guy loves a drama. Thrives on it. Thinks he's Bruce bloody Willis. Last thing we need is for him to get a head of steam up.' I was thinking back to our previous encounter. 'Or going off on one and taking a hostage.'

Wood was on the near end of the bridge, leaning back against the metal railings, his arms spread out in an arrogant sort of posture. Look at me. And screw you. He was pulling his shirt off. Everything about him suggested he was spoiling for a fight.

'Well, Jayne.' I'd stopped the car, barely fifty yards from him. 'I always say we should be fair and reasonable, but firm. I reckon this is a situation where firmness is called for. This youth is coming in. Now.'

He was in the road already, giving us two fingers, shouting and swearing. As soon I got out of the car he recognised me. 'You can f*** off, Pannett – and tek that ugly bitch with you.'

'If he wants to mess with me . . . ' Jayne had her hand on her Asp.

'Jayne,' I said, 'just play it straight down the line. No messing about. We've got enough on him already. He's coming in.'

I walked across the road towards him, the handcuffs at the ready. 'Right, Mr Wood, we've been watching you on the CCTV cameras and you need to calm down. We need to speak to you.'

'F*** off!'

'Well let me tell you right now, you're under arrest for being drunk and disorderly.' I chose at this stage not to mention the assault on his wife. The way he was looking it might send him into orbit. That could wait until he was cuffed and secure.

He stood there, fists clenched, his bare upper body glistening in the headlights of a bus which had just pulled out of the depot on the other side of the bridge. Maybe it was something in our manner, the fact that Jayne and I had approached him with confidence, knowing we had him, but he suddenly turned and ran across the bridge. Flight, not fight, I was thinking. We both gave chase, until he decided to vault the fence and go down onto the riverside.

'You prat,' I muttered. 'Why does he always have to do it the hard way?' This should've been a simple job: put the cuffs on, and take him away. Have him on CCTV evidence and then investigate the assault. But no, he had to take us on.

'Where the bloody hell does he think he's going?' Jayne said. We watched him stumble along the embankment to where it shelved steeply down to the water's edge. The river was high and fast under the bridge, cresting into a big wave as it sluiced around the pillars.

'He won't get far along there,' I said. Ahead of him was a tangle of dead undergrowth and brambles, and beyond that a little jetty at the bottom of someone's garden, with a blue and white fibreglass launch bobbing against it.

'Mr Wood,' I shouted. 'You are now unlawfully at large. Don't be bloody stupid. I'm telling you, if you go in that water the current will take you under. You could kill yourself.'

But he wasn't about to come back. His blood was up. And so was Jayne's. She was clambering over the railings. 'I'll have him,' she said.

'Whoa,' I shouted, 'whoa! You'll be in that river yourself if you aren't careful.'

'He managed it OK,' she said. 'And he's pissed.'

'Yeah but you can't be tussling with him on a slope like that. Just hold steady. He can't escape, can he? Where's he gonna go?' She turned back. 'He's no option but to come back to us.'

In the gathering gloom I was struggling to see him. I ran back to the car and grabbed my Dragon light. As I did so I gave control a quick update. I also asked Julie to call out the fire brigade, making sure they brought their inflatable boat. 'But Julie,' I added, 'ask them to approach silently. Wood's on a hair-trigger and we don't want to spook him.'

As I made my way back to where Jayne was I saw Ed getting out of his car. The best man for backup as far as I was concerned. I shone the light over the tangle of weeds below us. Wood seemed to have disappeared in the undergrowth. When he re-emerged my heart sank.

'What are you doing? Get yourself back over here,' I shouted. Somehow he'd reached the little jetty and was standing there, arms outstretched as he balanced himself.

'F*** off, you bunch of w***kers.'

Ed joined us on the bridge. 'Looks like he's got two chances,' he said.

'Little and none?'

'From where he is it's either come back to us or into the river.'

'And just how long do we think he'd last in there, that's the question?'

'Look at him, the prat.' Strange as it may seem, part of me actually felt sorry for him. He was one of life's losers, one of those lads Walt had talked about who just couldn't help themselves. When it came to it the last thing I wanted was to see him swept away.

But that was on the cards as he swayed to and fro, inching his way towards the little boat. As we watched, his foot slipped on the wet boards and he almost went in. 'Right,' I said, 'I'm going after him. I'll tackle him. You two be ready with the gas if he wants to fight. OK?'

'Your choice.'

'Cheers, Ed.'

I climbed over the fence and the other two followed. I pushed a path through the dead weeds, the brambles ripping at my trouser legs. I'd got within fifteen feet or so when Wood hurled the first rock at us.

'Bloody hell!' For a moment I thought Jayne had been hit. 'Come on, Mike, let's bleeding have him!'

I turned to face her and held my hands up. 'Just stay calm, Jayne.'

'He's not going anywhere,' Ed said. 'Let him come to us.'

She wasn't listening. She was ducking as another rock flew past her.

'Shit!' Wood was in the water now, up to his waist, trying to untie the boat from its mooring. The water was swirling past him, the current nudging him against the jetty as he struggled to grab the side of the little craft and haul himself on board.

'The bloody idiot. He'll freeze to death.' I scrambled a little closer, grabbing at a willow sapling to steady myself, and called out to him. 'Now come on,' I said. 'Don't be doing anything daft. You take off in that boat and it's next stop Kirkham weir. You won't stand a bloody chance, mate. Come on, it's not worth it.'

'I don't bloody care.' I realised then that he was about to crumble. The aggressive, snarling edge was starting to wear off. He was freezing, and feeling sorry for himself again. 'I might as well bloody die,' he said. 'F***ing wife. It's 'er you wanna be talking to. I've had enough, me.'

Jayne had fought her way through the weeds to join me. Behind me I could hear Ed talking to one of the fire officers who had arrived. Thank God they'd responded promptly. They'd managed to launch their boat on the other side of the bridge, nice and quietly. If the worst came to the worst and he did get swept away, they were in the perfect position to go after him.

You have mixed feelings in situations like this. You feel good because you've got everything in place. The situation is just about under control. And you're comforted by the support around you. But at the same time you're enraged to think of the waste of time and resources – and never mind the potential threat to everyone's safety – and all because some pillock has had too much to drink.

Wood had now turned his attention to Jayne. She was doing her best to be patient, but he was taking it as indecision. 'I'm telling you, I'm having the bloody boat – and then you'll never get me, you stupid cow. Teks more than a f***ing cockney bitch to bring me in.' I could see him struggling to untie the rope, still waist-deep in the swirling waters.

'You take that,' Jayne said, 'you'll be charged with stealing a boat as well.'

'You think I give a shit?'

She'd had enough. 'All right,' she said, 'you keep threatening you're gonna go in the river. Let's see you. Or are you just a bloody wimp? Come on, show us what yer made of.' She was out of order, of course, but I had every sympathy. It's hard work not responding when some drunken idiot is mouthing off at you and you have to stand there and take it. Sometimes you really would rather step in and belt them one and get the job over with.

'Don't you worry, bitch. I'm off, me, down t'bloody river. You won't see me again. Next stop bloody Hull.'

He turned to pick at the knotted rope, but even as he did so we could see he was slowing down, struggling to make his fingers do the work. He must have been freezing. He gave up, tugged at it, tried again, then threw the rope against the side of the boat, and tried to climb up onto the jetty. But his strength was deserting him, rapidly. Instead, he worked his way slowly along the edge towards the bank. When Jayne and I approached him, grabbed an arm apiece and pulled him onto dry land, he offered no resistance. He opened his mouth to speak but the only sound that came out was a stuttering of 'ff-ff-ffs' as his lips quivered uncontrollably. He whimpered with pain as he hobbled over the rough ground. He'd lost one of his trainers in the river. By the time we reached the bridge he was in tears. 'You wanna sort out that f***ing bitch I got married to. She's the one wants seeing to. She's the one.'

He barely had the strength to hold his arms out for the handcuffs. He staggered and almost fell as we put him into the back of the car and threw a blanket over him and put the heater on.

A moment or two later an ambulance pulled up and we transferred him into that. He sat in the back of the ambulance muttering 'She's the one' to himself while the paramedics checked him over. 'You'll live,' they said. I glanced at Jayne and knew what she was wanting to say.

'Jayne . . . '

'Yeah, I know. He had an unhappy childhood.'

When we'd got him back to the station I further arrested him for the assault. He was booked in and placed in the cell. It would take him a while to sober up, which was good news for us. We could get ourselves home. The late turn could deal with him.

As Jayne and I sat having a cuppa I had a few words about what she'd said to Wood on the bridge. 'I understand how you felt,' I said, 'but it's not very professional, is it?'

'Yeah, I know. But he's assaulted his wife, he's in my bleeding face. He's a worthless piece of . . . '

'I know, Jayne, but think about it. What if? You always have to ask yourself that question. What if he had gone in the river – deliberately or accidentally. And drowned. And just suppose a member of the public had heard you tell him to take a flying you-know-what. Where would that put us then? The newspapers would love it. "Police told drowning victim to jump!"'

She nodded, and looked at the ground. She saw my point OK. 'Listen,' I said, 'I've done and said things I regret, specially when I first started out. Luckily I had people around me who pointed out the errors of my ways. We all live and learn.'

I didn't see much of Jayne over the next few days, although she did approach me one more time to try to recruit me for her Christmas night out. 'Look,' I said, 'I've told you once. I'm otherwise engaged.'

'Oh, right. The Superintendent. Birmingham.'

'That's the one, Jayne. The secret lover.'

I was starting to enjoy the joke by now. When Chris overheard it and raised an enquiring eyebrow I winked at him, touched the side of my nose and gave him the old 'That's for me to know and you to find out' routine. As with any rumour, once I'd started it it had taken on a life of its own. It had even reached Ann's ears, although I didn't realise that until the evening of the twenty-third, when I set off to collect her for our night out. I was in full festive mood. I'd just done my last shift before a four-day break, and boy was I ready for it, even though it meant missing out on two days of overtime for Christmas and Boxing Day. I love having Christmas off. I'm like a child. I love the excitement, the presents, the turkey, even the tradition of watching City get thumped on Boxing Day.

'You do realise,' she said, as she got into the car, 'that you've never said where you're taking me.'

'You don't want to guess?'

'Well, word has reached my ear . . .'

'Go on. What you heard?'

'It's not a Travelodge on the M60 by any chance, is it?'

'Ha. That venue has been discussed, yes.'

'But it's a joke, right?'

'Course it's a joke. Where I'm taking you is a bit closer to home – and a bit more romantic. You should know it. Anyway,' I said, 'never mind the Malton gossip. What's the news from York? How'd it go this afternoon?'

'I think I did well. But . . . '

'But what? Did sommat go wrong?'

'No, I just mean that you can never really tell, can you? You know how it is. You come out thinking you've played a blinder – and they turn you down. Wouldn't be the first time.'

'But you feel confident?'

'Tell you the truth, when I came out of the interview I thought it was in the bag. There were only three of us. I'm hoping the fact that I've done the job before gave me the edge. I don't think the other two have the experience to slot straight in. But you know how it is. You start off thinking you've scored. Then the doubts creep in.'

'I tell you what though Ann. This is North Yorkshire. If they think they can save money by not having to train the others up, it'll be no contest.'

'Yeah thanks. I think!'

'So when are they going to let you know?'

'I've been waiting for a phone call but – well, it's almost seven. They aren't going to call me now, are they?'

'Don't see why not. We had a lad in Battersea, went for a job, came home, paced up and down for a couple of hours, gave it up and went to bed – and the phone rang at half past ten. Anyway, there's nowt you can do about it, so let's just relax and enjoy ourselves.'

Ann took out her mobile. 'You're right. I'm hardly getting a signal as it is. So even if they do ring . . . ' She snapped it shut and put it back in her bag. 'Anyway, where are we going? You still haven't said.'

I managed to keep her guessing until we'd driven through Brandsby and were following the lane that runs north to Crayke. 'Hey, you're not taking me back to my teenage haunts are you?' she laughed. 'The Durham Ox?'

'The very same,' I said as we drove up the hill into the village. 'I never knew you went there.'

'Oh, I used to be a regular – me and my little gang. That was when I was still young and foolish – before I went south and joined the Met.'

'Been in recently?'

She shook her head. 'No, must be ten years. More than that.'

'You'll like it. They've done it up really nice – and the food's out of this world.'

They'd found us a super table for two, tucked away on our own in a quiet corner. When the waiter took our coats and pulled out our seats I stood there for a few seconds, just gazing at Ann.

'Something the matter?' she asked, her eyes twinkling in the candlelight. She was wearing a sleeveless black dress to match her hair, and a beautiful silver necklace. She looked absolutely breathtaking.

'Tell you in a moment,' I said. Then, when the waiter had disappeared, I cleared my throat. 'I need a drink.'

'But just the one, right?'

'We'll talk about that later.' I sat down. 'God, you look gorgeous. Look,' I said, as the waiter returned with the wine menu, 'I may as well come clean. I was going to surprise you, but you need to know now. We're booked in for the night.'

'What, here?'

'No, the Travelodge.'

'Eh?'

'Yes, of course I mean here.'

She gave a little whistle. 'Last of the big spenders, eh? I won't ask what it cost.'

'No, don't. Just enjoy yourself.'

'Well, that eases the pressure. I was waiting for that delicate moment when you tell me I'm on one glass of wine because you want me to drive us home.'

I tapped the side of my nose. 'Forward planning, Ann – and before you bother with that wine list, I've already ordered a bottle of champagne to kick things off.'

We had a brilliant evening. The food was fabulous; the wine flowed; the service was superb. And all the time I was getting more and more tense. We were waiting for our coffee to arrive, and I was looking at Ann through the flickering light of the candles. She was sipping a glass of dessert wine, a sweet rosé, and smiling at me. I'd had something on my mind all evening and just knew that now was the time to say it. 'Ann?'

'Yes, Mike.'

'Er, just excuse me a moment. I need to pay a call.'

Chicken-hearted, that's me. Give me a madman with a sword and I'm as cool as you like, but putting a simple proposition to the woman I love? Well, ask any bloke. In the gents I threw cold water on my face and gave myself a stern talking-to, which was interrupted by a fellow diner who walked in and looked at me as though I was stark staring mad.

'Right,' I said, when I returned to my seat. 'There's something I've been wanting to ask you.'

She was just closing her handbag. 'Have I got a towel in here? That it?'

'Eh?'

'Your face is all wet.'

'Oh, right.' I wiped it with my napkin.

She shoved her bag under her seat and moved the candelabra to one side, reaching out a hand. 'Go on then.' She had a strange look on her face, what you'd call a knowing smile. I wondered whether she'd rumbled me. 'Fire away,' she said, 'I'm all yours.'

'Hey, careful what you say now.' I took her hand in mine, closed my eyes and gathered my thoughts. 'OK,' I said, 'it's like this. We've been seeing each other a full year now.'

'Almost to the day.'

'Almost, but not quite.' We were both silent for a moment. She was looking at me, waiting. I dried the sweat off my hand on the tablecloth.

'Ann, let's say you get this job in York.'

'I'm . . . hopeful,' she grinned.

'As you should be. I mean – you're a good candidate, and—'

'Mike, I told you earlier. I have a good feeling about it.'

'Right.'

'So you may continue.'

'Sorry.' The coffee had arrived. I waited while it was arranged on the table. And then waited some more while our waiter told us what blooming mountain it was grown on in Guatemala or some such. 'OK then. So, let's say you get it. It'll mean you're no longer a sergeant at Malton.'

'This is true.'

'And that means that we no longer have to be a well-kept secret.'

'Also true. And I tell you what, I'll be mightily relieved.'

'Well, how would it be if we decided that this was the time

to get a place of our own? I mean, how would you feel about us living together?'

'Goodness.' She paused halfway through pouring the coffee and looked into my eyes.

'Look,' I said, 'you don't need to answer me now. I mean, if you want time to think about it.'

'I don't,' she said. 'I don't need any time at all. I've been thinking about it for a while.'

'And?'

She put the glass down, held me hand in hers, and took a deep breath.

'Bleedin' hell! Look who it is!'

'Oh no. Surely not.' I'd felt a cold draught around my legs just a moment earlier. I'd put it down to the waiter popping outside for a breath of air. But no, there he was walking past us, and in his wake was a party of diners. Ed, Chris, the Scarborough WPCs, and Jayne, who was beaming at me and pointing at Ann.

'I knew it,' she said. 'I bleedin' knew it.'

'I beg your pardon?' Ann's hand was gripping mine. Jayne ignored her and addressed her reply to me. 'Gawd, you wanna be more careful, y'know. If word gets back there could be trouble . . . '

I was about to give her a mouthful when Ann spoke. 'Jayne, I know you pride yourself as having your finger on the pulse, but your sources have let you down badly this time.' I'd not seen Ann like this before. She was icy cool and seemed to be relishing the situation.

'Well, I mean . . . ' Jayne shrugged her shoulders. 'Just that you – well, you don't want word getting out, thass all.'

'Ah. You mean about dating a sergeant from your home station?'

'Well, no . . . I mean . . .' Jayne was wriggling like a fish on a hook.

Ann took out her mobile and flipped the lid open. 'Well Jayne, let me bring you up to speed. Mike and I are going to be moving in together and I am taking a posting as a sergeant at York, starting in the new year.'

'Oh, right. Well, I always said you two were well suited.' Beads of sweat were breaking out on her forehead. I thought she was about to crack – until Ed defused the situation. He stepped in and gave Ann a hug and a kiss. 'Well done, you two. This is fantastic news – and hey, if you're short of any furniture we're having a bit of a clearout at home . . .'

'Bloody hell,' I murmured as they were shown to a table across the far side of the room. 'That shut her up. What a carry on!'

'Seems to have shut you up too,' Ann said, drumming her fingers on the table.

'Oh, right. Yes. Congratulations. So what happened? Have you had a call?'

'Soon as you took off for the gents it beeped at me. I've heard of people being fired by text. Seems I've been appointed via my answering service. They're phoning with more details tomorrow morning.'

I picked up my glass, but it was empty. 'Er, waiter.'

'Yes sir?'

'What'll it be, Ann? Remy Martin?'

'That'll do nicely, thank you.'

'Make that two, will you?' I took hold of her hands and squeezed. 'God, that's brilliant. York, eh?'

'Back to working in the city then.'

'Ha. They won't know what's hit 'em.'

'Anyway, where were we?'

'You were about to answer my question. About getting a place together.'

'Yes.'

'And I take it from what you just said to Jayne that the answer is . . . ?'

'Yes.'

I banged the table with my hand. 'Fantastic. You've no idea how I was sweating on that.'

'Of course, we'll need somewhere that suits us both – me travelling to York, you to Malton.'

'Details,' I said as the brandies arrived. 'To be arranged later. Take your glass. And here's to us.'

'To us. In our own place.'

Acknowledgements

My thanks to the great people of North Yorkshire, without whose wit, warmth and character, this book could never have been written.

With thanks to my family and friends for their support and encouragement.

Thanks also to Joanna Devereux and Rupert Lancaster, whose continued faith and enthusiasm over the past five years has made this all possible.

Now read this exclusive extract from
Mike Pannett's next book:
Not on My Patch, Lad,
available soon from Hodder & Stoughton.

It's no laughing matter, I told myself as I drove down the steep wooded hillside towards the ruins of Kirkham Priory and bumped my way over the level crossing. No laughing matter at all. But when you're called out to investigate a sixty-year-old male who's been seen on the public highway, on a pedal cycle, stark naked – well, it's hard to keep a straight face. In this day and age, of course, we're all wary of any suggestion of behaviour that's in any way sexually threatening – or worse – so this could have been a serious matter. However, I was pretty sure I knew the man in question. It had to be Gerald. Who else could fit the caller's description? He was, according to the lady who'd rung in, 'riding along with his front basket full of old tin cans, smoking a pipe, and not a stitch on him but a straw hat.'

The thing with Gerald is, first and foremost, he's a Yorkshireman. And if you don't quite know what that means, let me say that amongst his many attributes, a real dyed-in-the-wool Yorkshireman is his own man. I always tell people a Yorkshireman is like Popeye. Remember him? 'I am what I am.' And he has a certain cussedness. Like Algy, the time he found out it was illegal to fly a Yorkshire flag within sight of the public highway. What did he do but go straight out, erect a thirty-foot high pole next to his front gate, then run the white rose ensign up it. Some people say that folk like Algy are just looking for confrontation, that they thrive on it. Others say he's standing up for his rights, and we should all take a leaf from his book. I remember a conversation we had in the Jolly Farmers around this time, when the first rumours were starting up that the government might try to enforce a ban on hunting with dogs. Algy had never mounted a horse in his life, let alone gone hunting, but he stood at the bar that night and told anyone who'd listen that the minute our elected representatives tried to tell him that he couldn't go hunting, he'd be straight out to buy a horse and ride with the Middleton hounds. 'And if anyone cares to write that down, by golly I'll sign it in my own blood,' he added for good measure. Fortunately for him, nobody had any blank paper on them at the time. Or if they did they weren't owning up to it.

However, I'm getting off the subject, which is our mate Gerald. I'm not sure what Gerald's background was. He didn't have much of an accent, but he was Yorkshire through and through. He was an educated man. According to Walt, he'd been an accountant in Harrogate years ago, and when you heard him speak you could imagine it. He'd been married and had a family, but for some reason or other he'd dropped out of what we call respectable life and gone off to live in the wilds as an ageing child of nature. Well, I suppose that's a slight exaggeration: what he'd done was build himself some sort of retreat in the woods, not far from Kirkham, but a long way off the road. It was part way between a caravan and a shed, it was static, and as such I suppose it wasn't exactly legal, but the farmer who owned the woods had never objected, and in any case Gerald only lived there part of the year. April to October, more or less. The rest of the time he stayed at his niece's house over Ripon way. But in the summer months I'd occasionally see him, puffing away on his pipe as he gathered armfuls of firewood, his bike leaning against a convenient hedge or a gate; or I'd spot him wheeling it home with a five-gallon container balanced on the handlebars. He had a couple of old Army jerry-cans that he used to fill with spring water he collected from the pipe that fed one of the drinking-troughs in a nearby cow pasture. He rarely had more than a pair of shorts on, but up until now I wasn't aware that he'd go the whole hog. Not within view of the public, at any rate.

I'd only been to his place once or twice, and each time I'd had difficulty finding it. But I'd decided it was time to seek him out and put him right about what the law did and didn't allow. These things are best nipped in the bud.

It was a cool, grey day but the rain that had been falling all morning had stopped at last, and the sky was brightening form the northwest. When I came to the green lane that led to his place I found it was thoroughly overgrown. There was no way I'd get my Puddle Hopper down there. So I parked on the old forestry track and set off on foot. 'Great,' I muttered to myself as the overhanging branches showered water down my neck and the rank grasses soaked my trouser legs.

I smelled the place before I actually spotted it. It wasn't the sweet smell of burning wood, rather the pungent aroma of charred plastic. And as I entered the little clearing where the old shed stood. there he was, naked as the day he was born, bent over an old dustbin and pulling out a tangle of electrical cable on the end of a garden fork. I watched as he dumped it into a brazier, then stepped back as black smoke and yellow flames swirled about him.

'Now then,' I said.

'Ah, good afternoon.' He didn't seem at all surprised by my

presence. He just stuck his fork into the ground and turned to face me.

'I'm PC Mike Pannett from Malton,' I said. 'I'm your rural beat officer.' It's hard to know where to look when a man's got nothing on, so I nodded at the fire instead. 'At least you've got a nice warm job.'

'Yes, I save them up for days like this.' He reached out with his fork and pulled a strand of copper wire from the blaze. 'Surprising how much this stuff fetches at the scrapyard.'

As he spoke, a gust of wind shook the trees and a shower of fat drops hissed on the glowing sides of the brazier.

'Listen,' I said, 'can I have a word – inside?' I looked across at the door of his little dwelling. It was a wooden-framed thing, painted yellow and glazed with that fluted glass they used to put in back doors back in the sixties and seventies. He must have rescued it from a builder's skip somewhere. It still had the original plastic numbers on it, 34.

'Yes, do come in.' Leaning beside the shed was a bike, a plastic bag tied over the fishtail saddle, its large wickerwork basket overflowing with crushed aluminium drinks cans. It certainly fitted the description the complainant had given us. Not that I'd doubted for a minute that Gerald was our man.

Inside he sank into an old leather-upholstered car seat and offered me a wooden rocker. There was barely room for both of us between a folding bed, a black pot-bellied stove and one of those glass-fronted kitchen cabinets, its front folded down to make a worktop. I doubt that Gerald's entire home measured more than about six feet by ten. And was it my imagination, or was the whole place tilted to one side?

I decided to get right down to it. I had little choice. He was sitting there, relaxed, at peace with the world, legs apart, wiping some mud off his foot on a square of old carpet before tamping a fresh wad of tobacco into his pipe.

'Mr Rodgers,' I said, pulling out a notepad and flicking it open, 'I'm afraid I've received a complaint which I believe may concern you.' I stared hard at the empty page as he crossed his legs and sucked on his pipe. Then I looked up at the ceiling, which seemed to be lined with a patchwork of yellow and blue fertiliser bags.

'Oh yes,' he said, through a fog of blue smoke. 'and what might that be about?'

'It's from a lady,' I said. 'Down in the village. She said she saw someone who answered your description cycling past the other morning dressed in – well, in not very much.'

Gerald took his pipe out of his mouth and balanced it on the edge of the glass-fronted dresser. 'And that's the point, is it? That I wasn't wearing very much?'

'Yes, it is.'

'I think you'll find, officer, that under British law a man has a perfect right to dress as he pleases. Or has something changed? It's been a while since I read what passes for a newspaper these days.'

'Her exact words were—' – I sought refuge in the empty notepad again – 'that you "had all your goods on display." She was quite upset.'

'Look, Constable . . . Pannett, did you say?' Gerald picked his pipe back up, flicked his lighter into life and sucked the flame into the bowl. 'I'm not a paid-up member of the Naturists' Society or whatever they call it, but I believe it is better for my mental and physical health to expose my skin to the sunlight during the summer months. That's the way I believe nature intended us to live.'

'Don't get me wrong,' I said. 'In the woods here, that's fine. But when you're out and about on your bike, would you just think about the public at large – especially the ladies – and try to . . .' I didn't mean to, but I couldn't help it: I gestured towards his nether regions. 'Try to keep things under wraps, eh?'

Cases like this can be difficult. Where does the law draw the line between self-expression and giving offence? We have naturist beaches now, even on the east coast of Yorkshire. And you have to believe that anyone who'll prance about naked on the beach at Fraisthorpe when that wind's coming off the North Sea has to believe in what they're doing. So when you're dealing with a character like Gerald – well, is he just a bit of a character, a determined individualist, or has he some sort of mental health issue? It's a tough call, and as a cop you have to do your best to make that judgement. You think of offences like 'being a public nuisance', 'indecent exposure', or perhaps general public order offences. But you also have to weigh up what's in the public interest – and the effect on the witness or victim. Having had my chat with Gerald, I decided that a gentle warning and a word of advice would, hopefully, sort things out. We would see if there were any more complaints over the next few weeks. I left him to his scrap metal reclamation. As I walked back through the dripping woods to my vehicle I thought about the endless variety of cases that comes your way as a copper. I certainly couldn't remember dealing with anything quite like it before.

I was debating whether to go back to the station or call in at Walt's for a cup of tea and a chance to dry my trousers when the mobile rang. I bumped to a halt in a gateway and took the call. It was Nick the gamekeeper. 'Now then, Mike, are you up to anything?'

'Not a lot, Nick. Just between calls at the moment. What's on your mind?' I was hoping he'd rung to tell me that his wife was baking. It wouldn't be the first occasion on which I'd timed a visit there to coincide with a fresh batch of rock buns coming out of the stove.

'You remember that feller Jenks I was telling you about the other week? At the Country Watch do?'

'Hmm – sommat about a barn with the windows sealed up?'

'Aye, that's it. Blacked out, they were.'

'What's up? Has sommat happened?'

'No no – just that I ran into him this morning down at Yates's in town, and he was asking me if you'd been and had a look.'

'Tell you the truth, Nick, I haven't had time yet. But I tell you what, it's not far out of my way. I'll maybe pop over there and have a look. Unless you're wanting help with them cakes your missus is baking.'

'*Sorry to disappoint you, son. She's in town herself. Market day, isn't it?*'

If you wanted directions to the main farm, the one that old Jenks lived in, I have to say I'd be struggling. Not that I was wanting to talk to him at this stage. For now I was just going to have a nose around the rented place. The main farmhouse, where he lived, was only really visible if you were out walking in the hills. I'd seen it a time or two from a track where I sometimes took [my dog] Henry to try and burn off some of his excess energy. It forms a part of a long-distance footpath, the Wolds Way, and looks out over one of those beautiful dry valleys the area's known for – dry because as soon as it rains any runoff tends to seep quickly through the chalk base and go underground. As to the rented place I was supposed to be looking for, well, Nick had tried to explain where it was, but as my vehicle bucked and swayed its way along the narrow track, splashing through a succession of milky puddles, I started to wonder whether I'd got it right. However, I knew that Nick knew his way around these parts. And there was at least one set of fresh wheel-ruts, so I ploughed on between the overgrown hawthorn hedges that lined my route.

I must have gone the best part of a mile by now and was starting to wonder whether I'd gone wrong. The hedge had given way to a dark copse, a tangle of ash and elder with ivy smothering the ground in between. Above me, through a gap in the trees, I could see the steep, bare Wolds, dotted with sheep. And then, around a bend, the track suddenly opened out into a large, well maintained lawn, to one side of which stood a handsome farm cottage, to the other a tall redbrick barn with a pantiled roof, its two rows of windows blacked out with some sort of sheeted material. From this distance it was hard to tell what it was exactly – and I had no intention of going any further. I'd seen all I needed to for now. Just in case I happened to be seen or challenged by the occupants, I had prepared a cover story, but there was no one around and so I backed up fifty yards or so to where there was a bit of a clearing, turned around, and headed to town. I needed to have a chat with a man called Des.

Des Carter was our CID man. He came from the West Country and he wore a suit. He was a detective constable. Unlike some DCs I have met, Des didn't assume that he was superior to every uniformed officer he came across. He was odd that way: if it wasn't for the fact that he would dish out gratuitous insults to us Plods as a matter of course – always with his tongue planted firmly in his cheek – you could be forgiven for thinking that he saw us as equals, allies in the fight against crime. I liked Des, and not just because his career had taken a similar course to mine. Like me, he'd started out in the Met, then started hankering for the open spaces he'd grown up with, although in his case he made the move to his wife's home territory, which was North Yorkshire, rather than back to his native Devon. We had another thing in common: we both loved fly-fishing. Not that we ever got much chance to talk about it. We didn't see a great deal of each other at work. The CID and the uniformed branch inhabit very different worlds most of the time.

People have funny ideas about the Criminal Investigation Department. They assume that a DC is superior in rank to a PC. Not so. All they are is specialists. As their name implies, they investigate crimes, rather than just policing an area. Whereas a PC deals with whatever comes his way, and may well have to break off from working on a burglary to attend to a road traffic accident or a domestic bust-up, a DC does not pound a beat and is therefore free to attend to the long and often laboured enquiries that are a routine part of investigation into a serious crime. They have the time to undertake the detailed interrogation of a suspect that is par for the course in cases like rape, murder, high-value robberies and so on. They can also advise the beat bobby in certain specialist areas, although in my case I rarely felt the need for guidance: during my time in London I had a dealt with pretty well every type of crime you can think of and was well clued up on the standard procedures. In this case, however, I had no hesitation in going straight to Des. Apart from anything else, he would have a handle on the latest intelligence.

'Now then, you idle bugger!' I'd found Des hunched over a

computer screen with a pile of box files on the desk beside him. 'What you skiving at this time?' Just because I'd marked his cards as one of the good guys, there was no reason why I shouldn't get my insults in first.

Des skidded his swivel chair away from the desk and tapped his finger to his head. 'Listen, you bloody woodentop, I could explain it to you, but you know what? You'd start complaining that your head hurts – and right now I've run out of aspirins. Just you stick to pounding the pavements, and leave the intellectual stuff to us, eh?'

'Don't you worry about the streets of our fair city,' I said, pulling up a chair. 'They're in good hands. Anyway, I wouldn't dream of sending you out there. Might get that nice new suit all mucky and crumpled. Can't have that, can we now?'

'And on a more serious note?' Des was doing his best not to laugh.

'Young couple, Des. He's working, they have a kid at school, right? They rent a farmhouse way out in the middle of nowhere with a big barn out the back – and they black the windows out. Any ideas?'

'No law against it.'

'No, but it's an odd thing to do, isn't it?'

'Depends what they're into. Not an artist, is he?'

'I doubt it.'

'His missus?'

'They like natural light, don't they?'

'Could be a photographer.'

'Des, this ain't a darkroom. The place is bloody huge. Size of a church.'

'Hm.' He scooted forward, took hold of the mouse and brought up a file on screen. 'Tell you what we have had,' he said. 'A bit of info from Crime Stoppers. Came in a few weeks ago. They reckon someone's growing cannabis in industrial quantities out our way.'

'Interesting. I came across something similar to this in the Met. It was in Clapham. An industrial unit with blacked-out windows. Turned out to be a huge cultivation site.'

'Yeah, they do it on an industrial scale. Use hydroponics. Most of the skunk that's out there these days, they grow it in tanks. You know, watering systems, artificial light. And, of course, invisible from the outside.' He turned away from the screen and leaned back in his chair, stretching, his hands behind his head. 'A big old barn miles from anywhere, you say? If I was looking for a place to grow some weed I'd say it's just the job, mate.'

People tend to assume that most of the drugs consumed in the U.K. are imported illegally, but research has shown that as much as 60 to 70 per cent of the cannabis supply is actually grown here. And making a very nice profit.

'Right,' I said, 'I'll take a closer look.'

'And I'll do some digging around, shall I?'

'You do that Des. Oh, by the way', I said as I headed out of the door, 'I hear that North Yorkshire CID have uncovered a new type of drug abuse.'

'Oh yeah?'

'Where the user injects ecstasy directly into the mouth.'

'I haven't heard about that one.'

'Yeah, it's called E by gum.'

'Pannett, get the hell out of here.'

Back on my rounds I thought about what I'd seen, and wondered whether it might indeed tie in with Des's intelligence reports.

If it did, I needed no further motivation. People have mixed views on drug use. Or drug abuse: you can take your pick. But I've always been dead against it. Having said that, I have to add that growing up in rural North Yorkshire in the 1970s I was never really exposed to anything in the illegal substance line. The nearest we got to it at school was when the big kids, the ones who fancied themselves as hard cases, used to go behind the bike sheds, take teabags apart and smoke the contents. I can't say it ever appealed to me, but they made a big play of it, and staggered around when they came back into the playground, pretending they were high. They impressed one or two first-years, but that was about it.

Later on, when I started going into York for a drink on a Friday and Saturday night, my mates and I became aware that there were one or two pubs where you could buy cannabis, if you knew who to talk to. But that was about it: rumours, whispers, a few loudmouths boasting about what they were up to. So going to work in South London, where the cannabis culture really had got hold, was quite a revelation. The stuff was everywhere, along with various harder drugs. Heroin was prevalent. And then along came crack cocaine: highly potent, very addictive, and bringing with it all sorts of other issues. For a start, the people who used it were permanently skint, and soon started funding their habit through street robbery, burglary and suchlike. It was a massive problem, and when I left London I was glad to think I'd seen the last of it. But these days, even in the market towns, you see heroin and, more recently, cocaine. But up to this point, in Ryedale, we'd only had a few drugs busts, mostly small-scale stuff. And I wanted it to stay that way.

Des and I agreed that I would take a further look at the place, but without announcing myself to the occupants. I'd team up with Jayne and investigate under cover of darkness, and Des would find out what information he could about the people associated with that address: who paid the utility bills and so on – and was there anything untoward about the amount of electricity or water being consumed?

As soon as I told Jayne what I had in mind her face lit up. 'Nothing I like better than a nice night-time operation,' she said. 'Plain clothes, is it? Unmarked cars?'

'Oh yes. We don't want the subjects spotting us, but if they do – hey, we'll be a courting couple looking for a quiet spot for romance.'

'Mike, I've heard some sad come-ons in my time, but that takes the biscuit.'

'All in the line of duty, Jayne.'

'Yeah, yeah, yeah – but joking aside, I mean, admit it. It's what we joined the force for, isn't it? Proper old-fashioned cops and robbers.'

Jayne was right, in a way. When you decide to go into the police, yes, you're thinking community service, upholding the law, doing a worthwhile job, making the world a safer place; but a part of you is also thinking high-speed car chases, big crime busts, and cloak-and-dagger operations. To be perfectly honest, the amount of routine work you have to do is a bit of a letdown when you first start out. At the age we were when we started, we wanted action, not admin. So, by the time Jayne and I had set the thing up we were like two kids the night before Christmas.

The shift began like any other. We patrolled the town, waiting impatiently for the pubs to close and the streets to empty. Then we checked out the villages before going back to the station for a coffee. It was getting on for two when we changed into plain clothes and set off in an old, nondescript Vauxhall Vectra. For backup we had Ed and Fordy parked a couple of miles away in another unmarked car. Hopefully we wouldn't need them, the objective of the operation being to gather more information rather than to confront anyone. But all the same, we had to be prepared. The higher the stakes, the greater the dangers. Preliminary checks had shown that it was a couple with a small child who resided in the farmhouse. Neither were known for violence and no firearms were registered to them.

We drove down the narrow track on sidelights, taking it very slowly and keeping the engine on low revs. We'd gone maybe three quarters of a mile before pulling up in a gateway and continuing on foot, barely able to make out more than the odd dark shape in front of us. The sky may have been clear, but there was no moon, so it was very, very dark. We'd have been better off if it had been overcast. The amount of light that's reflected from clouds, even when you're several miles from town, gives you far better visibility than you'll get on a starlit night such as we had.

I set the pace, creeping slowly towards the end of the track, with Jayne following a few paces behind. When I trod on a stick it seemed to go off like a pistol shot. Otherwise all we could hear was the sound of our own breathing, the rustle of our clothes against the low-hanging branches. I was thinking about Jayne behind me, and what was going through her mind. I had done stuff like this before, but the first few times you're out of uniform and in plain clothes – well, it's as if your armour is off. You feel exposed, vulnerable.

I whispered back to her, 'You OK?'

'Fine Mike, yeah. Exciting, innit?'

'Careful!' I whispered. I'd come to a stop and Jayne almost

ran into the back of me. I tugged her sleeve and pointed towards the house, its outline clearly visible even though there wasn't a single light on anywhere in the vicinity. We stood for a minute or so, listening. There was no sound save the distant yip of a fox. Somehow that made me even more apprehensive. My biggest fear was that there might be guard dogs on the premises. You only need to be attacked once to be very wary indeed. It happened to me years ago, before I ever joined the force. I was working on a demolition site. Sauntered in one morning and clean forgot about the Alsatian they kept there until it charged across the yard at me. It broke its chain and I had to jump in a skip to get away from it. I still have the scar to this day – although only a few close friends have seen it.

We crept along the edge of the copse towards the barn, which stood between us and the house. I was feeling more edgy by the minute. As we approached our target I was overcome with this odd feeling that we were doing wrong. It was the sort of feeling I might have had years ago on a scrumping expedition. I knew it was daft: we had a perfect right to investigate what we considered suspicious circumstances. Perhaps it was the darkness, the fear of discovery, the fact that we were on someone else's property.

'They got security lights?' Jayne asked.

'I'm not sure, but I couldn't see any when I recce'd the place.'

We walked slowly across the yard towards the barn, treading as lightly as we could over the loose stones. At this stage all I was interested in was getting some idea of what was going on in there. I was within a few yards of it when I stopped, held my breath and put my hand up to Jayne. I could have sworn I'd heard a low humming noise. I beckoned Jayne forward again and went right up to the wall. Up above us was a row of windows, all blackened out. There it was again, the humming, like a grain dryer but not as loud. It was more the sort of noise you'd hear from an old electricity substation. Jayne was right up beside me now, breathing hard.

'What the hell's that?' she whispered. 'Couldn't be radiation, could it?'

'I bloody hope not,' I said. And then, looking up, I saw a ventilator grille. Wafting down from it on a draught of warm, moist air was a familiar smell. 'Hey, recognise that?'

She sniffed. 'Cannabis.'

There was no doubt about it. It's one of those distinctive smells: once you've smelled it you never forget it. I edged forward a few yards to a ground-floor window. This one wasn't blacked out. Shining my Maglite through the dusty glass, I saw a room about twelve feet square and more or less entirely taken up with a large blackened container full of water, with a copper and plastic pipes running up through the ceiling and back down.

'Right, mate. That'll do me.'

'What's the plan?'

'Get out, quick as we can.'

Back at the car we radioed Ed and Fordy to tell them they were no longer needed, then drove back to the station, where Chris Cocks immediately wanted to know what we'd found.

'Plenty,' I told him. 'The place reeks of cannabis. They've got a sophisticated plumbing system on the go, extractor fans, all sorts. They'll be producing the stuff by the ton, mate.'

'So what you going to do next?'

I looked at the clock on the wall. It was turned half past four. 'Write up a few notes, leave a message for Des, and home to bed.'

I woke up early next day. I knew I would. Cases like this don't come along very often, and when they do you don't want to miss a thing. Your biggest fear is that some vital development will take place on your day off, or while you're on leave. I already felt proprietorial about this one. It was mine, and I was determined to follow it through. At the end of the day I didn't want this sort of thing happening on my patch, and if it did I wanted to be in on the bust. Still, I reminded myself as I picked up the phone to call Des, there really was no rush on this one. These people would have no idea we were onto them. There was no reason why they wouldn't carry on as normal.

Des and I agreed that the first step was to refer the matter to our inspector, Birdie, to bring him up to speed and get his authority to apply to a magistrate for a search warrant. It was a necessary first step before we applied to a magistrate for a warrant that would permit us to search the premises. Then the uniformed officers and the CID would sit down and plan a joint operation. Meanwhile Des would conduct enquiries with the utility suppliers to see if there was anything unusual with the bills or the supplies to the premises.

In doing this we had to tread carefully, in case these people were already being watched by the Regional Crime Squad, or the National Criminal Investigation Squad as part of a broader investigation. Back in the 1970s, Operation Julie, which netted a massive LSD production ring, brought scores of individuals under surveillance nationwide and resulted in over a hundred arrests. Confidentiality was the key throughout, but at the same time the officers involved needed to make sure that none of the suspects were picked up by some local branch, thus alerting the others in the ring. So Des and I searched the computer database to see whether anything was flagged up on the farmhouse or its occupants. There was nothing.

A few days after Jayne and I had been down to the farm we met with Des and a couple of his CID colleagues. Inspector Bird was with us, along with Ed, Jayne and Fordy. The young man who lived at the farmhouse was, we learned, known to Humberside police. He'd been arrested in Hull a couple of years ago for possession of drugs. But that was it. He now worked in a factory in Malton and was to all intents and purposes living a normal, law-abiding life. He and his partner had a five-year-old daughter. Des had checked on their electricity bills and reported back that they were no more than an average domestic consumer might run up. That certainly didn't make sense.

After our discussion I went to Pickering to see the magistrate. My application was held *in camera*, the only other person present being a clerk. I presented our case and obtained a warrant under Section 23 of the Misuse of Drugs Act, entitling us to search the barn and house or anyone on the premises for drugs or any equipment or paraphernalia used in the manufacture or supply of drugs. We had a month to execute it. If we didn't do so within that time we'd have to apply for a fresh one.

With that side of things sorted out, we met again and agreed that we might as well put our plan into operation as soon as possible.

Twenty-four hours later we met with a search team based at Scarborough. That consisted of a sergeant, four PCs trained in drug searches, a dog handler with a specially trained drugs dog, and a SOCO or Scene of Crime Officer.

The following morning we had a coffee with the briefing, which was held at Malton. It felt good to see the team assembled, to know that everything was in place and all the available resources were there for us. I went through the briefing sheet that Jayne and I had prepared. There was nothing dramatic about it. We simply described the location of the premises we were going to search, pinpointed it on the map, then outlined the intelligence we had gathered, mapped out the route we would take, and set out the strategy. Each unit would arrive in its own marked vehicle: CID, uniformed officers, and the search team with the search equipment, gloves and evidence bags.

We nominated Ed as the exhibits officer. He wasn't best pleased, but for such an important job you want an experienced cop. The exhibits officer is detailed to log everything that is seized, the time and date of seizure, the officer finding, a description of the item, where it was found, and the seal and exhibit number of each individual bag. Everyone always tried to avoid the job. It was a painstaking and laborious task, but it was absolutely vital should the case go to court.

It was agreed that if we took any prisoners they would go to Scarborough to be held in custody. Along with all that, there were certain other details to iron out: what radio channel we would communicate on, for example. We also made contact with a local vehicle hire company, and had them on standby to supply a large van to transport property should the raid prove successful.

The question of timing was important. For a drugs job, you'd either execute the search warrant very early in the morning, when people are asleep and less likely to offer resistance or have an opportunity to dispose of the goods, or you'd choose a key time, when they're fully stocked for, say, the weekend and in the process of distribution. That way there's more chance of catching some of the punters too, which provides additional evidence that the people concerned are supplying drugs. On this occasion, we had a five-year-old-child to consider. It was decided that we would go at nine thirty, when the child would, hopefully, be at school.

It didn't take long, but it was long enough. In the end it was a relief to be in our cars and heading out along the A64. In fact, it was more than a relief. As we swung off on the country road that would take us towards our quarry, it felt exhilarating. When you look in your rear-view mirror and see that you are part of a convoy of several fully marked police vehicles, and you know you have a sound plan and are fully equipped to implement it you feel . . . empowered. That's the word.

So, for the third time within a week, I made my way down the bumpy lane towards the farm. The puddles had dried up now, and when the vehicles fanned out across the yard in the morning sunlight we raised a cloud of white dust.

I went to the front door and gave it a good bang. There was no reply. I knocked a second time while Ed and Des checked around the back. Nothing. The windows were all shut, but there was a car parked in the shade of the house, the driver's side window open and the keys in the ignition. We went across to a stout-looking wooden door set in the wall of the barn. I had the door enforcer in the back of the car, but there was no need for that; as soon as I turned the handle it swung silently open. Inside was a set of wooden stairs with a stout metal handrail. The atmosphere was humid and laden with that same heavy scent we'd smelled a few nights earlier. Above the low humming of what had to be a pump, we could hear water gurgling through pipes, and an irregular ticking as the sun beat down on corrugated panels in the roof. Even as we stood there I felt my heart beating faster. It's the same feeling I've felt a hundred times, but it's still exciting. It's precisely what you expect policing to be about when you join up. It doesn't matter how many times you've felt it before or how many different jobs you've been on, it's still there. It's an adrenaline rush, and I think it's what most of us like best about the job.

We walked swiftly up to the first floor.

'Christ!' Ed was at my shoulder, shaking his head. 'Look at that.' In a space the size of a school gymnasium, illuminated by an array of overhead lights, was a sea of dark green. Hundreds upon hundreds of cannabis plants growing in densely packed rows. I jumped as a sudden click was followed by a sharp hissing sound, then felt my shoulders relax as a set of overhead nozzles started spraying water onto the foliage. The only time I've breathed air as warm and wet as that was in the tropical hothouse at Kew Gardens. As to the smell, it was almost nauseating. Even as I stood there I heard a whirring noise as a set of ventilators in the roof were cranked open by an electric motor.

'Bloody place is fully automated,' Ed said. 'They've probably got robots doing the weeding.'

We walked slowly along the rows on duckboards. I could feel the fine spray settling on my face. I'd just got to the end of the tanks when I stopped dead in my tracks. In front of me, lying face-up, topping up her tan on a sunbed, and wearing a set of headphones and a very skimpy bikini, was a dark-haired young woman, completely oblivious to our presence.

Someone had to say something, and I was first in line. 'Excuse me, Madam.' She didn't respond, so I repeated myself, a little louder. At that she turned towards me, pulled an earpiece out, sat bolt upright and said, 'Oh my God!'

'I'm PC Mike Pannett of North Yorkshire Police,' I said. 'I think you know why we're here, judging by all these plants. We'll be searching these premises under warrant for drugs or material used in the production of drugs. I do need to tell you that you are under arrest on suspicion of cultivation of cannabis,' I added. Then I cautioned her.

Sometimes it feels strange giving the formal spiel. You want to say, 'Look, lady, you're nicked.' But those days have long gone.

She said nothing. But when she took off her sunglasses it was so that she could wipe away a tear.

'Is your husband about the place?' I asked her.

'No. He's at work.' She had stood up now and was putting on a long towelling dressing gown.

'I understand you have a child.'

'She's at school. I just took her in half an hour ago.'

'I see. And what are these plants?'

'I don't know.' She glanced past me at the CID boys, standing there with Fordy. Jayne had stepped past me to stand by the woman's side.

'Well, just so you know what we're doing, we're going to crack on now and search the barn and seize all of the plants and equipment. I'm sorry to say that we are also going to have to search your house.'

'OK,' she said, 'I understand.'

While Des and the lads set about searching the rest of the place, Jayne led the woman across to the farmhouse to get dressed. By the time Ed and I had followed them across they were both in the kitchen, and the woman's mobile was ringing. I told her to go ahead and answer it.

I was hoping it was the husband so that we could get him back and sort everything out. You wouldn't normally let someone answer the phone in such circumstances, but it was a judgement call and I was banking on the fact that he wouldn't want to leave his wife and child to take the rap.

'Yes?' she said, her hand shaking as she held the phone to her ear. She listened to the voice on the other end for a moment, then said, 'Listen, the police are here.'

'Is that your husband?' I asked. She nodded, and I held out my hand. 'Can I have a quick word?'

She passed me the phone. 'Now then sir,' I said, 'we're at your house and we've found what we suspect to be cannabis plants under cultivation.' He said nothing, just gave out a long slow sigh. 'Your wife's under arrest. Best thing for you is to come home,' I said.

He seemed very calm. 'That's no problem, officer. I'll be there in twenty minutes.'

At this point the woman broke down in tears as the reality of what was happening hit home. 'What'll happen?' she sobbed. 'What about my daughter? Will I go to prison?'

'Look,' I said, 'it is fairly serious, but let's get everything sorted out first. Have you got anyone who can collect your daughter from school and look after her for a bit?'

'There's my mum.'

'Right, well don't worry. We'll sort that out.'

'Mike.' It was Des, who'd come across from the barn. 'You realise we have a huge find here.'

'I'd say it could be one for the record books, mate.'

'We're gonna have a problem shifting all those plants,' he said.

'Yeah, I'll get on to Mennel's for the hire van.'

I saw Fordy arrive at the kitchen door. 'You need to get yourself to town,' I said. 'The hire van needs collecting.'

A raid such as we were now involved in throws up a number of administrative and logistical problems. Before we shifted anything the SOCO had to photograph the whole place, and

Stuart only knew one way of working. He was thorough and painstaking, which meant that he wasn't one to be rushed. After he was through, every last scrap of relevant material had to be counted, logged and bagged up. It's no good showing up in court with vague estimations of 'lots of plants'. The prosecution want accurate numbers that can't be challenged by the opposition. So plants, lights, even the wiring system, the timers and valves, header tanks – it was all evidence and it would all have to be dismantled and taken back to the station store. So we now had two members of the search squad going from tank to tank, counting the plants in each row, multiplying them by the number of rows, and Ed complaining of writer's cramp as he logged all the figures. After they'd done that, it was on with the white paper suits and masks to start bagging everything up.

I was glad to leave that job to the search team. I wanted to meet the husband, see what kind of fellow he was. Criminals are rarely what you expect when you meet them face to face. Some of the worst ones look mild-mannered and inoffensive. When this chap drove up in his Astra van it was quite clear he knew what was coming. Some people have a defiant attitude when you tell them they're under arrest. Some will argue; some will fight; some are morose and silent. This guy was simply resigned. I have to say that he and his wife looked a sorry pair. Crestfallen, you might say. And you could understand it. They must have ploughed a fair bit of capital into setting up the growing system, and here it was being dismantled before their eyes. Funnily enough, a little part of me was troubled to think of a healthy crop bring destroyed. Living up in the country you learn to respect growing things. We would later establish that from a crop this size they could expect to recoup £100,000, in cash, tax-free. And they would harvest three times a year. It had me wondering why the lad still kept his full-time job in town, but that would be for the investigating officers to find out.

'We're going to have to search your house,' I said, after I'd put the handcuffs on him.

'Yeah, I s'pose you will,' he said, and led us inside.

I don't like searching people's homes. If you do it right it's a tedious business. And the worst part, for me, is bedrooms. It gets embarrassing. You see things you'd rather not know about. It was clear they ran their business from theirs – or he did. There was a computer, which of course we seized; there were notebooks with phone numbers, written orders, bank statements – all of which would be manna from heaven for the Intelligence Unit. There was even a collection of plastic bags used for packaging the cannabis, some of them already full, and scales for weighing it out. According to Des what we'd found was grade A skunk cannabis, twice as valuable on the street as the plain resin. It was clear that this fellow was supplying the stuff wholesale, and leaving it to others to distribute it to local dealers.

By the time we'd got everything dismantled and bagged up it was well past four o'clock and we were all starving hungry. It was at this stage that one of the CID boys called me over to a metal box that was fixed to the pole that brought the overhead power supply to the house.

'Remember we wondered why their electricity bills were so low?' He pointed at a black cable that ran out from the box and snaked across they yard towards the barn. 'Looks like they've short-circuited the meter and tapped straight into the mains supply, the crafty buggers.'

'Yeah, right. That'll be a further arrest for abstracting electricity. I'll get onto control to get the leccy board down to make it safe.'

While Fordy got on with packing all the seized material into the hired van, we took our prisoners to Scarborough, where they would wait to be interviewed.

By the time I got back to Malton we were well into overtime. Fordy had just arrived from the farm and was ready to unload the van. 'Birdie's told us to get all this in the property store.'

'Bloody hell, that's on the third floor!'

'Well, Jayne's been sent to help Des out with the interviews – gain a bit of experience. So it looks like it's you, me and Ed got the short straw.'

Fordy took me round to the back of the van and lifted the sliding door. Two lamps, a tangle of wires and a plastic header tank clattered onto the tarmac, exposing a pile of binbags stuffed to the top with cannabis plants. The van was totally chock-a-block, from floor to ceiling. It took us a full hour to get it all put away – even with the help of a couple of lads off the late turn. Last job was to sweep out the back of the van, which was covered with several hundreds of pounds' worth of cannabis leaves. And if I thought that was it, job done, I had another think coming. I had my jacket over my arm and was heading for the door when I bumped into the new chief superintendent.

She stopped and wrinkled up her nose, then looked at me. 'Mike, I've just come down from my office and the whole building stinks of cannabis.' She put her hand into her pocket and produced a small handful of leaves. 'And I found these on the stairs.' She looked at me, and my heart sank. 'Jacket off and get it sorted.'

'Will do, ma'am.'

She paused, then gave a hint of a smile. 'Good job, by the way.'

* * *

So after boxing off the paperwork and sweeping down the stairs, all I had to do was dodge the afternoon desk sergeant. But he collared me as I was opening the door to leave. 'Call from a lady out in the woods near Westow, Mike. Seen a man hanging his washing out on the trees.'

'And?'

'All his washing. Everything.'

'Oh no. You mean he was . . .'

'That's right, mate. Stark naked.'

'First call tomorrow, mate. I promise.'

Back home, after the dog had taken me for a walk, I had a shower and changed into some more comfortable clothes. As I finally sat down to a plate of grub and a bottle of beer with the ten o'clock news coming on the telly, Ann arrived from work. She leaned forward and kissed me, at the same time nicking a pickled onion off my plate. 'What's for supper then?' she asked. 'Supper?' I said. 'This is my lunch – and I'll thank you to keep your fingers out of it.'

Help raise £1 million for 'The Moors'

The North York Moors is one of the most beautiful parts of the UK, best enjoyed on board the North Yorkshire Moors Railway, with its magnificent steam engines, period rural stations and smartly uniformed staff. The railway runs through the heart of the National Park, and because it links Pickering with Whitby, is the perfect gateway to the moors and coast.

To help maintain the long-term future of the railway, the **Bridge & Wheels Appeal** has been launched, seeking to raise £1 million to fund the renewal of a 100 year old bridge between Goathland and Grosmont, and to fund much needed steam engine restoration.

If you would like to contribute to the appeal contact the **North Yorkshire Moors Railway** at **12 Park Street, Pickering, North Yorkshire, YO18 7AJ, Tel: 01751 473799** or visit the website **www.bridgeandwheels.co.uk**.

For more information about the North Yorkshire Moors Railway and train services, please visit www.nymr.co.uk.